READINGS IN ANTHROPOLOGY OF HUMAN MOVEMENT
Edited by Drid Williams

Anthropology and Human Movement

The Study of Dances

Drid Williams

Readings in Anthropology of Human Movement, No. 1

The Scarecrow Press, Inc.
Lanham, Md., & London
1997

SCARECROW PRESS, INC.

Published in the United States of Americ
by Scarecrow Press, Inc.
4720 Boston Way
Lanham, Maryland 20706

4 Pleydell Gardens, Folkestone
Kent CT20 2DN, England

Copyright © 1997 by Drid Williams

British Cataloguing-in-Publication Information Available

Library of Congress Cataloging-in-Publication Data

Anthropology and human movement : the study of dances / [edited by]
    Drid Williams.
        p.   cm. — (Readings in anthropology of human movement ; no. 1)
    Includes bibliographical references and index.
    ISBN 0–8108–3236–4 (cloth : alk. paper)
    1. Dance—Anthropological aspects. 2. Dance—Sociological aspects.
    3. Dance—Study and teaching. I. Williams, Drid, 1928–. II. Series.
    GV1588.6.A58   1997
    306.4'84—DC20   96-33151
                                                                    CIP

ISBN 0–8108–3236–4 (cloth : alk. paper)

 The paper used in this publication meets the minimum requirements of
American National Standard for Information Sciences—Permanence of
Paper for Printed Library Materials, ANSI Z39.48–1984.
Manufactured in the United States of America.

CONTENTS

PREFACE

This book of *Readings* is the first introductory textbook specifically designed for courses in the Anthropology of Human Movement Studies. It can be used for courses in the Anthropology of the Dance, Dance Anthropology, Dance Ethnography or Dance Ethnology courses. It is constructed for use in any course or set of lectures aiming to provide an anthropological perspective on the study of dances. It is designed to prove useful to mainstream anthropologists who are interested in the sub-field and its potential for elective readings connected with more standard courses.

The *Readings* can be used for graduate and/or third and fourth year undergraduate courses. Apart from reprinted articles, chapters and excerpts, it contains (1) short biographical notes of the authors of the selections and (2) précis exercises taken from the articles themselves. These exercises include questions about definitions of unusual words and relevant issues the author has tackled. Accompanying the précis exercises are questions about the particular societies whose dances are represented, or about specific theoretical issues relevant to the study of human movement.

Biographies of the authors of the articles are given with the text because students should be aware that such legitimate social scientific knowledge as we possess about the world's dances was generated by people who often spent many years carrying out research in order to produce the work. The essays chosen for the volume are based on serious study by highly qualified practitioners in the field.

Students also need to know that this field of study is relatively new: it started *circa* 1967 as a sub-field of sociocultural anthropology (see Williams 1986: 159-219 for further information). Four of the writers, i.e. Keali'inohomoku, Kaeppler, Williams and Royce were originators of the field with reference to (a) legitimate, mainstream anthropological qualifications, (b) general scholarly standards and (c) ethnographic description.

Précis exercises are placed at the end of the articles because we think teachers of the subject will welcome adequate benchmarks whereby a student's grasp of the material can accurately be assessed. Often, students who take dance anthropology or dance ethnography courses have had no instruction whatsoever in sociocultural anthropology. Because of this, they frequently encounter difficulties, not being aware that they enter a universe of discourse that is different from (and infinitely wider than) more familiar kinds of literature written about dances, dancing or the dance.[1]

Keali'inohomoku's contribution makes a point of this by contrasting anthropological writing about the dance with the writings of dance scholars who look at dances from general literary, journalistic or aesthetic points of view. Because of the difference in approach, students face technical terminologies and unfamiliar terms commonly used in anthropology. They need assistance fully to understand what anthropologists mean, for example, by the use of such ordinary words as 'culture', 'society', 'ethnic', 'kin', and many others.[2]

Précis exercises are also given to help students sort out the intellectual, political and scholarly issues relevant to the field of study. In fact, that is why this book begins with Keali'inohomoku's seminal article on the ethnic character of *all* dance forms. Her essay begins with a clear statement of a fundamental anthropological viewpoint: "It is good anthropology to think of ballet as a form of ethnic dance"(*infra* p. 16). It is also good anthropology to think of ourselves as ethnics, because our dances, no less than those of others, are culturally and linguistically derived.

From there, she outlines serious problems of categorization and classification that up to now, have been hardy perennials in this field of study. No author has done a better job of explaining the complications and presenting the issues than Keali'inohomoku has done. Her work in this area is so important that students aspiring to master the field couldn't be considered adequately educated if they remain unfamiliar with her writing.

The two sections of text that follow *An Anthropologist Looks At Ballet as a Form of Ethnic Dance* dwell on similar issues of definition and classification. Both Royce and Williams use slightly different approaches, but they can easily be seen to be talking about the same kinds of thing. Nevertheless, précis exercises are given for both, because there are important points to be learned to which each author draws attention.

It is assumed that the instructor for the course will devise more such exercises if he or she believes they are necessary. The Editor doesn't claim the précis exercises cover *every* important point in the chosen articles because the *Readings* are characterized by their richness of content. Fundamentally, they are there to help students learn to think and to develop a healthy anthropological sensibility.

The Exercises after each précis are designed so that students can discover for themselves what reading for a university course means — the many dimensions of 'knowing' that are required. Then too, Royce's and Williams's books are available in most college and university libraries for further study at the discretion of the lecturer. These books have a variety of useful applications outlined below.

Instructors who have used the *Readings* text in manuscript form have said, for example, that using the subject index of Williams's book, an instructor or the students themselves can easily find related materials, i.e.

dance (The): ambiguity of "origins," 32-33, 55-56, 76, 203; ... definitions of, 6, 58, 96, 105, 185, 88, 354-355; ... unilineal evolutionary theory of, 14, 26, 32, 88-89; ... origin of drama, 84 (Williams 1991: 411).

Apart from learning the rudiments of bibliographic searching, these references supplement, not only the first three readings, but those which follow very well. In the author index, students can find all the references Williams makes, for example, to Kaeppler's writings, i.e.

Kaeppler, A. xviii, 6, 133, 171-172, 180, 215-216; (1972) 16, 204, 214-215, 228, 323, 340, 360; (1978) 5, 59-60, 88-89, 157, 168, 360, 363; (1985) 204, 267, 364; (1986) 204, 241, 360, 380.

By looking in the Bibliography, students can find other articles by the same author. That is,

Kaeppler, A.
  1972. Method and Theory in Analyzing Dance Structure With an Analysis of Tongan Dance. *Ethnomusicology*, 16(2): 173-217.
  1978. The Dance in Anthropological Perspective. *Annual Review of Anthropology*, 7:31-39.
  1985. Structured Movement Systems in Tonga. *Society and the Dance*. (Ed. P. Spencer), Cambridge University Press, Cambridge, U.K., pp. 92-118.
  1986. Cultural Analysis, Linguistic Analogies and the Study of Dance in Anthropological Perspective. *Explorations in Ethnomusicology: Essays in Honor of David P. McAllester*. (Ed. Frisbie), Detroit Monographs on Musicology #9, Detroit, Michigan, pp. 25-33.

Royce's book offers similar bibliographic advantages. Her work is useful, too, because it introduces students to the differences in American styles of anthropological thinking and research, in contrast to Middleton's and Williams's essentially British social anthropological approach. In other words, not only are students introduced to the variety of dances in the world, the *Readings* text leads naturally and relatively painlessly to a more sophisticated understanding of anthropological authors and related works.

Philosophy

After the first three sections, dealing with general anthropological issues in the field, readers encounter the work of a Wittgensteinian philosopher, David Best, who spent the better part of a lifetime spelling out the philosophical issues related to the study of dances and dancing. Where the problem of definition is presented by the first three authors in anthropological contexts, students now have the benefit of a finely-honed philosophical analysis of the problem.

At more advanced levels, philosophical issues surrounding the study of dances (sign languages, martial arts, ceremonies, rituals, manual counting systems and the like) gradually assume greater importance. It is vital for students to familiarize themselves early on, not only with the chapter on 'definition', but with all of the arguments raised in Best's many books, for they are relevant to all writing in the field, regardless of theoretical approach or type of movement study.

Fieldwork

From the definitional problem in general anthropological and specific philosophical terms, the text moves on to the notion of definitions in ethnographic writing taken from the standpoint of participant-observation method and field notes, where authors use many native words and terms not easily translatable into English. Kaeppler handles these aspects of ethnography with apparent ease. The central point of her work on Tongan ceremony and dances, for example, turns around the word, *heliaki*.

> The most important element in this ceremonial pig presentation is the poetic text. The poetry conveys information through metaphor and allusion interwoven with the Tongan aesthetic principle *heliaki*. This concept usually translated as 'not going straight' or 'to say one thing and mean another', is characterised by never going straight to the point but alluding to it indirectly. *Heliaki* is poetically realised through the Tongan literary device of alluding to people and their genealogical connections with place names, flowers, and birds, metaphorically making reference to the occasion and those honoured by it (Kaeppler, p. 93).

The importance of being able to define, explain and clarify complex words and concepts from another language into English cannot be overstressed, because it is a characteristic feature of good anthropological writing. Kaeppler is especially good at this, although her work was chosen for other reasons as well. For example, in the beginning of her article she asks, "Is the concept 'dance' useful in studying either our own culture or others?" (see p. 89), concluding that "The concept 'dance' appears to be an unsatisfactory category imposed from a Western point of view because it tends to group together diverse activities that should be culturally separated".

Earlier on, she clearly indicates what she thinks an anthropologist of the dance and human movement should do, proposing that

> [O]ne of the tasks of an ethnographer is to study *all* human movement that formalises the non-formal and to elucidate what the movement dimensions of various activity systems are communicating and to whom. Such an analysis could delineate similarities and differences in the movement dimensions and their contexts as well as how these are regarded and categorised and the components by which they are grouped or separated. It might then be possible to illuminate cultural constructs that produce a cultural conception of 'dance' (see p. 90).

She follows her own suggestions through an admirable description and explanation of human movement systems in Tonga.

Fieldwork [East Africa]

From a Pacific oceanic culture (Tonga), readers travel halfway around the world to Uganda, East Africa, to the dances of the Lugbara people. Middleton begins his ethnography with comments on general themes that have been met in all of the sections of the *Readings* so far: definition, classification and categories. He says,

> My aim is not to understand what 'dance' is in itself, partly because I am uncertain whether it is a separate and meaningful category, but also because *it is its social context that gives it meaning.* So I first ask what is that context and its significance for the people who are involved in it. *I am concerned to study the Lugbara dance as a way of understanding Lugbara thought and the ways in which they order their experience* (p. 124 - italics added).

These are important anthropological ideas and aims of which students need to be aware from the outset, for there are many ways of describing a dance; many possible ways of interpreting what is going on in a danced event and numerous strategies available for organizing the final results of field work, whether in another culture or in one's own.

Middleton's work is a fine example of an anthropologist

writing about dances with specific anthropological aims in mind, for Lugbara dances (together with many others) provide an excellent means for studying the ways in which people order their social experience.

Moving From 'A Dance' to a Whole Society

Where Kaeppler's and Middleton's work introduce novices to ethnographies of *specific* dances and movement events, Schieffelin's work is an ethnography of a danced ceremony contained within an entire anthropological monograph. It is, therefore, the next logical step. The dancing and related activities in the Gisaro were so important in terms of Kaluli society as a whole that Schieffelin used the ceremony as a scenario through which he describes the whole society. His strategy is explained in Extract #3. The author asks

What, then, is Gisaro all about? The songs project the members of the audience back along their lives, through images of places they have known in the past. As a visiting government interpreter once remarked to me, "It is their memory". Tragic situations are renewed, allowing people to take account of them once more and settle them in their hearts and minds. It is not the nostalgic content of the songs, however, but the angered and anguished *taking of account* in Gisaro that is most striking to an outsider, and it is the taking of account, I believe, that to the Kaluli gives the ceremony its special character ...(p. 173).

Gisaro is a drama of opposition initiated by the dancers but played out by everyone. Within a structure of reciprocity, the action of the performers and the feelings of the audience are brought into a relation with each other that allows intelligibility and resolution (p. 173).

From the study of this ceremony, students can attempt reading Schieffelin's whole book from an advantageous position. They are better equipped to understand the nature and character of an entire anthropological monograph. The point is, not only are students expected to learn about *dances* through the use of this text, they are also expected to learn something about how anthropologists think.

For example, Schieffelin points out:

In social anthropology, when violence and antagonism are expressed ceremonially between two groups, it is customary to assume that they represent underlying stresses between the groups and thus to search for a deeper content to the opposition in the underlying tensions of social relationships (p. 174).

There are important features of anthropological theory and method to be gained from the *Readings*, which are useful in any future study students may undertake in the field.

Comparison, Movement Literacy and Theory

The text as a whole can be seen to lead students step-by-step towards an introduction to comparative method, opening with excerpts from Royce's book. Enlarging on the same theme, it moves into the issue of the *literacy* of dances and to the role of theory in human movement studies.

The section on comparative method includes work by contemporary anthropologists of the dance and human movement studies on the value of movement-literacy, and the values of having *movement texts* as evidence for events they have seen (and probably participated in) in the field. Regarding the role of theory, we read,

Without theories and hypotheses anthropological research could not be carried out, for one only finds things, or does not find them, if one is looking for them. Often one finds something other than what one is looking for. The whole history of scholarship, whether in the natural sciences or in the humanities, tells us that the mere collection of what are called facts unguided by theory in observation and selection is of little value (Evans-Pritchard 1951: 64).

The section on comparison, movement literacy and the role of theory in anthropology is meant to stimulate class discussion. By the time *Notes on Comparison* is reached, students have sufficient knowledge actively to contribute. Not only that, it is probable that an instructor will find it good practice to assign term papers asking students to compare and contrast two of the articles they have read — but there are many possible pedagogical approaches to the material.

The first volume of *Readings* closes with Franken's work on Swahili dances from the coast of Kenya that formed the ethnographic basis for her Doctoral work. Her article emphasizes class and gender differences among Swahili-speaking peoples located largely in and around Mombasa. They are predominantly Muslim and their language, *Kiswahili*, is a Bantu language having a large lexical content which reflects close trading and religious relationships between East Africans and Arabic-speakers from Middle Eastern peoples. An interesting contrast exists between the Swahili (an urban culture), and the Lugbara, who are mainly an agricultural and rural society.

Conclusion

The introduction to the anthropological study of dances represented by this text focuses on the wide diversity of types of dances and the characteristic subject-matter of dances among peoples of the world. At the same time, it identifies important issues in the anthropology of human movement studies, and, it attempts to acquaint students with relevant features of anthropological thinking and writing. The text provides examples and valuable commentary about dancing from the United States, Mexico, Tonga, East Africa and New Guinea.

In the final section, Reading X *(Signs and Symbols)*, the text provides for themes which can be used in connection with each essay that preceded it. For example, how do the representative authors deal with symbols — with signs?

In the second volume of the Series: *Anthropology and Human Movement, 2: Searching for Origins,* the focus changes from ethnography to prehistory, asking how the micro-histories of actual dance forms fit into the macro-history of the human race. In the third volume, readers again return to ethnography and themes of comparison along with the notion of action signs and symbols, developed at more advanced levels. That is, references are made to Brenda Farnell's edited collection (1995a) entitled *Human Action Signs in Cultural Context: The Visible and the Invisible in Movement and Dance,* which is on the leading edge of the field. However, Volume 3 also includes the work of E.E. Evans-Pritchard on Azande dances, published in 1928, and the efforts of other, earlier anthropologists, e.g. Stanner (1966) and Lienhardt (1957/58).

In other words, we feel it is important to document the fact that recent archæological discoveries in southern Africa are likely to change how we classify and categorize so-called 'primitive' dancing. We also believe it is important to point out that new approaches to human movement studies didn't emerge from an historical vacuum. Although relatively few in number, there is a distinguished group of writers to whom present-day authors and students can look for inspiration.

Since the late 'sixties, the Anthropology of Human Movement Studies has developed and it continues to progress through the efforts of first generation, then second and third generation sociocultural anthropologists who have taken keen interest in dances, the martial arts, signing, rituals and ceremonies of all kinds. Younger generations have had wider theoretical, linguistic, philosophical and historical resources upon which to draw regarding concepts of embodiment, causality and substance than earlier writers did, thus their work often transcends that of their predecessors, but it does so without minimizing or rejecting their overall vision.

The Editor

READING I

BIOGRAPHICAL NOTES: Joann Wheeler Keali'inohomoku, native of Missouri, after six years in Hawai'i returned to the mainland, where she completed a Master's degree at Northwestern University. Her Doctoral work was done at Indiana University under Alan P. Merriam's supervision. Although she worked on the anthropology of dances before Adrienne Kaeppler did, her Ph.D. is dated 1976—the same year that Judith Lynne Hanna (Columbia, N.Y.) and Drid Williams (Oxford, U.K.) completed their degrees. In 1969 Keali'inohomoku left Indiana University (six years before Anya Royce, who completed her Ph.D. at the University of California in 1974), joining the anthropology faculty at Indiana University in 1975. Keali'inohomoku taught modern dance for twenty years. Among other forms, she studied the dances of Polynesia and Micronesia for several years. She carried out research on the religious and recreational dances of African-Americans. Her field research among the Hopi Indians of Arizona began in 1965. She continues to research the dance cultures of both the Pacific and the Native Southwest. After 14 years on the anthropology faculty at Northern Arizona University she left the university to devote her time to independent scholarship. She is Executive Director for *Cross Cultural Dance Resources*, a non-profit organization she co-founded in 1981.

The text is a reproduction, with minor changes, of **Keali'inohomoku, J.W.1980[1969].** 'An Anthropologist Looks At Ballet as a Form of Ethnic Dance'. *JASHM*, 1(2): 83-97. Reprinted by permission of the *Journal for the Anthropological Study of Human Movement* [JASHM].

Introduction

It is good anthropology to think of ballet as a form of ethnic dance. Currently, that idea is unacceptable to most Western dance scholars. This lack of agreement shows clearly that something is amiss in the communication of ideas between the scholars of dance and those of anthropology, and this paper is an attempt to bridge that communication gap. The faults and errors of anthropologists in their approach to dance are many, but they are largely due to their hesitation to deal with something which seems esoteric and out of their field of competence. However, a handful of anthropologists of the dance are trying to rectify this by publishing in the social science journals and by participating in formal and informal meetings with other anthropologists.

By ethnic dance, anthropologists mean to convey the idea that all forms of dance reflect the cultural traditions within which they developed. Dancers and dance scholars, as this paper will show, use this term, and the related terms *ethnologic*, *primitive* and *folk dance*, differently and, in fact, in a way which reveals their limited knowledge of non-Western dance forms.

In preparing to formulate this paper, I re-read in an intense period pertinent writings by DeMille, Haskell, Holt, the Kinneys, Kirstein, LaMeri, Martin, Sachs, Sorell and Terry. In addition I carefully re-read the definitions pertaining to "dance" in *Webster's New International Dictionary*, the 2nd edition definitions which were written by Doris Humphrey and the 3rd edition definitions which were written by Gertrude Kurath. Although these and other sources are listed in the bibliography at the end of this paper, I name these scholars here to focus my frame of reference.

The experience of this intense re-reading, as an anthropologist rather than as a dancer, was both instructive and disturbing. The readings are rife with unsubstantiated deductive reasoning, poorly documented 'proofs', a plethora of half-truths, many out-and-out errors, and a pervasive ethnocentric bias. Where the writers championed non-Western dances and dancing, they were either apologists or patronistic. Most discouraging of all, these authors saw fit to change only the pictures and not the texts when they re-issued their books after as many as seventeen years later; they only updated the Euro-American dance scene.

This survey of the literature reveals an amazing divergence of opinions. We are able to read that the origin of the dance was in play and that it was not in play, that it was for magical and religious purposes, and that it was not for those things; that it was for courtship and that it was not for courtship; that it was the first form of communication and communication did not enter into dance until it became an 'art'. In addition we can read that it was serious and purposeful and that at the same time it was an outgrowth of exuberance, was totally spontaneous, and originated in the spirit of fun. Moreover, we can read that it was only a group activity for tribal solidarity and that it was strictly for the pleasure and self-expression of the one dancing. We can learn also, that animals danced before Man did, and yet that dance is a human activity.

It has been a long time since anthropologists concerned themselves with unknowable origins, and I will not add another origin theory for the dance, because I don't know anyone who was there. Our dance writers, however, suggest evidence for origins from archaeological finds, and from models exemplified by contemporary primitive groups. For the first, one must remember that Man had been on this earth for a long time before he made cave paintings and statuary, so that archaeological finds can hardly tell us about the beginnings of dances. For the second set of evidence, that of using models from contemporary "primitives", one must not confuse the word *primitive* with *primeval*, even though one author actually does equate these two terms (Sorell 1967: 14). About the dance of primeval Man we really know nothing. About *primitive* dances and dancing we know a great deal. The first thing that we know is that there is no such thing as *a* primitive dance. There *are* dances performed by primitives, and they are too varied to fit any stereotype. It is a gross error to think of groups of peoples or their dances as being monolithic wholes. "The African Dance" never existed; there are, however, Dahomean dances, Hausa dances, Maasai dances, and so forth. "The American Indian" is a fiction and so is a prototype of "Indian dance". There are, however, Iroquois, Kwakiutl, and Hopis, to name a few, and they all have dances.

Despite all anthropological evidence to the contrary, however, Western dance scholars set themselves up as authorities on the characteristics of "primitive" dance. Sorell combines most of these so-called characteristics of the primitive stereotype. He tells us that primitive dancers have no technique, and no artistry, but that they are "unfailing masters of their bodies"! He states that their dances are disorganized and frenzied, but that they are able to translate all their feelings and emotions into movement! He claims the dances are spontaneous but also purposeful! Primitive dances, he tells us, are serious but social! He claims that they have "complete freedom" but that men and women can't dance together. He qualifies that last statement by saying that men and women dance together after the dance degenerates into an orgy! Sorell also asserts that primitives cannot distinguish between the concrete and the symbolic, that they dance for every occasion, and that they stamp around a lot! Further, Sorell asserts that dance in primitive societies is a special prerogative of males, especially chieftains, shamans and witch doctors (Sorell 1967: 10-11). Kirstein also characterizes the dances of "natural, unfettered societies" (whatever that means). Although the whole body participates according to Kirstein, he claims that the emphasis of movement is with the lower half of the torso. He concludes that primitive dance is repetitious, limited, unconscious and with "retardative and closed expression"! Still, though it may be unconscious, Kirstein tells his readers that dance is useful to the tribe and that it is based on the seasons. Primitive dance, or as he phrases it, "earlier manifestations of human activity" is everywhere found to be "almost identically formulated". He never really tells us what these formulations are except that they have little to offer in methodology or structure, and that they are examples of "instinctive exuberance" (Kirstein 1942: 3-5). Terry describes the functions of primitive dance, and he uses American Indians as his model. In his book *The Dance in America* he writes sympathetically towards American Indians and "his primitive brothers". However, his paternalistic feelings on the one hand, and his sense of ethnocentricity on the other, prompt him to set aside any thought that the people with whom he identifies could share contemporarily those same dance characteristics, because he states "the white man's dance heritage, except for the most ancient of days, was wholly different (1956: 3-4, 195-198).

Another significant obstacle to the identification of Western dancers with non-Western dance forms, be they primitive or 'ethnologic' in the sense that Sorell uses the latter term as "the art expression of a race" which is "executed for the enjoyment and edification of the audience" (1967: 76), is the double myth that the dance grew out of some spontaneous mob action and that once formed, became frozen. American anthropologists and many folklorists have been most distressed about the popularity of these widespread misconceptions. Apparently it satisfies our own ethnocentric needs to believe in the uniqueness of our dance forms, and it is much more convenient to believe that primitive dances, like Topsy, just "growed", and that 'ethnological' dances are part of an unchanging tradition. Even books and articles which purport to be about the dances of the *world* devote three quarters of the text and photographs to Western dances. We explicate our historic eras, our royal patrons, dancing masters, choreographers, and performers. The rest of the world is condensed diachronically and synchronically to the remaining quarter of the book. This smaller portion, which must cover the rest of the world, is usually divided up so that the portions at the beginning imply that the ethnic portions at the end of the book for, say, American [black] dance, give the appearance of a postscript, as if they too "also ran". In short we treat Western dance, ballet particularly, as if it was the one great divinely ordained apogee of the performing arts. This notion is exemplified, and reinforced, by the way dance photos are published. Unless the non-Western performer has made a "hit" on our stages, we seldom bother to give him a name in the captions, even though he might be considered a fine artist among his peers (Martin is the exception). For example, see Claire Holt's article "Two Dance Worlds" (1969). The captions under the photos of Javanese dancers list no names, but you may be sure that we are always told when Martha Graham appears in a photo. A scholar friend of mine was looking over the books by our dance historians, and he observed that they were not interested in the whole world of dance, they were really only interested in *their* world of dance. Can anyone deny this allegation?

Let it be noted, once and for all, that within the various 'ethnologic' dance worlds there are also patrons, dancing masters, choreographers, and performers with names woven into a very real historical fabric.The bias which those dancers have toward their own dance [forms] and artists is just as strong as ours. The difference is that they usually don't pretend to be scholars of other dance forms, nor even very much interested in them. It is instructive, however, to remind ourselves that all dances are subject to change and development no matter how convenient we may find it to dismiss some form as practically unchanged for 2000 years (see DeMille 1963: 48). It is convenient to us, of course, because once having said that, we feel that our job is finished.

As for the presumed lack of creators of dance among primitive and folk groups, let us reconsider that assumption after reading Martin's statement; "In simpler cultures than ours we find a mass of art actually created and practiced by the people as a whole" (Martin 1939: 15).

The first question which such a statement raises is what is

a "mass of art"? Martin never really defines art, but if he means art as a refined aesthetic expression, then it can be asked how such could ever be a collective product. Does he mean that it appeared spontaneously? Does he really think there can be art without artists? And if he believes that there must be artists, does he mean to imply that a "people as a whole" are artists? If so, what a wonderful group of people they must be. Let us learn from them! Doubtless Martin probably will say that I have taken his statement to an absurd extension of his meaning, but I believe that such thoughtless statements deserve to be pushed to their extreme.

It is true that some cultures do not place the same value on preserving the names of their innovators as we do. That is a matter of tradition also. But we must not be deceived into believing that a few hundred people all got together and with one unanimous surge created a dance tradition which, having once been created, never changed from that day forward.

Among the Hopi Indians of Northern Arizona, for example, there is no tradition of naming a choreographer. Nevertheless they definitely know who, within a Kiva group or a society, made certain innovations and why. A dramatic example of the variety permitted in what is otherwise considered to be a static dance tradition is to see, as I have, the 'same' dance ceremonies performed in several different villages at several different times. To illustrate, I observed the important Hopi 'bean dances' which are held every February, in five different villages during the winters of 1965 and 1968. There were the distinguishing differences between villages which are predictable differences, once one becomes familiar with a village 'style'. But, in addition, there were creative and not necessarily predictable differences which occurred from one time to the next. The Hopis know clearly what the predictable differences are, and they also know who and what circumstances led to the timely innovations. Not only do they know these things, but they are quite free in their evaluation of the merits and demerits of these differences, with their own usually (but not always) coming out as being aesthetically more satisfying.

In Martin's *Introduction to the Dance* (1939) the first plate contains two reproductions of drawings of Hopi *kachinas*. Judging from its position among the [photographic] plates, this must be Martin's single example of dances from a primitive group. DeMille also shows Hopis as examples of primitive dancers (1963: 33, 35—the latter is a posed photo). Let us see how well the Hopis compare to generalities attributed to primitive dancers.

Paradigm

Hopi dances are immaculately organized, are never frenzied (not even, in fact, especially, in their famous snake dance), nor is there a desire to translate feelings and emotions into movement. The dances are indeed "serious", if this is synonymous with *purposeful*, but many dances are not serious if that word negates the fact that many dances are humorous, use clowns as personnel, and contain both derision and satire. Hopi dance is also "social" if one is speaking as a sociologist [or anthropologist], but they have only one prescribed genre of dance which the Hopis themselves consider "social" in the sense that they can be performed by uninitiated members of the society. Hopis would find the idea of "complete freedom" in their dance to be an alien idea, because much of the form and behavior is rigidly prescribed. Certainly they would never lapse into an orgy! Nor do they "hurl themselves on the ground and roll in the mud" after the rains begin (DeMille 1963: 35).

Hopis would be offended if you told them that they could not distinguish between the concrete and the symbolic. They are not children, after all. They certainly understand natural causes. But does it make them "primitive", by definition, if they ask their gods to help their crops grow by bringing rain? Don't farmers within the mainstream of America and Europe frequently pray to a Judeo-Christian God for the same thing? Are the Hopis more illogical than we are when they dance their prayers instead of attending religious services with responsive readings, and a variety of motor activities such as rising, sitting, folding hands and the like?

Once again assessing the Hopis in the light of the characteristics presumably found for primitive dancers, we find that Hopis don't dance for the three specific life events which supposedly are 'always' recognized in dance. That is, Hopis don't dance at births, marriages, or deaths.

Obviously, it cannot be said that they "dance on every occasion". Furthermore, the Hopi stamping would surely be a disappointment to Sorell if he expected the Hopis to "make the earth tremble under his feet" (1967: 15). DeMille might also be surprised that there is no "state of exaltation" or "ecstasy" in Hopi dance (*cf.* DeMille 1963: 34 and 67).

It is true that more Hopi dances are performed by males than by females, but females also dance under certain circumstances and for certain rituals which are the sole prerogative of females. What is more important is that women participate a great deal if one thinks of them as non-dancer participants, and one must, because it is the entire dance *event* which is important to the Hopis rather than just the actual rhythmic movement(s).

For the Hopis, it is meaningless to say that the primary dancers are the chieftains, witch doctors and shamans. Traditionally they have no real 'government' as such, and every clan has its own rituals and societies which are further divided according to the village in which they live. Thus everyone will participate to some degree or another in a variety of roles. There is no "shaman" as such, so of course there cannot be shamanistic dances. As for witch doctors, they do not dance in that role although they dance to fulfill some of their other roles in their clan and residence groups.

I do not know what is meant by a "natural, unfettered society", but whatever it is I am sure that description does not fit the Hopis. In their dance movements the whole body does not participate, and there is no pelvic movement as such. The dances are indeed repetitious, but that does not inter-

fere in the least with the real dramatic impact of the performance. Within the "limitations" of the dance culture, Hopi
dance still has an enormous range of variations, and this is
especially true because the dance event is so richly orches-
trated.

Far from being an "unconscious" dance form, Hopi dancing is a very conscious activity. And I cannot believe that it is
any more "retardative" or closed within its own framework
than any other dance form, bar none. Finally, I find nothing
in Hopi dance that can be called "instinctively exuberant",
but perhaps that is because I don't know what "instinctive
exuberance" is. If it is what I *think* it is, such a description is
inappropriate for Hopi dances.

Lest someone say that perhaps the Hopis are the exception
to prove the rule, or, perhaps, that they are not really "primitive", let me make two points. First, if they are not "primitive" they do not fit into any other category offered by the
dance scholars discussed in this article. Their dances are not
"folk dance" as described, nor do they have "ethnologic
dances" nor "art dances" nor "theater dance" as these terms
are used in the writings under consideration. Clearly in the
light of these writers' descriptions, they are a "primitive",
"ethnic" group with dances in kind. Second, I know of no
group anywhere which fits the descriptions for primitive
dance such as given by DeMille, Sorell, Terry and Martin.
Certainly I know of no justification for Haskell's statement
that "many dances of primitive tribes still living are said to
be identical with those of birds and apes" (1960: 9). Unfortunately, Haskell does not document any of his statements and
we cannot trace the source of such a blatant piece of misin-
formation.

It is necessary to hammer home the idea that there is no
such thing as "a primitive dance form". Those who teach
courses called "primitive dance" are perpetuating a dangerous myth. As a corollary to this let it be noted that no living
primitive group will reveal to us the way our European ancestors behaved. Every group has had its own unique his-

tory and has been subject to both internal and external modifications. Contemporary primitives are not children in fact, nor can they be pigeon-holed into some convenient slot on an evolutionary scale.

I suggest that one cause for so much inaccurate and shocking misunderstanding on the subject of primitive groups is due to an over dependence on the words of Sir James Frazer and Curt Sachs whose works have been outdated as source material for better than three decades. In their stead I would suggest that they read some of the works of Gertrude P. Kurath, whose bibliography appeared in the January, 1970, issue of *Ethnomusicology*. This and other suggested readings are given at the end of this article.

Definitions

It is disconcerting to discover that writers tend to use key words without attempting real definitions which are neither too exclusive nor too inclusive. Even the word "dance", itself, is never adequately defined to apply cross-culturally through time and space. Instead of definitions we are given descriptions, which are a different matter altogether. I have been closely questioned as to the need for definitions "as long as we all mean the same thing anyway", and I have even been asked what difference it makes what we call something as long as we all understand how some term is being used. The answers are two-fold: without the discipline of attempting to define specific terms we are not sure we do all mean the same thing or that we understand how a term is being used. On the other hand, the tacit agreement about frames of reference can distort the focus of emphasis rather than giving the broadly based objectivity which comes from using a term denotatively.

For seven years I pondered over a definition of [the word] *dance*, and in 1965 I tentatively set out the following definition which has since undergone some slight modifications. In its current form it reads

Dance is a transient mode of expression, performed in a given form and style by the human body moving in space. Dance occurs through purposefully selected and controlled rhythmic movements; the resulting phenomenon is recognized as dance both by the performer and the observing members of a given group (Keali'inohomoku, 1965: 6, revised, 1970).

The two crucial points which distinguish this definition from others are the limiting of dance to that of human behavior since there is no reason to believe that birds or apes perform with the intent to dance. Intent to dance and acknowledgment of the activity as dance by a given group is the second distinguishing feature of my definition. This is the crucial point for applying the definition cross-culturally as well as setting dance apart from other activities which might appear to be dance to the outsider but which are considered, say, sports or ritual to the participants. *Webster's International Dictionary* shows much contrast in the definitions of dance between the2nd and 3rd editions. The reason for the contrast is clear when it is understood that a performer-choreographer of Western dance wrote the dance entries for the2nd edition (Doris Humphrey), while an ethno-choreologist (Gertrude Kurath) wrote the entries for the 3rd edition.

We cannot accept Kirstein's contention that "it is apparent, … that the idea of tension, from the very beginning, has been foremost in people's minds when they have thought about dancing seriously enough to invent or adapt word-sounds for it" (1935: 1). Charles J. Alber in a personal communication in 1970, assured me that both Japanese and Mandarin Chinese have time-honored words for dance and related activities and that the idea of tension does not occur at all in these words. Clearly Kirstein's statement indicates that he has not looked beyond the models set out in Indo-European languages. Can we really believe that only white Europeans are "advanced" enough to speak about dances?

The notion of 'tension' through the etymology of European words for dance does reveal something about the Western aesthetic of dance which is apparent from the Western dance ideals of "pull-up", "body lift" and "bodily extensions". Elsewhere these things are not highly valued. Indeed my "good" Western-trained body alignment and resultant tension is a handicap in performing dances from other cultures. Martin seems to have the greatest insight in the relativity of dance aesthetics when he describes dance as a universal "urge" but without a universal form (1946: 12). Further, he states

It is impossible to say that any of these approaches is exclusively right or wrong, better or worse than any other ... They are all absolutely right, therefore, for the specific circumstances under which they have been created (Martin 1946: 17).

Indeed, Martin comes the closest to the kind of relativity which most American anthropologists feel is necessary for observing and analyzing any aspect of culture and human behavior (see 1939: 92, 93 and 108). It is true that Sorell and others speak of differences caused by environment and other pertinent circumstances, but Sorell also ascribes much of the difference to "race", to "racial memory", and to "innate" differences which are "in the blood" (Sorell 1967: 75, 76, 275, 282 and 283). These ideas are so outdated in current anthropology that I might believe his book was written at the end of the 19th century rather than in 1967.

It is true that many cross-cultural differences in dance styles and dance aesthetics are due, both to genetically determined physical differences and learned cultural patterns. In some cases, the differences are clear. For example, a heavy Mojave Indian woman could not, nor would not perform the jumps of the Maasai people of East Africa. Other differences are not clear because they are part of a chicken/egg argument until further research is done and until more of the right questions are asked. We do not know, for example, whether people who squat easily with both feet flat on the ground do so because their leg tendons are genetically different from non-squatters, or if anyone could have the same tendon configuration if they habitually assumed such postures (see discussion in Martin 1939: 97). As for "innate" qualities, we have almost no real evidence. There is nothing to support claims such as "barefoot savages have an ear for rhythms most Europeans lack" (DeMille 1963: 48). There is much we do not know about bodies and genetics and cultural dynamics, and in addition, we are especially ignorant about systems of aesthetics. It would be wiser for Western dance scholars to leave qualifying remarks and open-endedness in their discussions of these things, or else these scholars may have a lot of recanting to do.

Two terms which now require discussion are "primitive dance" and "folk dance". These comments are to be understood against the framework of my definition of "dance" which I have already given.

British, and especially American, folklorists are concerned with defining the "folk" in order to know what "folk dances" are. Our dance scholars, on the other hand, usually use "folk dance" as a kind of catch-all term. For example, DeMille lists Azuma Kabuki under her chapter on folk dance companies (1963: 74). To call this highly refined theatrical form "folk dance" doesn't agree with Sorell's argument that folk dance is dance that has not gone "through a process of refinement"; that has not been "tamed" (Sorell 1967: 73). Perhaps such discrepancies help to show why definitions are so important and what a state of confusion can exist when we presume we all "mean the same thing".

Rather than following Sachs's contention that the "folk" or the "peasant" is an evolutionary stage between primitive and civilized man (Sachs 1937: 216), I shall follow the more anthropologically sophisticated distinctions which are discussed by the anthropologist Redfield in his book *Peasant Society and Culture* (1969: 23 and 40-41). In brief, a primitive society is an autonomous and self-contained system with its own set of customs and institutions. It may be isolated or it may have more or less contact with other systems. It is usually economically independent and people are often, if not always, non-literate.[1] In contrast, peasant or folk societies are not autonomous. Economically and culturally such a community is in a symbiotic relationship with a larger society with which it constantly interacts. It is the "little tradition of the largely unreflective many" which is incomplete without the "great tradition of the reflective few". Often the people in peasant societies are more or less illiterate. If one adds the word *dance* to the above descriptions of *primitive* and *folk* (or peasant) there might be a more objective agreement on what is meant by "primitive dance" and by "folk dance".

Another troublesome term is that of 'ethnic dance', as I have already indicated. In the generally accepted anthropological view, *ethnic* means a group which holds in common genetic, linguistic and cultural ties, with special emphasis on cultural tradition. By definition, therefore, every dance form must be an ethnic form. Although claims have been made for universal dance forms (such as Wisnoe Wardhana has been attempting to develop in Java: personal communication in 1960), or international forms, such as has been claimed for ballet (see Terry 1956: 187), in actuality neither a universal form nor a truly international form of dance is in existence and it is doubtful whether any such dance form can ever exist except in theory.

DeMille says this, in effect, when she writes that "theater always reflects the culture that produces it" (1963: 74). However others insist on some special properties for ballet. La Meri insists that "the ballet is not an ethnic dance because it is the product of the social customs and artistic reflections of several widely-differing national cultures" (1967: 339). Nevertheless, ballet is a product of the Western world, and it is a dance form developed by Caucasians who speak Indo-European languages and who share a common European tradition. Granted that ballet is international in that it "belongs" to European countries plus groups of European descendants in the Americas.

But, when ballet appears in such countries as Japan or Korea it becomes a borrowed and alien form. Granted also that ballet has had a complex history of influences, this does not undermine its effectiveness as an ethnic form. Martin tells us this, although he probably could not guess that his statement would be used for such a proof:

> The great spectacular dance form of the Western world is, of course, the ballet ... Properly, the term ballet refers to a particular form of theater dance, which came into being in the Renaissance and which has a tradition, technic [sic] and an aesthetic basis all its own (1939: 173).

Further quotations could be made to show the ethnicity of ballet, such as Kirstein's opening remarks in (1935: vii).

Ethnicity of the Ballet

I have made listings of the themes and other characteristics of ballet and ballet performances, and these lists show over and over again just how "ethnic" ballet is. Consider for example, how Western is the tradition of the proscenium stage, the usual three part performance which lasts for about two hours, our star system, our use of curtain calls and applause, and our usage of French terminology. Think how culturally revealing it is to see the stylized Western customs enacted on the stage, such as the mannerisms from the age of chivalry, courting, weddings, christenings, burial and mourning customs. Think how our world view is revealed in the oft recurring themes of unrequited love, sorcery, self-sacrifice through long-suffering, mistaken identity, and misunderstandings which have tragic consequences. Think how our religious heritage is revealed through pre-Christian customs such as *Walpurgisnacht*, through the use of Biblical themes, Christian holidays such as Christmas, and the beliefs in life after death. Our cultural heritage is revealed also in the roles which appear repeatedly in our ballets such as humans transformed into animals, fairies, witches, gnomes, performers of evil magic, villains and seductresses in black, evil step-parents, royalty and peasants, and especially, beautiful pure young women and their consorts.

Our aesthetic values are shown in the long line of lifted,

extended bodies, in the total revealing of legs, of small heads and tiny feet for women, in slender bodies for both sexes, and in the coveted airy quality which is best shown in the lifts and carryings of the female [dancers]. To us this is tremendously pleasing aesthetically, but there are societies whose members would be shocked at the public display of the male touching the female's thighs! So distinctive is the "look" of ballet, that it is probably safe to say that ballet dances graphically rendered by silhouettes would never be mistaken for anything else. An interesting proof of this is the ballet *Koshare* which was based on a Hopi Indian story. In silhouettes of even still photos, the dance looked like ballet and not like a Hopi dance.

The ethnicity of ballet is revealed also in the kinds of flora and fauna which appear regularly. Horses and swans are esteemed fauna. In contrast we have no tradition of esteeming for theatrical purposes pigs, sharks, eagles, buffalo or crocodiles even though these are indeed highly esteemed animals used in dance themes elsewhere in the world. In ballet, grains, roses and lilies are suitable flora, but we would not likely find much call for taro, yams, coconuts, acorns or squash blossoms. Many economic pursuits are reflected in the roles played in ballet such as spinners, foresters, soldiers, even factory workers, sailors and filling station attendants. However, we would not expect to find pottery makers, canoe builders, grain pounders, llama herders, giraffe stalkers, or slash and burn agriculturists.

The question is not whether ballet reflects its own heritage. The question is why we seem to need to believe that ballet has somehow become a-cultural. Why are we afraid to call it an ethnic form?

The answer, I believe, is that Western dance scholars have not used the word *ethnic* in its objective sense, they have used it as a euphemism for such old-fashioned terms as *heathen*, *pagan*, *savage*, or the more recent term *exotic*. When the term *ethnic* began to be used widely in the 1930s, there apparently arose a problem in trying to refer to dance forms which came from "high" cultures such as India and Japan, and the term "ethnologic" gained its current meaning for dance scholars such as Sorell (1967: 72), Terry (1956: 187, 196), and La Meri (1949: 177-178).[2] I do not know why La Meri chose to discard this usage and substituted the word "ethnic" for "ethnologic" in her 1967 version of the *Dance Encyclopedia* article. She did not otherwise change her article, and since it was originally written with the above-mentioned dichotomy implicit in her discussion, her 1967 version becomes illogical.[3]

It is not clear to me who first created the dichotomy between *ethnic dance* and *ethnologic* dance. Certainly this dichotomy is meaningless to anthropologists. As a matter of fact, European cultural anthropologists often prefer to call themselves ethnologists, and for them the term "ethnologic" refers to the objects of their study (see Haselberger's discussion of 1961: 341). The term "ethnological" does not have much currency among American cultural anthropologists although they understand the term to mean "of or relating to ethnology", and "ethnology" deals with the comparative and analytical study of cultures. Because "culture", in a simplified anthropological sense, includes all of the learned behavior and customs of any given group of people, there is no such thing as a culture-less people. Therefore ethnological dances should refer to a variety of dance cultures subject to comparison and analysis. Ethnic dance should mean a dance form of a given group of people who share common genetic, linguistic and cultural ties, as mentioned before. In the most precise usage it is a redundancy to speak of an ethnic dance, since any dance could fit that description. The term is most valid when used in a collective and contrastive way.[4]

Apparently one pan-human trait is to divide the world into "we" and "they". The Greeks did this when "they" [non-Greeks] were called *barbarians*. Similarly, the Romans called [non-Romans] "they", i.e. *pagans*, Hawaiians call "they", *kanaka'e*, and Hopis call [non-Hopis] *bahana*. All of these terms imply not only foreign [beings] but creatures who are uncouth, unnatural, ignorant and, in short, less than human.

The yardstick for measuring humanity, of course, is the "we". "We" are always good, civilized, superior, in short, "we" are the only creatures worthy of being considered fully human. This phenomenon reveals the world view of the speakers in every language, so far as I know. Often the phenomenon is very dramatic. According to a scholar of Mandarin [Chinese] and Japanese languages, in Mandarin, "they" are truly "foreign devils", and in Japanese "they" are "outsiders".

I suggest that, due to the social climate which rejects the connotations with which our former words for "they" [and "them"] were invested, and because of a certain sophistication assumed by the apologists for these terms, English-speaking scholars were hard-pressed to find designators for the kinds of non-Western dance which they wished to discuss. Hence the euphemistic terms *ethnic* and *ethnologic* seemed to serve that purpose.

It is perfectly legitimate to use "ethnic" and "ethnologic" as long as we don't let those terms become connotative of the very things which caused us to abandon the other older terms. We should indeed speak of *ethnic dance forms*, and we should not believe that this term is derisive when it includes ballet since ballet reflects the cultural traditions from which it developed.

I must make it clear that I am critical of our foremost Western dance scholars only where they have stepped outside their field of authority. Within their fields they command my great respect, and I would not want to argue their relative merits. Scholars that they are, they will agree with me, I feel confident, that whatever are the rewards of scholarship, comfortable complacency cannot be one of them.

[JWK]

PRECIS EXERCISE 1

¹It is good anthropology to think of ballet as a form of ethnic ²dance. Currently, that idea is unacceptable to most Western ³dance scholars. This lack of agreement shows clearly that ⁴something is amiss ...
⁵By ethnic dance, anthropologists mean to convey the idea ⁶that all forms of dance reflect the cultural traditions within ⁷which they developed. Dancers and dance scholars ... use ⁸this term, and the related terms *ethnologic, primitive* and folk ⁹dance, differently and ... in a way which reveals their lim-¹⁰ited knowledge of non-Western dance forms.
¹¹This survey of the literature reveals an amazing divergence ¹²of opinions. We are able to read that the origin of dance ¹³was in play and that it was not in play, that it was for magi-¹⁴cal and religious purposes, and that it was not for those ¹⁵things; that it was for courtship and that it was not for court-¹⁶ship; that it was the first form of communication and com-¹⁷munication did not enter into dance until it became an 'art'. ¹⁸In addition we can read that it was serious and purposeful ¹⁹and that at the same time it was an outgrowth of exuber-²⁰ance, was totally spontaneous, and originated in the spirit ²¹of fun. Moreover, we can read that it was only a group ac-²²tivity for tribal solidarity and that it was strictly for the ²³pleasure and self-expression of the one dancing. We can ²⁴learn also, that animals danced before Man did, and yet ²⁵that dance is a human activity.
²⁶It has been a long time since anthropologists concerned ²⁷themselves with unknowable origins, and I will not add ²⁸another origin theory for the dance, because I don't know ²⁹anyone who was there. Our dance writers, however, sug-³⁰gest evidence for origins from archaeological finds, and ³¹from models exemplified by contemporary primitive ³²groups. For the first, one must remember that Man had ³³been on this earth for a long time before he made cave paint-³⁴ings and statuary, so that archaeological finds can hardly

[35]tell us about the beginnings of dances. For the second set [36]of evidence, that of using models from contemporary [37]"primitives", one must not confuse the word primitive with [38]primæval, even though one author actually does equate [39]these two terms. ... About the dances of primeval Man we [40]really know nothing. About *primitive* dances and dancing [41]we know a great deal. The first thing we know is that there [42]is no such thing as *a* primitive dance. There *are* dances [43]performed by primitives, and they are too varied to fit any stereotype. ...

[44]It is a gross error to think of groups of peoples or their [45]dances as being monolithic wholes. "The African Dance" [46]never existed; there are, however, Dahomean dances, Hausa [47]dances, Maasai dances, and so forth.

[48]"The American Indian" is a fiction and so is a prototype of [49]"Indian dance". There are, however, Iroquois, Kwakiutl, [50]and Hopis, to name a few, and they all have dances.

[51]Despite all anthropological evidence to the contrary, how-[52]ever, Western dance scholars set themselves up as authori-[53]ties on the characteristics of "primitive" dance. Sorell com-[54]bines most of these so-called characteristics of the primi-[55]tive stereotype. He tells us that primitive dancers have no [56]technique, and no artistry, but that they are "unfailing mas-[57]ters of their bodies"! He states that their dances are disor-[58]ganized and frenzied, but that they are able to translate all [59]their feelings and emotions into movement! He claims the [60]dances are spontaneous but also purposeful!

[61]Primitive dances, he tells us, are serious but social! He [62]claims that they have "complete freedom" but that men [63]and women can't dance together. He qualifies that last state-[64]ment by saying that men and women dance together after [65]the dance degenerates into an orgy! Sorell also asserts that [66]primitives cannot distinguish between the concrete and the [67]symbolic, that they dance for every occasion, and that they [68]stamp around a lot! Further, Sorell asserts that dance in [69]primitive societies is a special prerogative of males, espe-[70]cially chieftains, shamans and witch doctors.

Exercises

I. On a separate sheet of paper, define these terms:
•ethnic [lines 1 and 5]; •ethnologic [line 8]; •technique [56]; •primitive(s) [8, 31, 37, 42, 43, 53-4-5, 61, 66, 69]; •Kwakiutl [48]; •primæval [38, 39]; •exuberance [19-20]; •monolithic [45]; •spontaneous [20]; •stereotype [43, 53].

II. On a separate sheet of paper, answer the questions *in your own words* :
1. What do anthropologists mean by "ethnic dance"? [lines 5-7].
2. Dancers and dance scholars also use the terms *ethnic, ethnologic* and *primitive,* but in such a way that it proves what? [lines 8-10].
3. In lines 13 and 14, the author says her survey of literature showed a "divergence of opinions" about dances. Around what points do these divergences turn? [Lines 12-25].
4. [Lines 44-47] What would *you* say to someone who asked you to tell them about "African dance"?
5. "It has been a long time since anthropologists concerned themselves with unknowable origins, and I will not add another origin theory for the dance, because I don't know anyone who was there" [Lines 26-29]. In **200 words or less,** explain why you think the author said this about origins arguments.

III. Finally, in **150 words or less,** summarize (make a précis of) the main points the author made in the 70 lines above. Use your own words.

READING II

BIOGRAPHICAL NOTES: Anya Peterson Royce was born in California. She did both Master's and Doctoral work in anthropology at the University of California, Berkeley and her Doctoral degree was conferred in 1974. She had met Keali'inohomoku (before the latter went to Indiana) in Tucson, Arizona at a CORD [Congress on Research of Dance] conference. She subsequently met Kaeppler and Hanna in 1974 at a conference, *New Directions in the Anthropology of Dance* that she convened in Bloomington, Indiana for which there are no proceedings. The fact of the meeting is, however, recorded in Kaeppler (1978).

Royce danced professionally in ballet in San Francisco and New York City. Her particular area of interest is in Latin America, particularly Mexico. She conducted research into mime and ballet in Poland, France and Italy during the 'eighties ... Dr. Royce is a Professor of Anthropology at Indiana University and has also held administrative positions there such as Director of Latin American Studies and Vice Chancellor for Academic Affairs (updated from Williams 1986: 172-173).

The extracts below, with minor editorial changes, are taken from her book: **Royce, A. P. 1977.** *The Anthropology of Dance.* Indiana University Press, Bloomington. Reprinted by permission of Indiana University Press, Bloomington, Indiana.

Extract # 1

What we, as anthropologists, must consider are people's perceptions and explanations of the features that make up their particular universe. This, at least, is the starting point from which all further analysis, comparison, and generalization proceeds. Therefore, with dances, as with other aspects of human behavior, we look for the culturally relevant definition.

Let us take some examples of culturally relevant definitions of the dance which may not correspond to definitions derived from a basically Western point of view. In speaking of the Australian Aborigines of northeastern Arnhem Land, Waterman tells us that the word which comes closest to our word 'dance' is *bongol* but that this includes music as well as dance. At the same time, *bongol* may be used in a narrower sense than we would find comfortable where it excludes the patterned steps and movements of some of the sacred ceremonies and of certain activities of children's age groups.

The inclusion of music, dance, games, instruments, festivals, and so on within one word is not at all uncommon. In pre-Columbian Mexico, for example, music and dance were linked quite closely, both in thought and in practice, and this is still true of indigenous Mexico today. In Mixtec, the word *yaa* means "dance, game, and music". Further, the same adjectives are often applied to both music and dances. *Kaa / saa* means "high, loud, and strong" when applied to voices; it also means "to sound a high-pitched, loud, or metallic wind instrument", and "to jump" when applied to the dancing (Stanford 1966: 103). Isthmus Zapotec makes no distinction between "festival" and "music", both being translated as *saa*.

It is not only the non-Western languages and cultures that include several phenomena under one term. Take, for example, the phrase "going to a dance" as it is used in the U.S. The term "dance" here encompasses many things besides the actual physical activity. It includes the music, the interaction with other participants, the refreshments, indeed, the entire ambiance of the event. In fact, dancing may be the least important of the activities found at a dance.

The opposite kind of use also occurs, where 'dance' is used in a more exclusive sense than we might wish to define it. Generally this takes the form of more than one term for the activities we might classify simply as 'dance'. Frequently the several terms describe the different contexts of the dance. Spanish, for example, has two words for dance, *danza* and *baile*, which refer to dance as a ritual activity (*danza*) and secular dance (*baile*). Italian makes the same distinction with *danza* and *ballo*. In the classical dance traditions of India, a distinction is made between *nrtta*, 'pure dance', and *nrtya*, 'pantomimic dance'. The danger for the anthropologist looking at dances in unfamiliar cultures lies in the possibility of remaining unaware of the total range of danced activity. For example, should one formulate all questions regarding the dance using the term *ballo*, he or she would probably only learn about popular dances. ...

We have seen thus far that there are at least two possible kinds of definitions of the word 'dance'; those constructed by dance scholars and those meaningful to specific cultures. I have also indicated the problems in trying to reconcile the two kinds of definitions. Part of our difficulty in coming to terms with definitions is our tendency to separate the form of a dance from its context, and whether consciously or not, to use form as the primary basis for definitions. We can resolve much of this difficulty by thinking in terms of dance events (see Keali'inohomoku 1973) rather than of 'dances' and 'dancing'. To illustrate the advantages of taking whole events as the unit of analysis rather than individual dances, I will discuss weddings and the dances associated with them among the Isthmus Zapotec of Mexico.

The Zapotec [who] number around 250,000, are located almost exclusively in the state of Oaxaca. The Isthmus Zapotec live in the southern portion of Oaxaca along the Pacific coast portion of the Isthmus of Tehuantepec. Although they are primarily town and small city dwellers in a culturally heterogeneous area, they actively maintain an identity as Zapotec. One of the features of Zapotec identity is the dance form known as the *son* and one of the occasions that calls forth the dancing of *sones* is the wedding. By observing enough dance behavior at weddings, you can begin to say what is the minimal amount of dance essential, what is usual, and what are the outside limits. As a minimum, the sponsor of the young couple hires one band which can play both *sones* and *piezas* (these terms refer both to the music, the dance and the lyrics, if any; a *son* is a traditional dance form while a *pieza* is any Western social dance). *Sones* and *piezas* are played and danced alternately throughout the festivities. At a certain point during the afternoon the bride and groom must begin the *mediu xhiga*, a special *son* performed only at weddings. Without these kinds of dances, the *sones*, the *piezas*, and the *mediu xhiga*, the event is not considered a proper wedding.

There are additional dances which may be done but which do not figure in the minimal definition of wedding. These include *La Cola* and *La Escoba* (literally, The Tail and The Broom), both of which are non-couple dances, unlike *sones* and *piezas*. In certain weddings the political and social interests of the various parties may encourage a demonstration of Zapotec ethnic identity. In such circumstances the proportion of *sones* danced increases greatly in relation to the number of *piezas*. Weddings of wealthy persons usually involve a greater number of both kinds of dances, as well as of *La Cola* and *La Escoba*. Only the performance of the *mediu xhiga* remains invariable: it is performed once, and only once, at every wedding. The selection and sequence of dances at a Zapotec wedding make sense within the total context of Zapotec culture, and any changes in the selection or sequence give you information you would not have if you viewed each dance as an isolated occurrence.

One might argue that what I have described is not a dance event but a wedding event. First, since one cannot have a wedding without dances [in this context], the dance event and the wedding event are in a certain sense the same thing. Second, there are very few danced events where the dance is the only feature. Even where dances are performed in a theatrical setting, which is probably the closest thing to a pure dance event, there is the crucial factor of interaction between dancers and non-dancers. One simply has to observe those occasions where dances are performed and observe them in their entirety.

The real difficulty lies not in distinguishing the danced event *per se*, but rather in drawing boundaries around events or situations. Again, the analyst's divisions may be arbitrary and so once again we must discover the boundaries that are culturally meaningful. To the analyst a Zapotec wedding may be four days of feasting, dancing, processions, and religious and civil ceremonies. To a Zapotec, however, a wedding may have been a year in the making. If the wedding is by petition rather than by elopement, then it might begin with the asking for the bride by the groom's family and friends; it might include all the reciprocal visiting to settle matters; it would include the baking and distribution of the invitational bread without which one cannot have a wedding; it would include all the arrangements with the church and civil authorities; and, finally, it would culminate with the four days of *fiesta*.

In his article on Subunun religion Frake is concerned essentially with criteria for ethnographic adequacy. He holds that making an ethnographic statement includes at least the following tasks:

> 1. Discovering the major categories of events or 'scenes' of the culture; 2. Defining the scenes so that observed interactions, acts, objects, and places can be assigned to their proper scenes as roles, routines, paraphernalia, and settings; 3. Stating the distribution of scenes with respect to one another, that is, providing instructions for anticipating or planning for scenes (1964: 112).

Here Frake argues for defining major categories of events and thus is referring to categories which have meaning for the particular culture. A culture may or may not have a major category that corresponds to a dance event. It is the business of the researcher to discover that by observing and questioning rather than to create arbitrary dance event categories by the imposition of his or her own definitions or perceptions.

It may prove useful to proceed further to something Keali'inohomoku has called "dance culture". She defines this as

> [A]n entire configuration, rather than just a performance ... the implicit as well as explicit aspects of the dance and its reasons for being; the entire conception of the dance within the larger culture, both on a diachronic basis through time and on a synchronic basis of the several parts occurring at the same time (1974: 99).

It remains only to go one more step, as Merriam does, and conclude that "dance is culture and culture is dance" and the "entity of dance is not separable from the anthropological concept of culture" (1974: 17). This is the great strength of the anthropological approach to the dance. It is the only way of measuring the true significance of the dance in any group or society because it is the only approach that looks at the totality into which danced events fit. The difficulty is, of course, that in order to say anything at all about dances other than impressionistic statements one has to analyze them, that is, separate them from the rest of culture, as Merriam says, "take the phenomenon to pieces in the hope of finding out what makes it tick" (1974: 18). It is hoped that this can be accomplished without doing violence to the phenomenon.

Related to this process of separating the threads that comprise the fabric of culture, and related also to the danced event, is the problem of determining the significance of the dance in any particular society or culture. It is obvious that not all aspects of culture are given equal weight. As Benedict observed in 1934, there exists a metaphorical arc of possibilities from which each culture selects. Some cultures give prominence to the dance just as others puzzle endlessly over the complexities of a segmentary lineage system. It has been suggested that the dance is "most significant in societies that are least literate, i.e., non-literate" and further that "dance functions in some cultures, with as broad a spectrum of functions as the written word includes for others" (Snyder 1974: 213-214). I would amend this to say that I perceive differences in kinds of dance and in the functions of dance within literate and non-literate societies but that I cannot see a difference in significance that is correlated with the presence or absence of literacy. Why it is that some societies give a prominent role to the dance while others do not, I do not think we can say at this point. What we can do is to note the differing emphases and document the differing functions. ... (Royce 1977: 9-14).

Extract # 2

[The] dance has met various fates at the hands of anthropologists over the past one hundred years. Speaking very broadly, we can identify five approaches popular at different times in the United States which have dealt quite differently with the dance. In chronological order they are 1) the evolutionary approach; 2) the culture trait approach; 3) the culture and personality and culture configuration approach; 4) the problem-oriented approach in complex and plural societies, and 5) the approach that focuses on the dance as a unique phenomenon.

Evolutionists on both sides of the Atlantic, who posited a series of stages through which all societies progressed, viewed [the] dance as an essential part of primitive culture. As might be expected, they also held that primitive dances were just as rudimentary and lacking in symmetry and grace as the rest of primitive culture. Most dancing by primitives was thought to be associated with ritual, which in turn was seen as marking every important aspect of life. One has an image of primitive man weighed down by the awful burden of ritual, unable to take, or dance, a step without it. Sir James Frazer documented dances in various eras and locations as being part of homeopathic magic[al] rites; the latter, he suggests, belongs to an early stage of evolution. He tells us, for example, that in Transylvania dancers leap high in the air in order to make the crops grow tall; elsewhere women jump over newly planted crops to insure the latter's fertility; among the Omaha Indians the Buffalo Society held rainmaking rites which involved spilling containers of water. Similar to this view is the one that Martha Beckwith presents in her comparison of Moqui and Kwakiutl dances. She speaks of the imitative use of dancing to bring about a desired result, in this case the acquisition of power . ...

Edward Tylor associated possession dances with a primitive state of religion. ... Many of the early anthropologists and scholars in America dealt with the American Indian. By and large their view was that the Indian represented an early stage in the evolutionary schema. Dances of these people would predictably be primitive and integral to their culture. We also find the sentiment that as people progressed to the next stages their dances would be abandoned as a form of exercise not befitting civilized or rational man. One scholar holding such a view was Henry Schoolcraft, who was also responsible for the collecting of much dance data in the United States during the last half of the19th century. ... In the same year [1851] Lewis Henry Morgan, in his book on the League of the Iroquois, expressed much the same feelings as Schoolcraft when he commented:

> These amusements [music and dance] of our primitive inhabitants are not, in themselves, devoid of interest, although they indicate a tendency of mind unbefitting rational men (1962, originally published in 1851: 289-290).

[In America] the emphasis had shifted from the view that held that all societies and cultures progressed through the same series of stages to one which said that each society and culture was the result of a unique combination of history and environment. This was a view that encouraged the culture trait approach. Followers of this approach collected information about all cultural traits rather than selecting a small number which were identified as more significant than the others. Dance study fared quite well in this atmosphere. Some of the tenets of this school are revealed clearly in statements made about the dance; in particular, the belief which saw each culture as being a unique combination of traits and circumstances. Boas, for example, emphasized the importance of dance in Kwakiutl society:

> Song and dance accompany all events of Kwakiutl life ... and they are an essential part in the culture of the people. ... Although there are expert performers, everyone is obliged to take part in the singing and dancing, so that the separation between performer and audience that we find in our modern society does not occur in more primitive society such as that represented by the Kwakiutl Indians (1944: 10).

Leslie Spier argued for the uniqueness of cultures when he spoke of various manifestations of the Sun Dance:

> The [various] sun dances are not merely aggregates of diffused elements: the ideas locally injected to integrate the whole and the rituals originated have transformed them into something unique. How each tribe has made the ceremony peculiarly its own cannot be determined for want of precise historical data. But an approach is possible by recasting the question: in how far does the sun dance conform to preexisting ceremonial patterns? (in Mead and Bunzel 1960: 392; from Spier 1921: 505).

Along with the view that every culture was unique in some respect went the related belief that each culture should be valued for itself. The cultural relativism was, of course, also applied to the dances of cultures, thereby presenting an attitude very different from that voiced by the evolutionists. Paul Radin articulated this changed attitude in a statement about the Medicine Dance of the Winnebago:

> In other words, the Medicine Dance from the viewpoint of its leaders at least, was a drama depicting the ideal life and depicting it in terms of a myth from which all the coarser implications of its episodes had been completely obliterated. Such a highly artificial drama can manifestly represent the achievement only of men who have thought deeply on the meaning of life, who possessed the artistic skill to articulate their vision and leisure in which to do it, not to mention an audience that was willing to accept it ... (1957: 305).

With the influence of Freud and psychoanalysis in the early 1920s, anthropology in the United States took a new direction. The Culture and Personality school stands as an exemplar of the change in anthropology. Abandoned were the concerns with historical factors and with trait lists. Description was important only insofar as it illuminated theoretical concerns. Rather than being unique agglomerations of traits and history, cultures were seen through the lenses of pattern and configuration. Ruth Benedict's *Patterns of Culture*, published in 1934, typifies these concerns. She posits an arc of elements from which all cultures select. Cultures then combine these elements in certain ways so that the result is a configuration. Because of limited possibilities for combinations and elements, certain patterns are repeated over and over. Also, cultures can be characterized according to psychological set.

Benedict speaks in the very broadest sense of two psychological types, Apollonian and Dionysian. To illustrate she describes the Hopi as being essentially Apollonian and the Kwakiutl and Dobu as being Dionysian. ... Margaret Mead's *Coming of Age in Samoa*, first published in 1928, is an excellent example. Mead talks about Samoan dances because in Samoan society, where conformity is the norm, the dance provides the one area where individualism is tolerated. ... In studies of this kind, dances were discussed only if they contributed to an explanation of the personality structure of individuals within cultures or to psychologically oriented explanations of cultural patterns. The form of the dance was sketched briefly and in very general terms, if at all.

The notable exception to the overall pattern of psychologically-oriented research is the extensive body of literature on dissociational states and the dance that frequently accompanies them. Dance, both in form and in context, looms large in many of these studies. It is still viewed as a universal cultural phenomenon; we can say that the habit of looking for pattern above the level of individual societies that characterized the culture and personality school remained to distinguish these later studies as well. The comments of Erika Bourguignon are relevant here:

> Ecstatic dance ... represents a vital form of human expression in the context of particular, larger, cultural wholes. It must be seen in each instance within that cultural whole, yet we must be aware that it represents not merely a particular local invention, but a local utilization of a universal human capacity which has been used in many societies throughout human history (1968: 60).

Anthropologists began expanding their horizons after the 1930s to include the study of urban settings, plural societies, and Western industrialized societies. This was a gradual process of re-educating both scholars and the public, who carried in their minds an image of the anthropologist as that person who studied the exotic, the faraway, the primitive. ...

The new kinds of studies did not aim at simple description of small, relatively homogeneous situations, nor did they focus upon social structure as the key to unlock a treasure chest of general laws of society. Neither were they interested in cataloguing societies according to personality types. Anthropological investigations now were rapidly becoming problem-oriented. Many dealt with problems brought about by urbanization or industrialization. Others focused upon situations where formerly isolated groups were exposed to one another and were forced to develop strategies for coping with a radically different social setting. New methods appeared to deal with the change of subject matter, two of which were situational analysis and social drama. The first is a concept that isolates "temporally and spatially bounded series of events ... from the on-going flow of social life" (Garbett 1970: 215). It is useful, as Van Velsen has noted, "as a method of integrating variations, exceptions, and accidents into descriptions of regularities. ... Situational analysis, with its emphasis on process, might therefore be particularly suited for the study of unstable and non-homogeneous societies (Van Velsen 1967: 143).

The method of focusing upon drama is closely linked to

that of situational analysis. Dramatic events range from a
heated quarrel in the fish market to the pomp surrounding
the opening of a new bridge to actual dramatic, dance, or
musical performances. What all social drama shares is an
intensification or exaggeration of ordinary behavior. These
kinds of events allow an outsider to see values stated forcefully. On this basis one may then begin to say something
about priorities with regard to values and rules for behavior; one may order the cultural rules. Dances are frequently
the central activity in events of this nature. An example from
the Zapotec of Juchitán will illustrate the illumination and
ordering of cultural rules that one might observe in a danced
situation.

Every year the Zapotec of Juchitán send a delegation of
dancers to the Guelaguetza in Oaxaca City, the state capital.
Delegations from the various indigenous groups in the state
perform traditional dances and music on the occasion of the
Guelaguetza. The Juchitán delegation in the summer of 1972
consisted of twelve dancers, six women and six men. Selection of the dancers ... is always based on a number of factors. The women tend to come from the older, wealthier families. More specifically, they tend to come from families who
are currently aligned with the political powers in the city.
Dancing ability is also a factor, and, generally speaking, those
chosen are among the better dancers in the city. Men are selected after the women have been chosen, and their selection is primarily a function of friendship with the women
dancers, willingness to take part, and dancing ability.

Once the dancers have been chosen, rehearsals begin. It is
one of these rehearsals that I offer as an example of a dramatic event. The dancers were rehearsing the *fandango*, an
open couple dance that is regarded as one of the most traditional of the Zapotec dances. The music and the dance alternate between fast and slow sections. The beginning of each
section is marked by an exchange of places between the man
and the woman. As the *fandango* progressed, it became apparent that two couples were changing places when the

change in music occurred while four couples were beginning the exchange two measure before the change in the music. Maria Luisa (all names have been changed), an older dancer who has frequently been a delegate to the Guelaguetza and who is the acknowledged expert on the matter of dancing, corrected her young cousin, Elena, who was a member of one of the two couples. According to all the cultural rules about deference to age and expert knowledge, Elena should have accepted the correction. Instead, she contended that she and Julia were correct. Furthermore, she said that she was following the example of Beatrice, Maria Luisa's grandmother and a woman regarded as one of the finest dancers in Juchitán.

Elena became more and more excited and angry, and the rest of the dancers reacted more or less according to Zapotec standards of behavior. The men took themselves off to one corner of the courtyard, where they ignored the proceedings, smoking and talking among themselves. Julia from time to time supported Elena by comments and nods since Julia, too, would lose face if Maria Luisa's correction was accepted. Pilar, the second oldest woman and best friend of Maria Luisa, voiced her support of Maria Luisa's opinion. Antonia and Teresa stood to one side waiting for the outcome but prepared, if necessary, to support Maria Luisa since both … came from families with social status lower than that of Maria Luisa's family. Their families receive favors from the more prestigious family of Maria Luisa in return for support.

Everyone was embarrassed. When it became obvious that Elena only became more vocally adamant when subjected to pressure in front of the others, Maria Luisa and Pilar took her aside. This action was prompted by two Zapotec cultural values. One value holds that public disagreements and expressions of emotion should be limited to certain ritual kinds of situations. The second, and perhaps more crucial on this occasion, holds that one's allegiance belongs first to family. The women of the delegation represented two of the oldest families in Juchitán who have a long tradition of rivalry. One family, the Gómez, was represented by Maria Luisa, Pilar, Elena, and indirectly by Antonia and Teresa. The other family, the Martínez, was represented only by Julia. Her position was strengthened, however, by the fact that her cousin was the municipal president and she herself was the director of the *Casa de la Cultura*, an institution whose purpose is to celebrate Zapotec tradition. Nonetheless, the branch of the Martínez family represented by Julia was regarded by the Gómez as being relative newcomers to the city and therefore none of its members could be regarded as an authority on Zapotec tradition. Dances, and especially the *fandango*, are one of the most significant items of Zapotec tradition.

In the whispered dialogue Elena was reminded of all the great Gómez dancers in an attempt to prod her into doing the appropriate thing, namely acknowledging the Gómez superiority as represented by its oldest member on that occasion, Maria Luisa. Elena stubbornly refused. She said she would not be satisfied until Beatrice herself supported changing places two measures before the musical change. This put an end to the afternoon's rehearsal. Gómez and Gómez supporters went to consult Beatrice. Everyone agreed to meet for another rehearsal within the next few days. ... At the next rehearsal the Gómez family presented a united front for their version of the *fandango*. Julia argued for her version tacitly using the weight of her position with the *Casa de la Cultura*. She quickly abandoned her cause when it was suggested that all the dancers adopt Julia's version since the Gómez version admittedly was much more difficult, and the object was to have dances that all the dancers could perform well ... it became obvious to me that both versions were acceptable variants of the *fandango*. The cultural values being upheld on the occasion of the rehearsal were those of Gómez superiority and the necessity to show family allegiance and unity. That Elena was the youngest Gómez involved in the dispute made the resolution simpler because age brings with it respect and authority. Youth is accorded little of either. Elena's

protest was the protest of youth against age and authority.
That she made it in a public situation where a rival family
was involved caused the result to be as firm as it was inevi-
table. ... (Royce 1977: 19-31).

[APR]

PRECIS EXERCISE 2

[1][In the U. S.] the emphasis had shifted from the view
[2]that held that all societies and cultures progressed through
[3]the same series of stages to one which said that each society
[4]and culture was the result of a unique combination of his-
[5]tory and environment. This was a view that encouraged the
[6]culture trait approach. Followers of this approach collected
[7]information about all cultural traits rather than selecting a
[8]small number which were identified as more significant than
[9]the others. Dance study fared quite well in this atmosphere.
[10]Some of the tenets of this school are revealed clearly in
[11]statements made about the dance; in particular, the belief
[12]which saw each culture as being a unique combination of
[13]traits and circumstances. Boas, for example, emphasized
[14]the importance of dance in Kwakiutl society. ...
[15]With the influence of Freud and psychoanalysis in the early
[16]1920s, anthropology in the United States took a new di-
[17]rection. The Culture and Personality school stands as an
[18]exemplar of the change in anthropology. Abandoned were
[19]the concerns with historical factors and with trait lists. De-
[20]scription was important only insofar as it illuminated theo-
[21]retical concerns. Rather than being unique agglomerations
[22]of traits and history, cultures were seen through the lenses
[23]of pattern and configuration. Ruth Benedict's *Patterns of*
[24]*Culture*, published in 1934, typifies these concerns. She pos-
[25]its an arc of elements from which all cultures select. Cul-
[26]tures then combine these elements in certain ways so that
[27]the result is a configuration. Because of limited possibili-
[28]ties for combinations and elements, certain patterns are re-

[29]peated over and over. Also, cultures can be characterized [30]according to psychological set. Benedict speaks in the very [31]broadest sense of two psychological types, Apollonian and [32]Dionysian. To illustrate she describes the Hopi as being es-[33]sentially Apollonian and the Kwakiutl and Dobu as being [34]Dionysian. ...

[35]Margaret Mead's *Coming of Age in Samoa*, first published [36]in 1928, is an excellent example. Mead talks about Samoan [37]dances because in Samoan society, where conformity is the [38]norm, the dance provides the one area where individual-[39]ism is tolerated. ... In studies of this kind, dances were [40]discussed only if they contributed to an explanation of the [41]personality structure of individuals within cultures or to [42]psychologically oriented explanations of cultural patterns. [43]The form of the dance was sketched briefly and in very [44]general terms, if at all.

[45]The notable exception to the overall pattern of psychologi-[46]cally-oriented research is the extensive body of literature [47]on dissociational states and the dance that frequently ac-[48]companies them. Dance, both in form and in context, looms [49]large in many of these studies. It is still viewed as a univer-[50]sal cultural phenomenon; we can say that the habit of look-[51]ing for pattern above the level of individual societies that [52]characterized the culture and personality school remained [53]to distinguish these later studies as well.

[54]Anthropologists began expanding their horizons after the [55]1930s to include the study of urban settings, plural societ-[56]ies, and Western industrialized societies. This was a gradual [57]process of re-educating both scholars and the public, who [58]carried in their minds an image of the anthropologist as [59]that person who studied the exotic, the faraway, the primi-[60]tive. ... The new kinds of studies did not aim at simple [61]description of small, relatively homogeneous situations, nor [62]did they focus upon social structure as the key to unlock a [63]treasure chest of general laws of society. Neither were they [64]interested in cataloguing societies according to personal-[65]ity types. Anthropological investigations now were rap-

[66]idly becoming problem-oriented. Many dealt with prob-
[67]lems brought about by urbanization or industrialization.
[68]Others focused upon situations where formerly isolated
[69]groups were exposed to one another and were forced to
[70]develop strategies for coping with a radically different so-
[71]cial setting. New methods appeared to deal with the change
[72]of subject matter, two of which were situational analysis
[73]and social drama. The first is a concept that isolates "tem-
[74]porally and spatially bounded series of events ... from the
[75]on-going flow of social life" ... It is useful, as Van Velsen
[76]has noted, "as a method of integrating variations, excep-
[77]tions, and accidents into descriptions of regularities ... Situ-
[78]ational analysis, with its emphasis on process, might there-
[79]fore be particularly suited for the study of unstable and
[80]non-homogeneous societies.

Exercises

I. Do you know what these words mean?
   •trait(s) [lines 6, 7, 13, 19, 22]; •exemplar [line 18]; •agglom-
erations [21]; •configuration [23, 27]; •Apollonian [31, 33];
•Dionysian [32, 34]; •individualism [38-9]; •process [57, 78];
•pattern [23, 28, 42, 45, 51]; •norm [38]; •dissociation (-al) [47];
•temporal (-ally) [73-4]; •homogeneous [61, 80];

II. On a separate sheet of paper, answer these questions in your
own words:
   1. How many different changes of theoretical perspective in
   American anthropology does Royce talk about? [lines 1-73].
   2. What was the main idea Benedict put forward? [lines 21-34].
   3. What distinguished the culture-personality school in
   America? [lines 15-21].
   4. What was the anthropologist's popular image around the
   1930's? [lines 57-60].
   5. Two new methods appeared to deal with changes in subject
   matter. What were they? [lines 71-80].

III. (a): In **100 words or less,** state what is the main point of the whole passage [lines 1-80].

(b): Why is the passage important to students of the anthropology of the dance and human movement?

IV. In **200-250 words or less,** summarize (write a précis of) the whole passage.

READING III

BIOGRAPHICAL NOTES: Drid Williams, a native Oregonian, completed three post-graduate degrees, including a D.Phil., at the Institute of Social Anthropology, Oxford, U.K., from St. Hughes College. She met Keali'inohomoku, Kaeppler and Hanna for the first time in 1974 at a CORD/SEM Conference in San Francisco, California, and Royce for the first time in 1983 at a semiotics conference at Indiana University.

Williams was a professional modern dancer, she had a company in New York City, and she has performed and taught in the idioms of ballroom dancing, modern concert dancing, Afro-Caribbean forms, North Indian Kathak dancing, and ballet. She was the director of a graduate program in the anthropology of the dance and human movement studies at New York University ... and is founder and senior editor of the *Journal for the Anthropological Study of Human Movement* [JASHM], which still continues publication (from Williams 1986: 173). She is the architect of a theory of human actions called *semasiology*. She taught *Anthropology of the Dance and Human Movement Studies* at the University of Sydney in Australia (1986-1990) and at Moi University in Kenya (1991-1993). She has done field research in England, the United States, Cape York Peninsula, Australia, and in Eldoret, Kenya. She is presently teaching courses for the Dance Program at the University of Minnesota.

The following text, with minor editorial changes, is comprised of extracts from **Williams, D. 1991.** *Ten Lectures on Theories of the Dance.* Metuchen, New Jersey: Scarecrow Press. Reprinted by permission of Scarecrow Press.

Extract #1

It is not easy to define what it is that we are to understand by the dance for the purposes of these lectures. Were the emphasis to be on the question "*why* do people dance?" then we might accept some of the minimal answers that have been given in the past; 1. they dance because they want to have fun and relax — dancing is basically a vehicle for leisure and entertainment; 2. they dance because of biological, organic, or instinctive needs of some kind — the dance as a precursor to spoken language, perhaps; 3. they dance because they want to express themselves — dances as *symbolic* activities divorced from real life; 4. they dance because they feel sexy, happy or sad, or something — the dance as a prime repository of emotions; 5. they dance because a spirit has possessed them, whether good or evil — dances as hysterical, neurotic or *quasi*-religious manifestations; 6. they dance to show off or to relieve their overburdened feelings — the dance as *catharsis* or as one of the governors on a *steam valve* theory of human emotion ...

All of the above answers are inadequate. They all connote theories of human actions and, indeed theories of the nature of human be-ing, but since the emphasis here is rather on theories of the dance, I am not free to choose one of these answers over another, nor am I free to choose one of the definitions of dancing that they imply, since I shall have to discuss not only these, but a number of other hypotheses which go beyond these and other minimal definitions. ...It is well to remember that the word 'dance' in our culture alone includes an extraordinary variety of activities: disco-dancing, classical ballet, ballroom dancing, so-called 'ethnic' dancing, the New York City Rockettes, folk dancing — the lot. Just about anything that cannot be classified as ordinary movement can be (or has been) called dancing. I'll be obliged to make references to all of these forms of dancing (1991: 6-7).

Furthermore, I shall have to try to untangle the often confused statements about dancing, *per se*, that were made in the larger contexts of arguments about evolutionary or developmental theories of humankind, theories of human nature, cross-cultural surveys, and the like. Victorian scholars were intensely interested, for example, in the origins of the dance, largely because, one might imagine, they were preoccupied with the origins of nearly everything. Many books and articles have been written on the subject and were I to refer to all of them, these lectures would be cluttered up with little more than a recitation of names and book titles, because we can read that the dance has its origins in sex (Ellis 1920), or in play (Huizinga and Jenson 1949); in animal behavior (Sachs 1937), in magic (Frazer 1911), or that it represents the "childhood of man" (Frobenius 1908). We can read that its most vital expression and its *essence* is to be found in ancient Greek culture (Flitch 1912), in religion (van der Leeuw 1963), or that it exists largely as a function of an inability to speak (Kris 1952). In short, the dance could have begun in nearly any *primordium* that anyone cares to postulate and its essence has been located nearly everywhere.

None of the above explanations are adequate. There is no way of telling whether they are right or wrong because some of what is said by each author might apply to some forms of dancing, but not to others. About the best that we can do is to ask if the explanations are *plausible*, then try to see their limitations, and find out upon what grounds such claims are being made. … It is a remarkable fact that many of the explanations of the dance were expounded by people who knew relatively little about the activity in any of its manifestations, and who had to depend, as did Sir James Frazer's wife (penname, Lilly Grove) for her information on accounts given by missionaries, travelers, and others, thereby rendering her evidence highly suspect. We simply have no way of knowing how much of it was fabricated and how much was not.

The same might be said of many early accounts of American Indian dancing, for even though officers in the American Army or missionaries might have reported other aspects of social life with care, we have reason to believe that much

of what was said about dances and ritual practices was unreliable. By modern anthropological standards of professional
research, it was casual, out of context, superficial and ethnocentric. Statements made about the dances of any so-called
"aboriginal" or "simpler" peoples usually cannot be taken
at face value, and they should *never* be accepted without a
critical examination of sources and heavy corroborative evidence.

Because so much of what goes on in a dance *cannot be observed*, it is especially the case that great care must be taken
by the investigator to represent the beliefs, values, and ide-
ologies of the peoples concerned as truthfully and accurately
as is possible. Even professional anthropologists have had
trouble with *gesture*, although most of them recognize the
problems and some have provided us with valuable insights
because of their difficulties. I have in mind a Dutch anthropologist, Jan Pouwer, who was puzzled by a set of ordinary
gestures with which he was confronted every day. Part of
the puzzle was a gesture that he thought was "beckoning":

> If one were to travel through various parts of West New Guinea, one
> might observe the following gestures by Papuans who notice you.
> They might put a hand to their navel, their breasts, or their armpit;
> they might also beckon you. If you are lured into approaching the
> beckoner, he will be quite surprised for his hand simply said 'hello',
> and so did the navel and the breasts and the armpit and so on. All of
> them are visible, observable signs of an invisible message which has
> to be inferred (Pouwer 1973: 4).

He tells us that

> To these Papuans each individual person has a number of substan-
> tive *ipu*. English equivalents such as spirit or principle of life or for
> that matter *mana* hardly convey the meaning of *ipu*. Small wonder so
> many anthropological monographs are littered with native terms
> (1973: 3).

Pouwer refers to the *visible* and *invisible* characteristics of
human actions, and it cannot be overstressed that while we
may indeed see the *movement* that is made, it does not follow

that we have an understanding of those movements as human *actions* until we possess an understanding of subtleties like *ipu* (as in the above case). And the word alone is not enough either, as any graduate student who is a dancer will testify, whether it is one word or one gesture (Williams 1991: 8-9).

Extract #2

An instructive exercise that I have sometimes resorted to when training graduate students in the anthropology of human movement consists of the demand that they read all of the definitions of *dance* and *dancing* which have been given in the *Encyclopædia Britannica* since 1768 and in the *Encyclopedia Americana* since 1830. It is possible, through the use of this pedagogical device, for potential theorists and describers of the world's dances to comprehend not only the power and influence that such books of reference have in technologically advanced societies, but to comprehend the semantic difficulties involved in attempts to translate the body languages and conceptual structures of one people into the concepts of another people.

Considerable insights can be gained at a beginning level by trying to translate the English word 'dance' (meaning movement to music) into Fr. 'danse', f.; Ger. 'Tanz', m; Ital. 'danza', f.; Span. 'baile', m; Swed. 'dans', nn; or Yiddish, 'tants', m, and we might perform the same translations for the notion of 'dance' (meaning a party) or the infinitive 'to dance', but we know perfectly well there are considerable difficulties connected with the semantics involved among the above-mentioned languages, far less the difficulties that one faces when the language is Swahili, Japanese, Hindi, Yap, Eskimo or Kiowa. Furthermore,

> It is commonplace to separate dance, along with music, from other forms of human behavior and label it 'art'. Once it has been so separated, it is often felt that it need not be dealt with. This ethnocentric view does not take into consideration the possibility that dance may not be 'art' (whateverthatis) to the people of the culture concerned, or

that there may not even be a cultural category comparable to what Westerners call 'dance' (Kaeppler 1978: 46).

It is well known that the Hopi, for example, have no term for 'art' in their language, and this is not a "mere semantic problem" (as some would like to say, as if semantics were a 'mere' problem in any case). There are no *mere* semantic problems involved in the business of cultural translation, there are only *real* semantic problems (see Williams 1986 for further discussion). For example,

> [T]here can be powerful and dissonant side effects from the insistence of including art as an interface to dance. The manipulative attitudes of superordinate peoples can force adaptation by subordinate peoples that is not the same as an internally developed evolution. We may, for example, force the Hopi *kachinas* onto the proscenium stage and Hopi 'dance' may become an 'art'. If this happens, the world will lose at least as much as it gains (Keali'inohomoku, 1980: 42).

These semantic predicaments have great importance for the understanding of theories of the dance. One may, it is true, find some word or phrase in one's own language by which to translate a concept native to another language, as Kaeppler indicated, but we are then ... *obliged to ask what the word means to the native speaker*, and what the word means to the translator and his or her readers. Always and everywhere we have to deal with *double* levels of meaning, even if we consider the spoken language alone. We are faced with *triple*, even *quadruple* levels of meaning if we want to deal sensibly with gestures, dances or dancing. At best, there is only a partial overlap of meaning and so far, we have only been able partially to overcome the difficulties. ... (Williams 1991: 58-60).

Extract #3

There has emerged a probably largely unconscious format for books on dancing that exists even now and that apparently takes its shape from the same diffusionist theoretical sources that inspired Curt Sachs's book (see Evans-Pritchard

1962 for a discussion of diffusionist theory), because they are all based on a unilineal evolutionary continuum.

I refer to what were at one time thought to be "coffee table books" on the dance, i.e. Haskell (1960), Kirstein (1924), DeMille (1963), Terry (1956), Martin (1939 and 1963) and Lange (1975). Unfortunately, given that dance departments are now fairly common in the United States and are becoming so in Great Britain and in Australia, these books no longer repose solely on sitting-room tables. They are solemnly quoted on examination papers and cited as references for degrees. They are quoted in dance history and theory classes, as if they were something other than imaginative flights of fancy. They are all *quasi*-anthropological and it is regrettable that dance scholars seem unaware of the development of anthropology itself, especially if so much of what is written about the dance by this group is going to be laid (by implication or otherwise), at anthropology's door.

The interesting thing is, perhaps, that while one may find all manner of anthropological gobbledygook about origins of the dance in the published literature on dancing, nowhere can there be found histories of the development of dance departments in the United States or historically sensitive accounts of the development of, say, American modern dance or jazz dancing and the like. And if all this sounds a bit like 'overkill' or an indulgence on my part in over-emphasizing the disastrous effects of our ethnocentrisms upon ourselves and others, let me recall an experience that I had at the University of Ghana, Legon, in 1968, where I was asked to teach dance history to twenty-three young Ghanaian men at the Institute of African Studies.

The reference books I had to depend upon were the set I have mentioned above, plus a few others, including the *Dance Encyclopedia* (Chujoy and Manchester 1967). The experience to which I refer involved, among other things, trying to explain why these books were designed the way they were. I shall always remember my ultimately futile attempts to explain what the western dance world means by the phrase "primitive dancing".

I have had equal difficulties trying to explain to students from Asian or Middle Eastern ethnicities why their dances usually fall into the middle of this standard format of dance book, between "primitive" and "civilized" dancing. It is an impossible job, really, because I could find no more justification then than I can now for the ethnocentrisms that are so glaringly obvious in so much of western dance literature. Because of all this, and because I, too, tried to do research into other dance forms before I became an anthropologist, I appended, [in Williams 1991: 287-321], an essay entitled *An Exercise in Applied Personal Anthropology.*

Extract #4

"But how", students have asked, "can I begin to understand all that?" My reply? The process begins with the quality of reading and thinking that one does from the outset regarding the literature on dancing, and with the skill one develops over a period of years with reference to the articulation of one's ideas. Individual success in this kind of study, as well as the future success of the field of study itself, depends upon people who can read and write clearly, articulately, and cogently about the dance, dances, and the act of dancing. It is essential that students recognize theories and theorizing from the beginning and that they develop their capacities to think in these ways.[1]

It is with some regret that I am forced to say that the prevailing intellectual climate of these times is not very hospitable to these ideas. It certainly isn't conducive to the kinds of thinking that are required, because it isn't the kind of thinking that is useful in passing multiple choice and true-false examinations. The knowledge of language required in these cases, of course, amounts to little more than the ability to write check-marks that are equivalents of verbal grunts. One hopes this is merely a passing fashion in the educational world, of course, but it is well for aspiring students to recognize what they are up against.

The practical advice that I would want to leave with these students of anthropology and the dance is this: from the beginnings (whatever those may be in specific, individual cases), LEARN TO READ DIFFERENTLY. Follow Dutton's advice (1979) regarding ethnographies and their levels of explanation, criticizing Titiev's explanation of Hopi ceremony,

> So all of Hopi sacred drama—those moving texts and elaborate ceremonies, those magnificent dances—can be seen merely as an apparatus to cope with the threat of hostile desert environment. Here is yet another example: in her discussion of Hopi socialization, Goldfrank tells us that "large scale cooperation" seen among members of the Pueblo tribes is "no spontaneous expression of good will or sociability", but results from a "long process of conditioning" required by trying to engage in irrigation agriculture in a desert environment. To achieve the cooperation necessary for a functioning irrigated agriculture, the Zunis and Hopis strive from infancy for "a yielding disposition. From early childhood, quarreling, even in play is discouraged " (1945: 527) ... And so it goes.
>
> Why are the Navaho so concerned with witchcraft? asks an anthropologist, who learnedly informs us that it is because of the strain of living in a hostile desert environment. Why this vast and rich spectacle of Hopi sacred life? asks another, who wisely tells us that it is all just a device intended to counteract the hostile desert environment ... (Dutton 1979: 204).

Dutton focused his criticism on one type of meta-explanation—an environmental explanation, although there are several others. The reason that his short paper is so good is that he elucidates very clearly the fact that *anthropological writing requires more than one level of description*: Crick's discussion of fieldwork problems and techniques (1982) is apposite.

Novice anthropologists of human movement tend not to understand what is required of them at first, thus, when they are asked, for example, to give a précis of some anthropologist's arguments, say, regarding Hopi dances or ceremonies, they mistakenly offer a discussion of what the anthropologist has *described* about features of the dance or ceremony itself, usually with negative results. That is, the answer will rate a "B-" or "C" on an essay examination. Often, the student does not understand why, especially if the "ethnographic facts" that were presented by him or her about the anthropologist's description are accurate.

The simple explanation is this: a précis of a writer's *argument* concerning any set of facts is not the same as a descriptive rendering of the ethnographic facts.

Students should learn to read asking at least three questions:

1) What is being talked about here?

2) How is this material *interpreted*? and

3) What is the disciplinary or private *explanation* for that which is being talked about?

If students are encouraged to interact honestly and sensibly with received authorities and if he or she is encouraged to examine his or her privately held convictions, beliefs and such as part of the process, the results are usually extremely satisfying, both to students and teachers (Williams 1991: 281-284).

[DW]

PRECIS EXERCISE 3

[1]It is not easy to define what it is that we are to understand [2]by the dance for the purposes of these lectures. Were the [3]emphasis to be on the question "why do people dance?" [4]then we might accept some of the minimal answers that [5]have been given in the past; 1. they dance because they want [6]to have fun and relax — dancing is basically a vehicle for [7]leisure and entertainment; 2. they dance because of biologi-[8]cal, organic, or instinctive needs of some kind — dances as [9]precursors to spoken language, perhaps; 3. they dance be-[10]cause they want to express themselves — dances as *sym*-[11]*bolic* activities divorced from real life; 4. they dance because [12]they feel sexy, happy or sad, or something — dancing as [13]a prime repository of emotions; 5. they dance because a [14]spirit has possessed them, whether good or evil — dances [15]as hysterical, neurotic or *quasi*-religious manifestations;

16they dance to show off or to relieve their overburdened
17feelings — the dance as *catharsis* or as one of the governors
18on a *steam valve* theory of human emotion … *All of the above*
19*answers are inadequate.* They all connote theories of human
20actions and, indeed theories of the nature of human be-
21ing, but since the emphasis here is rather on theories of the
22dance, I am not free to choose one of these answers over
23another, nor am I free to choose one of the definitions of
24dancing that they imply, since I shall have to discuss not
25only these, but a number of other hypotheses which go
26beyond these and other minimal definitions. Moreover, it
27is well to remember that the word 'dance' in our culture
28alone includes an extraordinary variety of activities: disco-
29dancing, classical ballet, ballroom dancing, so-called 'eth-
30nic' dancing, the New York City Rockettes, folk dancing,
31the lot. Just about anything that cannot be classified as or-
32dinary movement can be (and has been) called dancing. I
33shall be obliged to make references to all of these forms of
34dancing …
35Furthermore, I shall have to try to untangle the often con-
36fused statements about dancing, *per se*, that were made in
37the larger contexts of arguments about evolutionary or de-
38velopmental theories of humankind, theories of human na-
39ture, cross-cultural surveys, and the like. Victorian schol-
40ars were intensely interested, for example, in the origins of
41the dance, largely because, one might imagine, they were
42preoccupied with the origins of nearly everything. Many
43books and articles have been written on the subject and
44were I to refer to all of them, these lectures would be clut-
45tered up with little more than a recitation of names and
46book titles, because we can read that the dance has its ori-
47gins in sex … or in play … in animal behavior… in magic
48…or that it represents the "childhood of man"…We can
49read that its most vital expression and its *essence* is to be
50found in ancient Greek culture … in religion … or that it
51exists largely as a function of an inability to speak…. In
52short, the dance could have begun in nearly any *primor-*

[53]*dium* that anyone cares to postulate and its essence has been
[54]located nearly everywhere.

[55]None of the above-mentioned explanations are adequate.
[56]There is no way of telling whether they are right or wrong
[57]because some of what is said by each author might apply
[58]to some forms of dancing, but not to others. About the best
[59]that we can do is to ask if the explanations are plausible,
[60]then try to see their limitations, and find out upon what
[61]grounds such claims are being made. ... It is a remarkable
[62]fact that many of the explanations of the dance were ex-
[63]pounded by people who knew relatively little about the
[64]activity in any of its manifestations, and who had to de-
[65]pend, as did Sir James Frazer's wife for her information on
[66]accounts given by missionaries, travellers, and others,
[67]thereby rendering her evidence highly suspect. We simply
[68]have no way of knowing how much was fabricated...

[69]The same might be said of many early accounts of Ameri-
[70]can Indian dancing, for even though officers in the Ameri-
[71]can Army or missionaries might have reported other
[72]aspects of social life with care, we have reason to believe
[73]that much of what was said about dances and ritual prac-
[74]tices was unreliable. By modern anthropological standards
[75]of professional research, it was casual, out of context, su-
[76]perficial and ethnocentric. Statements made about the
[77]dances of any so-called "aboriginal" or "simpler" peoples
[78]usually cannot be taken at face value, and they should *never*
[79]be accepted without a critical examination of sources and
[80]heavy corroborative evidence. ...

Exercises

I. Do you understand these words/phrases?
•minimal [lines 4, 26]; •organic [line 8]; •precursor [9]; •*quasi*
[15]; •catharsis [19]; •hypothesis (-ses) [25]; •evolutionary
theory [37-8]; •developmental theory [37-8]; •primordium [52-
3]; •fabricated [68]; •aspect(s) [72]; •ethnocentric [76]; •cor-
roborative [80].

II. On a separate sheet of paper, *using your own words,* answer these questions:

1. Williams says the 6 common answers about why people dance [lines 5-18] are "inadequate". Do you think they are inadequate? If yes, why? If no, why?

2. Why do you think the author says "the word 'dance' in our culture alone includes an extraordinary variety of actitivities" [lines 27-30]. What difference does it make what is included?

3. In lines 46-54, several sources are given for the origins of dancing. What are they?

4. Are *reasons for* dancing and *explanations of* dancing the same as *opinions about* dancing? If yes, why? If no, why?

5. Do you agree with this author that corroborative evidence is needed for early accounts of dancing? [lines 76-80]. What is the point of "having evidence" or "providing evidence" with regard to dancing and dances anyway?

6. This author is critical of much of the writing about dances that we inherit from the past. [The words 'critical' and 'criticism' are what we are interested in here.]

A. In general, what do you think of (and about) criticism?

B. Students ask, "if an author can be criticized negatively, what's the point of reading the book?" How would you answer that question?

C. Is there a difference between critical writing and being personally destructive? If there is, explain the difference and give at least two examples. If you think otherwise, explain and give at least two examples.

III. Choose *one* of the four extracts in this chapter, then write a 100-120 word précis of the extract. Use your own words.

ADDITIONAL THOUGHT EXERCISES

1. Keali'inohomoku, Royce and Williams all talk about definitions of 'dance', but there are points upon which they agree and disagree. What are those points? How would you describe the similarities and differences in what these authors say about the problems of definition?

2. What is the point of knowing about what Royce calls the "shifting emphasis in views" about societies and culture?

3. Choose any dance form with which you are familiar (and which you *like*) through practise, reading, and/or observation. Briefly describe the form, then explain how and in what ways it is 'ethnic'.

4. Carry out exercise number 3, with one difference: change the word, 'like' in the parenthesis, to 'dislike'. Does *liking or disliking* affect your ability to describe dance forms accurately? Discuss.

5. Imagine that you are going to carry out research on a dance form of your choice. You can begin your research by asking, *"What are people doing* when they dance?" Or, you begin by asking *"Why* do people dance?" Discuss the advantages and disadvantages of each question and its possible influence on the research.

READING IV

BIOGRAPHICAL NOTES: David Best is Professor in the Department of Philosophy, University of Wales, Swansea; Visiting Professor, School of Theatre, Manchester Metropolitan University; Senior Academic Fellow and Honorary Professor, DeMontfort University; Visiting Professor, International Centre for the Study of Drama in Education and Consultant to Bretton Hall College of the Arts. He holds various honorary appointments. Recently, he was Professor of Philosophy at Birmingham Institute of Art and Design. He acted as consultant for the National Department of Education and Science for England and Wales. He has written numerous articles and his books include: *Expression in the Arts* (Lepus Books, H. Kimpton Publishers, 1974); *Philosophy and Human Movement* (cited below); *Feeling and Reason in the Arts* (Allen & Unwin, London, 1985) and *The Rationality of Feeling* (Falmer Press, London, 1993). He frequently speaks at conferences and lectures in several countries. In 1992, he was invited to become a member of the International Association of leading academics and artists, based in *The Hermitage* in St. Petersburg, Russia. His philosophical interests are wide, but he is best known for his work in philosophy of the arts and the arts in education.

The chapter reproduced below, with minor editorial deletions and additions, retaining original English spellings and punctuation, is taken from **Best, D. 1978.** *Philosophy and Human Movement.* Allen & Unwin, New York Reprinted by permission of Allen & Unwin.

Introduction
[Ch. 6: *The Essence of Movement*]

The importance of recognising the limitations of empirical investigation resides not only in revealing the conceptual confusions of some scientific inquiry but also in exposing plausible misconceptions of an opposite extreme which are often encountered among non-scientists. Some phenomenologists misconstrue their recognition of those limitations by denying that empirical methodology can explain anything that really matters about human movement. They assume that only a close concentration on the movement itself will reveal its essential character, and that empirical examination is inevitably restricted to relatively superficial external aspects of it. The assumption that there must be such an underlying essence can lead to damaging misconceptions about the nature of human movement and its study. Such an assumption stems partly from a failure to provide an adequate account of those aspects of behaviour to which empirical investigation is inappropriate ... [T]here is a danger of misconception in the assumption that the truth is always to be found by digging *deeply*. Wittgenstein (1953) expresses the point in this way:

> The aspects of things that are most important for us are hidden because of their simplicity and familiarity. One is unable to notice something—because it is always before one's eyes. We fail to be struck by what, once seen, is most striking and most powerful.

The Definitional Fallacy

A common fallacy which is sometimes related to that adumbrated above is the general demand for definitions, i.e. the tendency to assume that one may be said to understand the meaning of a word only if one can define it verbally. Although I have considered this issue in another book (1974) it is worth repeating the main outlines here since the misconception is so prevalent. The assumption is, then, that to know the meaning of any general term is to be able to state those conditions which are separately necessary and together sufficient for all correct instances of its use.

It is important, first, to be clear about precisely what is required of a definition. It can be said that 'D' is a definition of 'A' only if the two terms are logically equivalent, by which I mean that all cases of 'A' are necessarily cases of 'D', and conversely, or, to put the point another way, that in all contexts 'D' can be substituted for 'A' and 'A' for 'D', without change of meaning. Now I do not wish to deny that precise definitions can be given of some terms. For example, a bachelor can be defined as an unmarried man, and a triangle can be defined as a plane figure bounded by three straight sides. What I do deny is that definitions can be given of all or even the great majority of terms, despite the common assumption that, in general, one cannot be said to have a clear understanding of the meaning of a term unless one can define it.

…[I]t is important to be clear about the meanings of the terms we employ, but it is equally important to recognise that being clear about meaning is by no means the same as being able to produce a verbal definition. There is a great deal that could be said on this topic, but I shall restrict myself to three arguments, each of which is sufficient to show that the general demand for definitions is misconceived.

(1) We are in practice unable to produce definitions of most of the words we use, although we are well aware of their meanings. For example, we are unable to define verbally the names of the primary colours, but this does not prevent our knowing what 'red' means and using it correctly. Moreover, it is significant that we certainly learned, as children, the meanings of most words without being provided with definitions.

(2) The person who says he must search for a definition before he can legitimately be said to know the meaning of a term, in practice inevitably contradicts himself. He puts the cart before the horse, since the ability to recognise that a definition is correct, or to raise counter-examples and objections to it, presupposes that he must know the meaning of the term *before* he finds the definition, even if he should succeed.

(3) Even the simple case of the triangle which we have considered depends upon an understanding of the *non* - defined meanings of the words used in the definition—words such as 'plane', 'bounded', 'straight', and so on. In short, if a definition had to be provided before we could understand the meaning of *every* word then we should never be able to understand the meaning of *any* word. Every word in the definition would have to be defined in words, each of which would have to be defined in words, each of which would have to be defined in words, each of which ... and so on to infinity.

This is another example of a vicious infinite regress ...[A]n argument which can be shown to depend upon such a regress has *ipso facto* been shown to be invalid, since it can never even begin. So the ability to give a definition presupposes that the words which comprise it are understood *without* definition.

This should be sufficient to explode the surprisingly pervasive and tenacious myth that it should be possible in general to provide definitions of the terms we use. An example is provided by Lange (1970) who, in an article entitled "The nature of dance", considers some of the better-known definitions of dance, and remarks that it is striking how much they vary. Yet this variety reveals not so much the difficulty of defining *dance* specifically as the more fundamental misconception concerning definitions. In short, the problem is created not by the nature of dance but by the common confusion of meaning with definition.

It is to be hoped, then, that enough has been said at least to induce considerable caution about the demand for definitions. It is a common experience, in discussion, to be asked to define one's terms, yet *it is ironic that those who ask are usually unclear about what is required of a definition* (italics supplied). So it may be a good ploy to ask the questioner to define 'definition'. Such a definition is provided above, but since he has asked such a question it is unlikely that he will be aware of it.

Nevertheless, it should not be thought that the search for definitions is always pointless. In some cases it may be possible to find one, and even where it is not, the attempt to find one may bring out salient features of the concept in question. The danger of misconception arises from the unquestioned assumption that there *must* be such a definition to be found.

The Movement Itself

The article by Spencer and White (1972) ... reveals a clear general position not only about the study of human movement but about the substantiation of any assertion. The authors make two major points: (1) They complain that there are many unsupported claims made for dance; (2) They insist that such claims, like any other statement, in order to be meaningful should be substantiated by empirical examination and quantification. For instance, they write: "The position taken in this paper is that dance is a form of behaviour, and, as such is open to empirical examination. That is, if something exists, it exists in quantity".

In order to understand the source of the misconception which is our primary concern in this chapter, we need to remind ourselves of the plausibility of the case proposed by Spencer and White. It could be argued as follows: "Dance is a form of behaviour. All forms of behaviour can be scientifically examined. Therefore dance can be scientifically examined". This argument is undeniably valid, yet ... although all behaviour can be scientifically examined that is certainly not to say that the only legitimate explanations of behaviour are scientific. Spencer and White fail to recognise this point and clearly do regard this as the only way in which statements made about human behaviour may be genuinely verified, since no aspect of it which is not open to empirical quantification can, in their view, be said even to exist.

Yet, in order to reject this sort of conclusion, some writers feel constrained to adopt an equally misconceived attitude, which in fact turns out to be the opposite side of precisely the same coin, in that they inadvertently share with their opponents the most damaging underlying assumption. A classic example occurs in an article by Harper (1973), significantly entitled "Movement and measurement: the case of the incompatible marriage". Harper is well aware that there is something particularly important about human movement to which the notion of empirical examination is inappropriate, yet he seriously misconceives the point. "Implicit in nearly all of the human movement literature is the following presupposition: Human movement is accessible in sense experience, i.e. the movement of one person can be perceived by another".

He goes on to state that this presupposition is patently false because it fails to take account of the important distinction between the possibility of sensing *things* which move or are moved, and the impossibility of sensing the *movements* of them. He agrees that we can see horses running, birds flying, rocks falling, and human beings walking, but he insists that we cannot see the movements themselves: "... what one actually comes upon in sense experience are various objects in the world, including human beings, which are moving or are moved, *and not the movements of them*".

This part of his argument is so immediately implausible that one already suspects that it is a consequence of a more significant, underlying misconception concerning sense-perception and objectivity. For clearly, to speak of the movement of John is just another way of speaking of John's moving. However, Harper produces a more plausible argument by reference to the distinction between what is experienced, and the experiencing of it. He writes:

> Regardless of how the researcher reasons, however, if he takes up the empirical methodology, he is caught in a flat contradiction. It is essential to empirical techniques that knowledge is to be ultimately grounded in sense experience. If the human movement researcher is willing to assume movement to be available in sense experience, then adoption of empirical techniques may be appropriate to the object. But, as we have pointed out, human movement is not of the nature to be sensed by another. And thus the researcher appears to be caught choosing a method which relies upon what is studied to be sense

given, but turning it towards an object which is not sensible. Under these imperfect conditions the nature of human movement could not ever be known.

This quotation clearly reveals that Harper assumes there is an essential nature which underlies human movement yet which, since it cannot be perceived, is beyond the scope of empirical methodology. This leads him to conclude that in this sphere such methodology can yield *no* positive knowledge and is therefore irrelevant to the study of human movement since it can only presuppose its essential nature:

With regard to ... the [experienced] movement, empirical research must fail to yield positive results as the *essential natures* of the various movements under examination are presupposed in order for empirical procedures to even be employed. In order even to find individual instances of an activity, one must already have presupposed an *essential knowledge* of the activity to be analyzed. Otherwise how could one know he is studying leaping and not running, tennis and not golf, wrestling and not eating? One knows what each of these activities are or he could never find reliable instances of them. And thus, the empiricist is caught presupposing the *essential nature* of what he is analyzing and thereby cannot inspect or clarify that *essential nature*. The *essential differences* between activities remain unnoticed and therefore unexamined (italics supplied).

Spencer and White insist that any statement made about human movement, to make sense at all, must be open to empirical examination. In order to reject that kind of misconception Harper succumbs to another by insisting that, on the contrary, since empirical investigation cannot explain the essence it is altogether irrelevant to our understanding of human movement. But the assumption on which he bases the conclusion, namely that the essence of movement is not available to sense perception, leads him to the startling conclusion that movement cannot even exist. In his own words: "In itself, a movement cannot exist, that is, cannot be in time and space. Therefore it cannot be available to sense experience as it is not anywhere at any time". One can, perhaps, already begin to appreciate that this is in fact the opposite side of the *same* coin as Spencer and White's, since, it will be recalled, they also insisted that "if something exists, it exists in quantity". But this is to anticipate the argument, and I shall return to the point.

Harper concludes that the reason for the unsatisfactory state of human-movement studies is that empirical techniques have prevented human-movement researchers from understanding clearly the essential nature of the subject matter. If he were right, those who study movement from, for example, psychological, sociological and physiological points of view are obviously wasting their time, since what they are attempting to examine cannot even be perceived.

A major source of his extraordinary conclusion is Harper's assumption that there must be an essence of movement to be found, and since it cannot be perceived he can presume only that it must lie outside the realm of sense-experience altogether. This is a clear case of the kind of misconception [considered elsewhere], of assuming that the truth about an action or movement is to be found by concentrating *closely* upon it. Such a misapprehension is also at the heart of much phenomenological thought, which mistakenly assumes that it makes sense to suggest that it is possible to exclude contextual and therefore conceptual factors in order to concentrate on what it supposes to be the movement *itself*. Wittgenstein (1953) puts the point in this way: "In order to find the real artichoke we divested it of its leaves". Similarly, in order to find the essence of human movement, Harper and such phenomenologists try to divest it of all that is available to sense-perception. But instead of finding the essence we discover that there is nothing left.

Of course it is true ...that empirical methodology cannot tell us *everything* about movement. Moreover, it is true that where the scientist is concerned to examine intentional action, *what* that action is has to be presupposed, and therefore it cannot itself be explained by scientific examination. Hence to imagine that empirical methodology can comprehensively explain human action or movement is to be fundamentally mistaken. Yet that is certainly not to say that the empirical sciences cannot explain what really matters, or anything that really matters, about human movement. There are many aspects of human movement to which the notion of scientific explanation is unintelligible, but only an essentialist presupposition will lead to the conclusion that therefore the sciences have *nothing* significant to say about it. On the contrary, there are also many important aspects of human movement which *do* lie within the scope of scientific explanation.

Experience and Observable Criteria

Although Spencer and White on the one hand, and Harper on the other, appear to be diametrically opposed, we have already had reason to suspect that in fact their extremes of opposition stem from a shared underlying presupposition. And further examination confirms that suspicion, for it can be shown that their respective positions are in fact opposite sides of the same misconceived coin. The point can be brought out in this way:

Spencer and White: If an aspect of human movement is not open to empirical investigation then it is not answerable to sense-perception, in which case it cannot be said to exist.

Harper: If an aspect of human movement is not open to empirical investigation then it is not answerable to sense-perception, in which case it cannot be said to exist. Since the essential nature of human movement is not open to empirical investigation, it must be beyond sense-perception and thus cannot be said to exist in time and space.

It is the agreed presupposition which, although commonly encountered, and central to much phenomenology, is the source of confusion ... there are many aspects of behaviour which are not open to empirical investigation but which are nevertheless objectively perceivable ...[A]n empirical investigation could not determine the character of the intentional action performed by the physical movement involved in signing one's name. But not even the most hard-headed scientist who received by cheque a gift of £100 as a result would, presumably, want to deny its objective existence on the grounds that it could not be empirically verified.

As I conceded above, Harper's most plausible argument rests on the distinction he draws between what is experienced and the experiencing of it. He adduces this distinction in order to show that the *experiencing* cannot be objectively perceivable. This carries plausibility because it is true that no sense can be made of the suggestion that someone else could observe my *experiencing*, even if he can observe *what* I am experiencing. But this argument does not achieve what Harper wants, and indeed it can be shown to undermine his whole position. As we have seen, he clearly regards the experiencing as the essence of an action or movement, and that which determines its character. Yet even given a coherent philosophical account of experiencing, namely as identified by typical manifestation in observable behaviour, it is unintelligible to suppose that it can be this which determines the character of the action. That is, it cannot coherently be supposed that simply having an experience while performing it is what determines what an action is. In fact, the opposite is true. It is not that the experience determines the action, but that the context of occurrence determines not only the character of the action but also the character of the experience. Nothing could amount to the action, and therefore the experiencing, of a checkmate move without the context of chess. Thus, although Harper is right to point out that empirical investigation has to presuppose, and therefore cannot determine, whether an action is "leaping and not running, tennis and not golf, wrestling and not eating", to appeal to the *experiencing* as that which explains the character of an action is equally misconceived since in fact it can explain nothing. For, in his terms, the experiencing cannot coherently be regarded as logically distinct from what is experienced.

To explain what is meant by this last remark will also allow me to expose the misconception inherent in an objection which is sometimes raised against some of my own work

...that I do not distinguish between the spectator and the performer, or that I concentrate my attention too much on the spectator and do not adequately consider the experience of the performer. Such an objection is based upon deep confusions about mental concepts. ... However, the argument of this chapter already reveals an outline of the fundamental misconception in this way of thinking, since implicit in the objection is the notion that it makes sense to suppose that while the context may be important for the spectator, it is the experience *itself* which is important for the performer, and this is a purely subjective matter which can be understood solely by the performer in isolation from any contextual considerations. And this, of course, is why Harper assumes that the experiencing, and therefore, on his view, the character of the intentional action, cannot be answerable to sense-perception.

Yet the notion of the experience *itself*, in isolation from its normal, perceivable context is unintelligible. For again, no experience could possibly *count* as that of making a checkmate move in isolation from the context of the rules and conventions of chess. Precisely similar considerations apply to Harper's examples of experiencing the movements involved in playing tennis and golf. Apart from the relevant rules and conventions, whatever movements were performed, nothing could possibly count as having the same experiences. As Wittgenstein (1953) puts it:

> The very fact that we should so much like to say: "This is the important thing—while we point privately to the sensation—is enough to shew how much we are inclined to say something which *gives no information*" (italics supplied).

Elsewhere (1969) he writes: "What is the proof that I *know* something? Most certainly not my saying that I know it ... An inner experience cannot show me that I know something". On the contrary, it is the characteristic external circumstance of its occurrence which, as it were, tells *me* what experience I am having. This is not to deny that one could have the experience in different circumstances and outside the normal context. It is to insist that the experience could not be *identified*, and therefore that nothing could possibly count as the same *'experiencing'*, without reference to the normal context of its occurrence. For example, on producing a convincing argument in a debate, someone might say: "It felt exactly like making a checkmate move". Although the experience now occurs in a debate, the normal context is necessary for such a characterisation of it. Moreover, even in these different circumstances it must be possible to offer in justification some link with the normal context in order for such an assertion to be intelligible.

To put the point another way, if the mover should refer to the experience by saying, while performing the movement: "It feels like *this*", there is no way of distinguishing the 'it' from the 'this'. That is, the performer's experience is determined *for him too* by the perceivable movement in the context of its occurrence. It is for this reason that it is necessary to concentrate a philosophical examination of experience on such *observable* criteria. But to assume that this reveals a concern solely or predominantly with the spectator shows a failure to appreciate why it is necessary. I insist on the central place of personal experience, and therefore I am equally concerned with the performer. To concentrate attention of perceivable behaviour is certainly not to denigrate the 'experiencing' but, on the contrary, is the only intelligible way to provide an account of it. As we have seen, a consequence of misconstruing the importance of such observable criteria is that the experience of movement disappears altogether. (I explain more fully in another book (Best 1974) the crucial relation of observable criteria to personal experience).

Harper's misconception, then, stems from two erroneous assumptions: (1) that there must be an underlying essential nature of human movement; and (2) that to be objectively answerable to sense-perception is to be open to empirical investigation. With these presuppositions he can hardly avoid the conclusion that the essential nature of movement cannot exist in space and time, for otherwise it would be available to sense-perception and thus, on his second assumption, open to empirical investigation.

It is most important to see not so much that his conclusion is mistaken as what led him to it, for it is based on plausible assumptions which are widely accepted without question in the field of human movement. I shall say a little more about the danger inherent in the former assumption in a moment. In relation to the latter, it is strange how persistent and pervasive is the misconception that 'objective' necessarily implies 'scientific', i.e. that *only* scientific explanations can be objective. I hope that enough has been said ... to expose that misconception, and to show how it almost inexorably leads to unintelligible subjectivism. To repeat the point, an account of an intentional action such as signing a cheque is as objective as an account of a physical movement, even although the former is not open to scientific explanation.

Each of the theses about the study of human movement which have been considered in this and the previous chapter is drawing attention, even if misguidedly, to an important aspect overlooked by the other. Thus it should not be thought that the mistakes which have been revealed are simple or stupid mistakes. On the contrary, such misconceptions are frequently encountered, and usually not so thoroughly worked out. The ... implausible conclusions are a consequence of taking a valid point to an invalid extreme.

To revert to the notion of an underlying essential nature of human movement, I was once involved in negotiations with a validating committee which was considering proposals for a degree in human-movement studies. At one point the suspicion was voiced that such a subject of study amounted to what was called a 'conceptually arbitrary topic'. So far as it was possible to discover what was meant by this, it appeared to reveal a vague feeling that there was no essential nature, central core, or unitary methodology here. Yet in that case the study of human movement is no more conceptually arbitrary than sociology, which inevitably incorporates the insights of disciplines such as history, geography, anthropology, psychology and philosophy in order to provide an understanding of human society and social relationships. If we were to divest the artichoke of sociology of the leaves of its contributory disciplines in order to discover its central core, or essential nature, there would be nothing left. Indeed, if the academic credentials of a subject of study depended upon its employing a unitary methodology, the only possible survivor of the exodus from universities would be pure mathematics. The sciences, for example, inevitably employ mathematics; geography involves the methodology of history, mathematics and the sciences; history involves the sciences and geography. A subject is none the less legitimately academic if it needs to call upon various contributory disciplines for enlightenment.

The article which has been the principal concern of this chapter was entitled: *Movement and Measurement: the Case of the Incompatible Marriage* (Harper 1973). As I have tried to show, the marriage is not in the least incompatible. ... Eternal wedded bliss is assured as long as each partner clearly understands the character of the other.

What is time? St. Augustine confessed that if no one asked him he knew, but when he tried to explain it, then he became puzzled. I suggest that we are in a similar case with human movement. It is what we see it is. There is no underlying essential nature, and no over-ridingly important academic methodology for its study.

What is human movement *in itself*?

Such a loaded question, as we have seen, may tend to such an excessive and misguided determination to uncover its essence that human movement will disappear altogether.

[DB]

PRECIS EXERCISE 4

[1]The importance of recognising the limitations of empirical [2]investigation resides not only in revealing the conceptual [3]confusions of some scientific inquiry but also in exposing [4]plausible misconceptions of an opposite extreme which are [5]often encountered among non-scientists. Some phe-[6]nomenologists misconstrue their recognition of those limi-[7]tations by denying that empirical methodology can explain [8]anything that really matters about human movement. They [9]assume that only a close concentration on the movement [10]itself will reveal its essential character, and that empirical [11]examination is inevitably restricted to relatively superfi-[12]cial external aspects of it. The assumption that there must [13]be such an underlying essence can lead to damaging mis-[14]conceptions about the nature of human movement and its [15]study. Such an assumption stems partly from a failure to [16]provide an adequate account of those aspects of behaviour [17]to which empirical investigation is inappropriate. ... [T]here [18]is a danger of misconception in the assumption that the [19]truth is always to be found by digging *deeply*. Wittgenstein [20]expresses the point in this way:

> [21]The aspects of things that are most important for us are hidden
> [22] because of their simplicity and familiarity. One is unable to no-
> [23]tice something because it is always before one's eyes. We fail to
> [24] be struck by what, once seen, is most striking and powerful.

[25]A common fallacy which is sometimes related to that ad-[26]umbrated above is the general demand for definitions, i.e. [27]the tendency to assume that one may be said to under-[28]stand the meaning of a word only if one can define it ver-[29]bally. Although I have considered this issue in another book, [30]it is worth repeating the main outlines here since the mis-[31]conception is so prevalent. The assumption is, then, that to [32]know the meaning of any general term is to be able to state [33]those conditions which are separately necessary and to-[34]gether sufficient for all correct instances of its use.

[35]It is important, first, to be clear about precisely what is re-
[36]quired of a definition. It can be said that 'D' is a definition
[37]of 'A' only if the two terms are logically equivalent, by
[38]which I mean that all cases of 'A' are necessarily cases of
[39]'D', and conversely, or, to put the point another way, that
[40]in all contexts 'D' can be substituted for 'A' and 'A' for 'D',
[41]without change of meaning. Now I do not wish to deny
[42]that precise definitions can be given of *some* terms. For ex-
[43]ample, a bachelor can be defined as an unmarried man,
[44]and a triangle can be defined as a plane figure bounded by
[45]three straight sides. What I do deny is that definitions can
[46]be given of all or even the great majority of terms, despite
[47]the common assumption that, in general, one cannot be
[48]said to have a clear understanding of the meaning of a term
[49]unless one can define it. ... [I]t is important to be clear about
[50]the meanings of the terms we employ, but it is equally im-
[51]portant to recognise that being clear about meaning is by
[52]no means the same as being able to produce a verbal defi-
[53]nition. There is a great deal that could be said on this topic,
[54]but I shall restrict myself to three arguments, each of which
[55]is sufficient to show that the general demand for defini-
[56]tions is misconceived.

[57]**(1)** We are in practice unable to produce definitions of most
[58]of the words we use, although we are well aware of their
[59]meanings. For example, we are unable to define verbally
[60]the names of the primary colours, but this does not pre-
[61]vent our knowing what 'red' means and using it correctly.
[62]Moreover, it is significant that we certainly learned, as chil-
[63]dren, the meanings of most words without being provided
[64]with definitions.

[65]**(2)** The person who says he must search for a definition
[66]before he can legitimately be said to know the meaning of
[67]a term, in practice inevitably contradicts himself. He puts
[68]the cart before the horse, since the ability to recognise that
[69]a definition is correct, or to raise counterexamples and ob-
[70]jections to it, presupposes that he must know the meaning
[71]of the term *before* he finds the definition, even if he should
succeed.

[72](3) Even the simple case of the triangle which we have con-
[73]sidered depends upon an understanding of the *non*-defined
[74]meanings of the words used in the definition—words such
[75]as 'plane', 'bounded', 'straight', and so on. In short, if a
[76]definition had to be provided before we could understand
[77]the meaning of *every* word then we should never be able to
[78]understand the meaning of *any* word. Every word in the
[79]definition would have to be defined in words, each of which
[80]would have to be defined in words, each of which would
[81]have to be defined in words, each of which … and so on to
[82]infinity. This is another example of a vicious infinite re-
[83]gress … an argument which can be shown to depend upon
[84]such a regress has *ipso facto* been shown to be invalid, since
[85]it can never even begin. So the ability to give a definition
[86]presupposes that the words which comprise it are under-
[87]stood *without* definition. This should be sufficient to ex-
[88]plode the surprisingly pervasive and tenacious myth that
[89]it should be possible in general to provide definitions of
[90]the terms we use. An example is provided by Lange, who,
[91]in an article entitled "The nature of dance" considers some
[92]of the better-known definitions of dance, and remarks that
[93]it is striking how much they vary. Yet this variety reveals
[94]not so much the difficulty of defining *dance* specifically as
[95]the more fundamental misconception concerning defini-
[96]tions. In short, the problem is created not by the nature of
[97]dance but by the common confusion of meaning with definition.

[98]It is to be hoped, then, that enough has been said at least
[99]to induce considerable caution about the demand for defi-
[100]nitions. It is a common experience, in discussion, to be
[101]asked to define one's terms, yet it is ironic that those who
[102]ask are usually unclear about what is required of a defini-
[103]tion. So it may be a good ploy to ask the questioner to
[104]define 'definition'. Such a definition is provided above,
[105]but since he has asked such a question it is unlikely that
[106]he will be aware of it.

[107]Nevertheless, it should not be thought that the search for

[108]definitions is always pointless. In some cases it may be [109]possible to find one, and even where it is not, the attempt [110]to find one may bring out salient features of the concept [111]in question. The danger of misconception arises from the [112]unquestioned assumption that there *must* be such a defi-[113]nition to be found.

Exercises

I. Find working definitions for these words:

•empirical [1, 7, 10, 17]; •phenomenologist [5-6]; •miscon-strue [6]; •misconception (-ceived) [4, 13-14, 18, 30-1, 56, 95, 111]; •assume/assumption [15, 18, 47, 112]; •inappropriate [17]; ploy [103]; •fallacy [25]; •adumbrated [25-6]; •*ipso facto* [84]; •contradict [67]; •pervasive [88]; •tenacious [88]; induce [99]; •ironic [101]; •salient [110].

II. On a separate sheet of paper, answer these questions:

1. [Lines 49-53] Here, the author says that being clear about meaning isn't the same as being able to produce a verbal defi-nition. What do you think he means? How would you ex-plain what he means in your own words, using examples from your own life experience?

2. In lines 96-97, what does the author conclude?

3. Does Best consider searches for definitions to be pointless? [Lines 107-111]. Do *you* consider searches for definitions to be pointless? If yes or no, explain why.

4. A. Summarize one (and only one) of the arguments in lines 57-87. **B.** After you have done that, **write a précis** of the argu-ment of the whole chapter, **using no more than 250 words.**

READING V

BIOGRAPHICAL NOTES: For a long time in the field of anthropology, the dance and human movement studies, Adrienne Kaeppler stood alone. Born in Wisconsin and having studied dancing since age five, she lived in Hawaii for many years and was connected, first as a student, later as a faculty member, with the University of Hawaii. She was a research anthropologist with the Bishop Museum. She went to Tonga in 1964, but not to study dances. She wanted to do an anthropological study of aesthetics and the relationship between social structure and the arts. As it happened, the major arts of Tonga were dancing and bark cloth-making. Her thesis on the structure of Tongan dancing brought her interests in anthropology and the dance together. Her Doctoral degree was conferred in 1967 from the University of Hawaii. She is curator of Oceanic Ethnology at the Smithsonian Institution. She has done extensive work on Tongan and Hawaiian dances and the dances of Korea, Japan, Malaysia, Polynesia, Micronesia and the Philippines (updated from Williams 1986: 173).

The following text is a reproduction with minor corrections, retaining the original English spelling and punctuation, of **Kaeppler, A. 1985.** Structured Movement Systems in Tonga. *Society and the Dance.* (Ed. P. Spencer), Cambridge University Press, U.K., Chapter 3, pp. 92-118.[1] Reprinted by permission of Cambridge University Press.

Introduction

Cultural forms that result from the creative use of human bodies in time and space are often glossed in English as 'dance'. These cultural forms can be said to formalise human movement into structured systems in much the same way that poetry formalises language. Such forms, though transient, have structured content, are often visual manifestations of social relations, and may be part of an elaborate aesthetic system. In many societies, however, there is no indigenous concept that can adequately be translated for 'dance'. These formalised movement sequences, in which human bodies are used or manipulated in time and space, may be considered by the society as different when performed for the gods from when performed for a human audience. Structured movements when performed as presentation pieces (for an audience) may be viewed as quite distinct activities from performances that are primarily participatory. Or social activities and social duties that include similar structured movements may be categorised quite differently from an indigenous point of view.

Western notions tend to classify all such movement dimensions together as 'dance', but culturally it would seem more appropriate to analyse them more objectively as movement dimensions of separate activities. The concept 'dance' may be masking the importance and usefulness of analysing human movement systems by introducing a Western category. From a more holistic and objective point of view the movement dimension of various activities should be recognised as an integral part of that activity. They should be described, analysed, and used in formulations about the form, function, and meaning of the activity, as well as in constructs about the cultural philosophy and deep structure.

Much social or religious ritual includes the manipulation of human bodies in time and space and may have a similar kind of structured content. Trance or other altered states of consciousness are often associated with structured movement systems. Indeed it seems almost impossible (and perhaps culturally inappropriate) to separate dance from other structured movement systems except by native categories. The Tasaday of the Philippines apparently do not have what would be categorised as 'dance' from a Western point of view. Yet when they sing they usually strike a pose with one hand placed to the side of the head. What are the components in our society that make it possible to classify together ballet, rock and roll, square dancing, and the waltz but separate them from ice skating, cheerleading, and a church processional? Is the concept 'dance' useful in studying either our own culture or others?

Every society has cultural forms in which human bodies are manipulated in time and space. How these forms are regarded by the society itself seems a crucial question for an understanding of that society. Can we isolate components that will either group or separate the various movement dimensions or the activities they project into visual form? An ideal study of a movement system would analyse the cultural forms in which human bodies are manipulated in time and space, the social processes that produce them according to the aesthetic precepts of a specific group of people at a specific point in time, and the components that differentiate activities that include movement. Discovering the structure and content of such forms, as well as the creative processes and philosophies from the indigenous point of view, are difficult tasks, but detailed empirical studies of movement systems including both *etic* and *emic* analyses will be necessary both for significant cross-cultural research and for understanding the deep structure of a society.

The concept 'dance' appears to be an unsatisfactory category imposed from a Western point of view because it tends to group together diverse activities that should be culturally separated. Yet a number of activities in many societies have enough common characteristics that outside observers describe certain sets of movement dimensions as dance. Many observers will describe dance and then describe other movement sequences as being 'like dancing'. Supporters of the idea that ice skating is dancing will agree that there is a difference between simply ice skating and dancing on ice skates. On the other hand, some purists may not agree that even dancing on ice skates is dancing. What is it that we have in our heads when we decide if something is dancing or not? I have not yet found a definition of 'dance' that satisfies me.[2] Apparently it has something to do with structured movement that is somehow further elaborated — perhaps by something as simple as having a definite beginning and ending.

I propose that one of the tasks of an ethnographer is to study all human movement that formalises the nonformal and to elucidate what the movement dimensions of various activity systems are communicating and to whom. Such an analysis could delineate similarities and differences in the movement dimensions and their contexts as well as how these are regarded and categorised and the components by which they are grouped or separated. It might then be possible to illuminate cultural constructs that produce a cultural conception of dance.

This chapter will explore some aspects of the movement dimensions of various activities in Tonga and I will attempt to delineate cultural constructs that might produce a cultural conception of the dance for that society. In previous articles on Tongan dance I have examined kinemic and morphokinemic structure, change in form and function of dance forms, aesthetics, underlying principles, and the communication of social values (Kaeppler 1967b, 1971a, 1972, 1976a, 1978b). I did not, however, really address the abstract conceptualisation of what dance is or whether the varied manifestations I described as dance can be grouped together in a way that implies that they have something in common that separates them from nondance.

Some activities in Tonga today that include structured movement are the ceremonial presentation of pigs; the ceremonial enumeration of pigs, kava roots, and baskets of food; the ceremonial mixing of kava; group speeches with choreographed movements; and movements performed in conjunction with *hiva kakala* (sweet songs - also see Glossary of Tongan Terms, p. 118), which may have preset choreography or may be choreographed spontaneously. The first four of these activities often occur as part of a larger ceremonial occasion known as *kātoanga* while the fifth is usually part of a less formal occasion. An examination of each of these activities will illustrate some of the important characteristics of the contexts and the movement.

Presentation of Pigs

Ceremonial presentation of pigs today is usually part of the prelude to an important kava ceremony, especially the *taumafa kava*, kava drinking in which the king partakes. The drinking of kava, an infusion of the root of a pepper plant (*Piper methysticum*), serves important functions in Tongan society ranging from informal get-togethers to an assembly of all the titled men of the kingdom. The *taumafa kava* is a representation of rank in action. It illustrates the relative ranking of titles and their proximity to the line of the individual holding the ceremony by the floor plan in which the title holders are seated and the order in which they are served. Important ceremonial occasions for the drinking of kava are associated with weddings, funerals, and the bestowal of titles. The actual mixing of the kava is usually preceded by the ceremonial presentation and enumeration of pigs, kava roots, and baskets of food. The largest pigs are pulled on sledges into the ceremonial receiving area. Although these sledges can easily be pulled by a few strong men, a large number of men and women may ceremonially pull the pig. Ostensibly this performance illustrates that the pig is so large that a large group is required to pull it — culturally, of course, it does much more than that. A number of persons dragging the pig distribute the burden and it is appropriate that the movements be coordinated. Sometimes, however, a number of associated individuals make no pretence of pulling but simply move in consort with those who do. Such presentations are done in conjunction with the singing of *tau'a'alo*, work songs. The function of *tau'a'alo* is to lighten the heart and strengthen the muscles as well as to synchronise movements that need to be done together by a number of people, such as rowing a canoe, dragging a canoe, or dragging a pig for presentation. Apparently many *tau'a'alo* traditionally functioned in precisely this way.

Today, however, the pig presentation and associated *tau'a'alo* performed by specific villages (usually the village of Holonga) on specific occasions (such as the validation of the title of the king or crown prince) go far beyond what is necessary for pulling and coordination. This formalized pig presentation has become a *faiva* of Holonga. *Faiva* refers to any kind of task, feat, craft, or performance requiring skill or ability, or anything at which an individual or group is clever. *Faiva* is an important concept because of the cultural implication that some things require cleverness while others do not.

The necessary requirements for the performance of Holonga's *faiva*,[3] which is categorised as a *tau'a'alo* (although in many ways it is quite different from more traditional *tau'a'alo*), are an appropriate ceremonial occasion; a poetic text, either newly composed or a previous text appropriate to the occasion; someone who can add the melodic and rhythmic setting to the poetry — characteristically sung by two groups of men and women, each group having up to six-part polyphony; someone who knows how to do the formalised walking movements; a pig of the largest category (*puaka toho*) for presentation; and a large number of men and women to pull and accompany the pig. The movements are basically formalised walking, pulling, and pushing. The actual movement of the group with the pig into the receiving area may take half an hour. The observers listen to the poetry (which is sung several times), critically analyse who the individuals are and what chiefly lines they represent, and, most important, note the presentation.

The most important element in this ceremonial pig presentation is the poetic text. The poetry conveys information through metaphor and allusion interwoven with the Tongan aesthetic principle *heliaki*. This concept, usually translated as 'not going straight' or 'to say one thing and mean another', is characterised by never going straight to the point but alluding to it indirectly. *Heliaki* is poetically realised through the Tongan literary device of alluding to people and their genealogical connections with place names, flowers, and birds, metaphorically making reference to the occasion and those honoured by it. By formalising the walking movements, the movement dimension itself becomes public and an appropriate medium for communicating the poetic information to the observers. Thus the presentation publicly acknowledges the occasion and the status of the receiver, and proclaims that the presentation should be noted as a symbol of support for the established social order by the audience as well as by the receiver. Although this formalised presentation is made by only one village, it is in effect symbolic for the presentations of all the villages. The formalised movements underscore and emphasise what is being communicated by the text in a direct (rather than abstract) manner.

Enumeration of Foodstuffs

The prelude to the kava mixing during which the pig presentation takes place also includes an enumeration of the foodstuffs presented, including pigs, kava, and baskets of *'ufi* (yams). This enumeration is done by designated men as a stylised oral proclamation while touching the foodstuffs, which are counted with formalised movements. The movements include bending the knees, touching the object or the basket with the right hand, raising the head to look at the person being honoured or the *matāpule* (a special ceremonial attendant who directs the proceedings), and shouting the number. The counter then moves to the next basket, bends, touches the basket with the left hand, looks, and shouts the next number. After counting each ten a second man holding a long stick shouts 'one' and keeps track by tens. This counting is done for each category by foodstuff and size. Some of the subtle, but important, movements include raising the head to look at the person being honoured or the *matāpule*, as if for acknowledgement, and which hand is used to touch the baskets. For example, one method is right, left, left, right, left, left, right, left, left, right. While touching a basket with the right hand the left hand touches the right thigh and vice versa.

If the *matāpule* does not like the way this enumeration is carried out — that is, if the oral counting or the movements are not to his liking — he will command them to stop. The counters will then sit down, the *matāpule* will chastise them, and then the counting begins again. It can therefore be said that the movement dimension of enumerating foodstuffs has formalised the nonformal into a structured system, and this system differs according to the line of chiefs honoured. Like ritualised pig presentation, ritualised food enumeration communicates support for the occasion by proclaiming it publicly in a direct (rather than abstract) manner.[4]

Kava Mixing and Drinking

The main part of the kava ceremony is the kava mixing and drinking itself and is the most important institution in Tongan society. It is the Tongan public occasion where various dimensions of rank are proclaimed, legitimised, and solemnised; where deviations involve calculated manipulation of chiefly lines; and where rites of passage of societal importance are celebrated. The most dignified and formalised rendering of the kava ceremony is the *taumafa kava*, which takes place as part of certain state *kātoanga*, especially those associated with the bestowal of titles of nobility. During these occasions elaborate formalised movements are performed in a precise order in response to directions of the officiating *matāpule*. During less formal kava mixing, the movements

are less elaborate, less verbose, less structured, but use similar movements — often in a nonformalised manner.

There are different styles of mixing kava depending on
which major chiefly line is being honoured. The right and
the duty to prepare kava for these chiefly lines is inherited.
For example, the right to prepare kava for the Tu'i
Kanokupolu line (the line of the present king) is held by certain individuals of the Ha'a Ngata chiefs. Thus, when a ceremony requiring *taumafa kava* is planned, it is understood
who the mixers will be — that is, designated people from
the village of Kolovai, who, under chief Ata, carry this re-
sponsibility. In many ways the mixers are as important as
the receivers. Often the mixers come in their own good time,
especially if they think they have been slighted for some reason. For example, the *taumafa kava* for the public validation
of the title of the present king had to be delayed for several
hours because the mixers did not come.[5]

The two main styles of kava mixing still in use are the styles
associated with the Tu'i Kanokupolu and the Tu'i Tonga (the
original line of chiefs of celestial origin and from which the
Tu'i Kanokupolu line is a second segmentation). The differences are minimal, including such refinements as whether
the lug of the kava bowl faces the mixer (for the Tu'i
Kanokupolu) or the person being honoured (for the Tu'i
Tonga), as well as differences in the movement motifs. The
mixing is considered a *faiva* and it is recognised that skill is a
necessity, especially for performing the *haka*— arm movements combined into recognised sequences.

Tongans are well aware of the differences between similar
activities when performed in public or nonpublic venues.
Nonpublic activities are not necessarily private, but rather
have a restricted sphere of recognition. That is, they are of
relevance primarily to the actors and not to an audience. Such
nonpublic activities, although they are expected and may be
observed, are not formalised into a public display. Thus although the preparation and drinking of kava is an everyday
activity, it is usually an event of participation. Only on cer-

tain occasions does the ceremony become primarily an event of presentation to an audience. To be more precise, the participants perform primarily for each other and by extension to announce to any observers that they are carrying out the ritual and acknowledging each other's participation. It thus becomes public, for what the titled men are communicating to each other is relevant to the entire society or specific portions of it. The very act of participation communicates the support of each individual concerned for the individual holding the kava ceremony and illustrates the social solidarity of those participating. It does this publicly with formalised movements and therefore is expected to be acknowledged by those for whom it is relevant. Thus the bestowal of Catholic priesthood on a man from the village of Lapaha is of relevance to his family, to his friends, to the village of Lapaha including its chiefly lines, and to the Catholic church in general. The bestowal of a title of nobility on the crown prince is of relevance to every Tongan individually and collectively, at home or abroad. The kava ceremonies in both cases, however, are public because they do not simply concern those partaking of the kava. The differences between the two ceremonies are in style and degree rather than kind.

For the kava ceremony titled men (chiefs and *matāpule*) or individuals who are included for some other reason are seated in an elongated, broken, near rectangular ellipse, the mixer and associates (and designated titled men) sit at the far end (*tou'a*) and face the person of honour who sits at the midpoint of the opposite end flanked by two *matāpule*, who call the commands and direct the proceedings.

The mixing of the kava entails a series of movements.[6] The mixer and his helpers enter and are seated crosslegged with the bowl placed behind the mixer. A large kava root is brought to the front and broken up by striking it with a large sharpened stake. The movements are quite straightforward, except that a side head tilt (*fakateki*) is added, which in effect formalises the striking movements. The pieces of kava root are placed on a pandanus mat along with two stones. Pieces of the root are then placed on the larger stone and the mixer raises the smaller stone in his right hand to the right side high above his head and looks at the officiating *matāpule*. The root is then pulverised, accompanied by judiciously placed *fakateki*, which again formalise the movements into a structured sequence.[7] The bowl is placed before the mixer, the pulverised root and water are placed into it, and the mixer performs a series of arm movements (*haka*) above the bowl. These movement sequences form motifs, some of which are named, and are punctuated by *fakateki* side head tilts. The mixer kneads the pounded kava root fragments with water, and is then handed a *fau* fibre strainer, with which he performs movement sequences. He clears the liquid of the pieces of root by entrapping them in the *fau*, and with a studied movement flings the *fau* to one of the helpers, who shakes out the kava bits. The *fau* is given back to the mixer to remove more pieces of the root. On occasion the mixer holds the *fau* at shoulder level, poses, looking at the honoured end of the kava circle, and does a *fakateki*. There are two named styles in which the wringing of kava with the *fau* may then be carried out, *milolua* and *fakamuifonua*, which emphasise different movement motifs.

When all bits of kava root have been removed, one of the men or women who will serve the kava brings a coconut-shell cup, stoops to hold it over the kava bowl, and the liquid is wrung into it with the *fau*. The mixer then proclaims '*koe kava kuo heka*' (the kava is lifted) in a stylised call and the *matāpule* answers '*ave ia ma`a X*' (carry it to X). The person called claps his hands in acknowledgement, and the server carries the cup of kava to him. By drinking the kava the drinker acknowledges to himself, to those in the kava circle, and to any other onlookers that he is indeed the holder of that title. The next cup is lifted with the mixer calling again '*koe kava kuo heka*', and the *matāpule* calls the name of the next person authorised to drink, following a specified order. This is repeated until each person in the circle is called, claps, is served the kava, drinks it, and hands the cup back to the server. These serving movements are done in a prescribed manner. For example, the server carries the cup with both hands and, stooping, hands it to the drinker; the drinker takes the cup and drinks while the server turns away from the drinker and takes a few steps as if to go back to the *tou`a*, but instead turns back again to the drinker (who has by this time drunk the kava), takes the cup, and returns to the *tou`a*.

Meanwhile, during the straining of the kava, one of the large pigs is removed, cut up, and a piece distributed with yams to each person in the kava circle as a 'relish' (*fono*) to be eaten with the kava. They do not, however, eat the *fono* but it is ritually taken away from each one by someone (called *kai fono*) who is `*eiki* (higher in rank) to them according to *kāinga* rank (that is, rank within his ego-based kindred. Such individuals include children of a sister (especially the oldest female child) or *mokopuna `eiki* (a grandchild of higher rank because of a son's elevated marriage). This taking of the *fono*, within a formal state ceremony, demonstrates that rank operates on more than one level simultaneously. In this case it shows that every individual regardless of his rank within the overall societal structure is outranked within his *kāinga* (see Kaeppler 1971 for details). Although it is forbidden to cross into the kava circle, those taking the *fono* do so with immunity. Their movements are not formalised, they simply enter the circle, take the *fono*, and leave. These movements are not considered public. The observers visually see them, of course, but because they are nonpublic and are not relevant to them, they are not acknowledged: the taking of the *fono* is relevant only to the *kāinga* of the individual from whom it is taken. Thus the proscription against entering into the kava circle is not broken because from a societal point of view it is not public and can be disregarded.

In short, the formalisation of movements within the kava ceremony communicates that those movements are public and should be acknowledged as such. Which set of formalised movements is used during the kava preparation indicates affiliation with the lineage of specified chiefs. The clapping of hands and drinking of the kava in a prescribed manner proclaims title and rank publicly and is thereby acknowledged by those to whom the particular kava ceremony is relevant. The occasion is a public and nonpublic event where information is communicated selectively by the movement dimensions of various activities within the ceremony.

Formalised movements in the distribution of kava are also used to communicate other information that cannot be communicated orally. For example, at the *taumafa kava* that validated the bestowal of the title of the present king, his new title was called and the first cup of kava was taken to him. Without being announced a second cup of kava was taken to the king's younger brother, Tu'i Pelehake. This was said to publicly proclaim that Tu'i Pelehake should be considered as the king's equal because he has exactly the same genealogy and according to the traditional reckoning, the Tu'i Pelehake title (of Tu'i Faleua) is more elevated than that of the Tu'i Kanokupolu.

Formalised movements have yet another function at state kava ceremonies — to emphasise taboos by having someone who is immune break them. For example, when the king is seated in his place in the kava circle it is forbidden for a Tongan to walk behind him. During the *taumafa kava* for the validation of the king's title, a Fijian of the title Tu'i Soso broke this taboo on several occasions during the ceremony while performing formalised Fijian movements behind the small pavilion in which the king sat — a silent reminder that Tongans may not do this. Tu'i Soso also took the *fono* of the king. When he did so, he emerged from the *tou'a* where the kava was prepared and advanced through the entire length of the kava ring performing Fijian dance motifs with spear and fan. He then speared a piece of pig and ate it in front of the king. These formalised movements communicated several sorts of information. They illustrated that Tu'i Soso's actions were public and relevant to all observers. Because no Tongan outranked the king in an appropriate way to take his *fono* this had to be done by a foreigner — not just any foreigner, but a foreigner of rank. It also demonstrated a difference between the king and other titled men — the *kāinga* rank of the others was nonpublic but the rank of the king is relevant to all.

Group Speeches With Choreographed Movements

The major public activity of a large-scale *kātoanga* in terms of the preparation and involvement of large numbers of people consists of group speeches with choreographed movements. Through these group speeches the same kind of information that is communicated through a kava ceremony is communicated by hundreds of people organised by village. These performances communicate the participants' support for the occasion, while at the same time they glorify their own villages with their histories, traditions, and genealogical lines. One might consider a *kātoanga* as a metaphor of a great kava ceremony in which villages take the place of individuals and in which the act of drinking kava is replaced by what would be called in English 'dancing'.

Large-scale *kātoanga* are rare. The seven given during the reign of Queen Sālote Tupou III (1918-65) were listed in the Tongan edition of the newspaper *Kolonikali* (*Chronicle*) shortly after the queen's death. These were the centennial celebration of the coming of Christianity (1926), the centennial celebration of the installation of Tupou I (1945), the double wedding of the present king and his brother (1947), the golden jubilee of the treaty between Tonga and Great Britain (1951), the travelling of Queen Sālote to London for the coronation of Queen Elizabeth II (1953), the visit of Queen Elizabeth and the Duke of Edinburgh to Tonga (1953), and the centennial celebration of the 'emancipation' (1962). The coronation of Queen Sālote in 1918 was not considered a *kātoanga*, probably because it was held too soon after the death of Tupou II and the kingdom was in mourning, which prohibits festivity. On the other hand, the *kātoanga* celebrating coronation week of Tupou IV in 1967 was primarily a public display.

Tupou IV had actually been king since December 1965. The 4 July 1967, European-style coronation on the king's forty-ninth birthday, as well as the 6 July *taumafa kava*, and the group speeches with choreographed movements on 5 and 7 July were a public validation of the title. During this week the king's title was validated by all the titled men of the kingdom (that is, all the chiefs and *matāpule*, not just the nobles) as well as by all the villages and their people. This occasion was meant to be acknowledged by the world.

The 1962 emancipation *kātoanga* was the most elaborate in living memory and included seventy-one group speeches with choreographed movements each lasting fifteen minutes to half an hour. These performances were spread over seven days and took place in three locations in the island group. It was easier to transport the royal party to the central and northern group of islands (Ha'apai and Vava'u), where four days of performances were held, than to bring the hundreds of performers to Tongatapu, where the sovereign resides. The group speeches, rendered melodically and rhythmically and accompanied by choreographed movements, included several types. There is no inclusive term for these performances except *faiva*, which as noted above also includes *tau'a'alo* and other things. If *faiva* is qualified as *faiva* with *haka*, *tau'a'alo* and the enumeration of foodstuffs are excluded, but kava mixing and the *tau'olunga* (dance) are included. *Tau'olunga*, however, is considered by Tongans to be something quite different.

The types of choreographed speeches included in the 1962 *kātoanga* were *lakalaka*, *mā'ulu'ulu*, *sōkē*, *taufakaniua*, and *meke*. *Me'etu'upaki* and *tafi* were also included in the 1967 *kātoanga*. The most important of these types today is *lakalaka*, which can be considered the classic type of this unnamed category of performances.

A *lakalaka* is composed according to the structure of a formal Tongan speech. Formal speeches have an introductory section known as *fakatapu*, which acknowledges the important genealogical lines and in effect asks their permission to speak. Although individuals of each chiefly line may not be in attendance, the *fakatapu* announces to whom this speech is relevant. The body of the speech may include information about the speaker and his comments and attitudes about the occasion. It is usually congratulatory to the occasion, the individual to whom it is addressed, and often to the speechmaker himself. Speeches usually end with a closing statement that expresses thanks to the listeners and again acknowledges the chiefs. Speechmaking is a highly respected *faiva*, requiring a knowledge of history and tradition, of honorific and elegant language, of poetic meter and *heliaki*, and stage presence.

Lakalaka texts follow a similar pattern but depend on the status of the composer and which group is going to perform. For example, if composed by Queen Sālote, the *fakatapu* need not make all the acknowledgements and ask permission to speak, nor would this be necessary if one of the king's children were to perform in it. Nevertheless, there would still be a *fakatapu* that would convey appropriate information and retain the structure.

As an example of a *lakalaka* appropriate to this chapter let us examine a *lakalaka* of the village of Kolovai that deals with *taumafa kava*. The poetry was composed by E. Vanisi in 1931.

Ko e Lakalaka 'A Kolovai Ko e 'Milolua'

I

1 Ko 'eku tu'u ni ke u fakahā
2 'A e anga 'o 'eku fiefia

3 Si'i 'aho ' e māhina

4 Ne fakakoloa ai ho ta fonua
5 Fakahifo ai e mo'onia
6 Ne ngatūtū he 'a natula

7 Pea me'eme'e manu e
　　'ata

I

1 Here I am standing to show
2 The manner of my happiness

3 The dear fourth day of the month

4 Our land has been enriched
5 Giving birth to the *mo'onia*
6 The land of Tonga was trembling

7 The birds of the air were dancing

8 He kuo huhulu mai e
la'ā .

II

9 'Oi Hala-ki-'ūmata mo e
kolo kakala
10 Ne mahikihiki 'a e
Taungapeka
11 'E Tuku mo Tafa he mo
'ahokata
12 'E Ha'a Havea he mo Ha'a
Ngata
13 Mo hono kotoa 'o e ngaahi
ha'a
14 Kuo lonuku he loto'ā
maka
15 Kuo tau fakataha ko e
fakana'ana'a
16 'Aki e faiva ko e lakalaka.
17 Kae tuku mu'a 'a e
fakahoha'a
18 Ho'o 'akafisi mo ke
'aka'aka
19 Ka ke 'ilo ko e me'a
māsila.

III

20 'Oi fanongo e Tonga mo e
Ha'apai
21 Kae 'uma'ā 'a Vava'u Lahi
22 Pea 'ilo 'ehe Piu 'o
Tafahi
23 Mo e maka ko
Finetoupalangi
24 'Alele pea mo motu '
A'ali
25 Kuo tau katoa 'i Palasi

26 Ke fakamanatu 'a e 'aho
lahi

8 The sun shows forth its
light.

II

9 Oh, rainbow way and sweet
smelling village
10 Kolovai was overjoyed

11 The boundaries of the
happy day
12 Ha'a Havea and
Ha'a Ngata
13 And all the other lin-
eages
14 Are assembled at the stone
fence [palace]
15 We are coming together to
praise [comfort]
16 With the performance of
lakalaka.
17 Please stop the disturbance
18 And your rolling about and
kicking
19 And note that it is a sharp
thing.

III

20 Oh, listen to me Tonga and
Ha'apai
21 And even you, big Vava'u
22 And the Piu of Tafahi
knows
23 And the rock of
Finetoupalangi
24 The islands of 'Alele and
'A'ali
25 We have all gathered at the
palace
26 To commemorate the great
day

27 Ta'u tahatolu kuo ne 'iai.

IV

28 Ke 'ilo 'e he sola pea mo e taka

29 'Ae 'alofi tapu ke tatala

30 Kau nofo hifo 'o ngaohi kava

31 Ke vakai na'a ke laka hala

32 Ka ke nofo pe mu'a 'o mamata

33 Ka mau milolua mo fakamuifonua.

V

34 He 'oi , ´Kuo holo´, ´tuku atu´, ´tuku mālie pe kae palu´

35 'Tafoki kimoua' pea ´ui ha`a mo vai´. ´Vai´.

36 '`Oi vai taha', 'ta`ofi `a e vai'

37 'Palu pea fakatatau´ pea 'tui ha`o fakama`u´

38 'Palu ki lalo´ pea '`ai ange `a e fau.´

VI

39 He 'oi, pea te u milolua, milolua mo fakamuifonua

40 He 'oi, mo fakamuifonua, He 'oi mo fakamuifonua.

VII

41 Ko e ngata e holo taumafa

42 Hiki e tou'a kau foki ange

27 Thirteen years he has.

IV

28 I want the stranger and the roamer to know

29 That the kava ring is forbidden to walking and moving

30 I will sit and make the kava

31 Beware of any wrong moves

32 Be content to sit and watch

33 We will perform the *milolua* and *fakamuifonua* [styles of making kava].

V

34 'It has been pounded', 'put it down', 'put it slowly and mix it'

35 'Face inward' and 'call for your water'. 'Water!'

36 'Stop one water', 'stop the water'

37 'Mix and squeeze', 'circle and squeeze with one hand'

38 'Mix it low' and 'put in the *fau.*'

VI

39 And now I will wring the kava in *milolua* style

40 And wring it in the *faka-muifonua* style.

VII

41 This is the end of our royal kava mixing

42 Kava mixers and helpers move and return

43 'O 'eva he Fala 'o Sētane

43 To walk upon the Mat of
Satan

44 'O kahoa hono loumaile

44 And wear the *maile*
leaves

45 Mo ta sei hono lou siale

45 And the ear ornament of
siale [flowers]

46 Mo e kotone ko fakavale

46 And the *kotone* [trees] which
bring foolishness

47 Si'ene maki'i kae tauele

47 Her giggling and beguiling

48 Fakalavetala kia te koe

48 To attract your attention

49 Ka ke ha'u kau 'ave
'a koe

49 If you come I'll take you

50 Ki homou hala ko
Fine'ehe

50 To your road, Fine'ehe

51 Hala sili mo e
tūkungapale

51 Road of the net fishers and
place of the prize

52 'Uta'anga 'o e manu
fefine.

52 The inland haunt of female
birds.

The first stanza of a *lakalaka* speech is usually the *fakatapu*.
Here, however, because of the subject and the performers,
this composition does not have a well-defined *fakatapu*, but
the first two stanzas serve as one.[8] The body of the text or
lakalaka proper gives information about the performers and
their village, comments on the occasion by alluding to the
genealogy of the person honoured and his association with
the village of the performers, and conveys other relevant information. The last stanza is the *tatau*— the closing counterpart of the *fakatapu* in which the performers say goodbye
and again defer to the chiefs. In addition to the three divisions of a speech, a *lakalaka* text often includes a section
known as the *tau*, which contains the essence of the speech.
The *tau* is a stanza or part of a stanza which elicits the performers' best efforts and during which the audience is encouraged to pay strict attention. The *tau* of this *lakalaka* is
stanza six, which formalises the wringing of kava. The wringing of the kava is not only the essence of this *lakalaka* but also
the essence of the village of Kolovai, giving them their im-

portance in the Ha'a Ngata. By extension the *taumafa kava* is metaphorically the essence of the sociopolitical system, which cements the relationships between the king, his nobles, the chiefs, *matāpule*, and the people in general. Performance of this *lakalaka* formalises and underscores that relationship for performers and audience, and thereby demonstrates their allegiance to the king and his government.

The translation of the text given here[9] is a quite literal translation in order to illustrate the aesthetic principle *heliaki*, 'not going straight'. Although the *lakalaka* is ostensibly about *taumafa kava* and stanzas five and six reiterate the directions and movements for mixing and wringing the kava, the real object of the poetry to which the *heliaki* alludes in the overall sense is the thirteenth birthday of the present king. This can be deduced from line 3 (he was born on 4 July) and from line 27, referring to the thirteenth year. A line-by-line analysis of the text is not relevant to this chapter, but a few verses are of interest to it. That *lakalaka* is a kind of *faiva* is shown in line 16. The literary device of alluding to people with flowers is found in line 5, where Tupou IV is alluded to by *mo'onia*, a specific way of sewing or stringing flowers. Kolovai, the home of flying foxes, is alluded to in lines 9 and especially 10, as an ancestral place of the Ha'a Ngata. The meaning to which the *heliaki* of lines 17-19 alludes is that it is the duty of the Ha'a Ngata chiefs (to whom the people of Kolovai belong) to protect the king and they will not accept any disturbance. And, of course, it is also the duty and privilege of the Ha'a Ngata to prepare the *taumafa kava*. Stanza four points out that it is forbidden to cross into the kava circle, but the *heliaki* implication is that according to Tongan tradition there are right and wrong ways to do things and one learns the correct way by observing. The last stanza glorifies Kolovai with place names such as the sandy beach called 'mat of Satan'. Plants such as *maile, siale,* and *kotone* and a specific kind of net fishing used in Kolovai are further references to the performers. The *heliaki* contends that Kolovai is such a marvellous place that it can lure one away supernaturally like that specifically Tongan affliction called *'āvanga* in which a spirit calls one to follow and one obeys as if possessed.

The movements that go with such a speech would be choreographed from beginning to end by a specialist (*pulotu haka*)[10] at the request of the chief of Kolovai for performance on a specific occasion. This particular version was performed for the thirteenth birthday of the prince. It could be performed at other times to commemorate that occasion, or by simply changing line 27 it could honour some other occasion specific to the king. Although the poetry should only have minor changes, the movements and musical setting might be changed each time the composition is performed.

Movements for this sort of *faiva* are based on three sections of the body — legs and feet, arms and hands, and the head.[11] *Lakalaka* literally means to keep on walking or to 'step it out' and figuratively means to advance or make progress. Foot and leg movements are basically a continuous walking by stepping to one side, bringing the other foot to touch next to it ('place'), stepping to the opposite side, and touching the opposite foot to place. The function of the foot movements is primarily to keep time. The most important movements in a *lakalaka* are the movements of the arms and hands. These movements form motifs, which are strung together in such a way that they can be said to 'comment' on a word or concept of the verse of poetry that they accompany. In effect, they make visual some aspect of the text by alluding to it — another form of *heliaki*. The arm movements form a secondary abstraction, alluding to selected words of the text that themselves allude to a deeper meaning. Or the arm movements, instead of alluding to the poetry, may allude to the deeper meaning, giving the superficial appearance that they have little if anything to do with the text. That is, the arm movements say one thing, but mean another. In short, the arm movements are the *heliaki* of the poetry while the poetry is the *heliaki* of the text. The third bodypart important in *lakalaka*, the head, is used primarily in the side head tilt *fakateki*. Although sometimes choreographed, the *fakateki* is

usually added by individual performers to attract and hold
the attention of the spectators. Aesthetic and decorative, the
fakateki emphasises the publicness of the performance and
proclaims that this presentation is meant for an audience.
Fakateki is par excellence the movement that compels a
Tongan to watch.

Lakalaka is performed by all the men and women of a village who care to perform, often as many as two hundred.
The performers are arranged in two or more long rows facing the audience — the men forming the right half, the
women forming the left half (from the observer's point of
view). Men and women perform two separate sets of movements, illustrating the Tongan view that in public different
kinds of actions are appropriate for men and women. Men's
movements are strong and virile while women's movements
are soft and graceful. Two sets of movements also make it
possible to allude to the text or its underlying meaning in
two different ways, adding another dimension of *heliaki*.

Next to *lakalaka* the most appropriate performing medium
for *kātoanga* is *māʻuluʻulu*, a group speech with choreographed
movements performed sitting down. Although the *māʻuluʻulu*
are often performed on semiformal occasions as a showpiece
and need not have a strict formal structure, when performed
for a *kātoanga* they too incorporate the formal speech-making divisions of *fakatapu*, body of the text, and the *tatau* closing statement. The overall structure has one of two forms —
a through-composed form similar to its prototype (the seated
ʻotu haka section of a *faʻahiula*) or a verse-refrain form adapted
from Christian hymn tunes. The latter is now the more usual
and in it the refrain or chorus is a *tau* that contains the essence of the composition. During the *tau* the performers do
their best in order to compel the audience to pay strict attention. Although strophic in form (that is, verse/refrain, verse/
refrain) the verses need not have the same melody or the
same number of phrases per verse.

Seated crosslegged in one or more rows or with the rows
gradually elevated in various ways — kneeling, sitting on

chairs or benches, or standing — the performers are accompanied by one or more skin-covered drums. The arm movements are similar to those used for mixing kava and for *lakalaka* but more varied and precise. The poetry is preceded and followed by *haka fakalongolongo*, silent *haka*, performed in conjunction with drumming but no text. As in *lakalaka* the *fakateki* head tilt rises from inner feelings of exhilaration and emphasises that the performance is directed to an audience. Usually the performers are all of one sex, preferably female, and often comprise all the students of a sex-segregated secondary school. During the *kātoanga* of 1962, *māʻuluʻulu* were performed by Queen Sālote College, Pilolevu College, Siuʻilikutapu College (all girls' schools), St. Andrew's College, the old women of Tongoleleka, and by the villages of Holonga, Teʻekiu, ʻUiha, and ʻOvaka.

As in *lakalaka* the poetry is basic and composed first with the specific performing genre in mind. The poetry is rendered rhythmically and melodically and visually enhanced by movements. Both the text and the movement incorporate the aesthetic principle *heliaki* by alluding to deeper meanings with formalised speech and movement motifs. Metaphorically each group delivers a speech in which poetry and movements point out and comment upon the occasion and the society.

Other *faiva* that have been performed as part of large-scale *kātoanga* were not entirely appropriate in their original forms, but were made appropriate by giving them a speechlike structure. Primarily this involves adding a *fakatapu* or altering a stanza of poetry to serve as one. During the 1962 *kātoanga* there were performances of two *sōkē*, two *meke*, and a *taufakaniua*. The latter is a performance local to one of the northern islands of the Tongan group and is considered their *faiva*. *Sōkē*, and *meke* are considered to be non-Tongan, having come from ʻUvea and Fiji, but for various historical reasons were appropriate to the group that performed them.

During the 1967 *kātoanga*, a *meʻetuʻupaki* and a *tafi* were performed as specialities of the villages of Lapaha and

Fua'amotu. These *faiva* were particularly appropriate on that occasion because they are associated with the two senior lines of chiefs. Their performance demonstrated visually that these two chiefly lines were part of the genealogy of the king, that these lineages were still powerful forces in the society, and that the people and chiefs of these villages were proud of those affiliations. The performances also demonstrated that, although higher in ceremonial prestige, these lines acknowledged Tupou IV as head of government, and gave their allegiance to him as king of Tonga.

In short the performances of *lakalaka*, *mā'ulu'ulu* and other *faiva* at a *kātoanga* can be considered as an enlarged and extended kava ceremony in which the whole society takes part. Just as the *taumafa kava* demonstrates the allegiance of the individual titled men to the king and indicates their support of the sociopolitical system, so the performance of the *faiva* demonstrates similar sentiments village by village as well as those of every individual performer regardless of his or her place in society. Many villages have a special title by which they are called when it is time to perform — just like a man who is to drink kava is called by his title. These titles, like the titles of chief and *matāpule*, are based on history and tradition. For example, when the inhabitants of the village of Lapaha perform *lakalaka*, they are known as 'Lomipeau' — this refers to a large semimythical canoe associated with Lapaha and its chiefs; when the inhabitants of the village of Kolovai perform *lakalaka*, they are known as Milolua — even if performing a *lakalaka* that is not based on kava mixing. During kava mixing and its prelude of food presentation and enumeration, *the use of structured movement makes information public* (italics supplied). Group speeches with choreographed movements are also preceded by the giving of food and other gifts when they are presented in the receiving ground behind the palace before the actual day of the *kātoanga*. It is on this earlier occasion that the king and his *matāpule* note the support and allegiance of the village nonpublicly. This support is then presented publicly on the day of the *kātoanga* in a festive celebratory context. The social order is upheld poetically and visually in a nonpublic village-by-village treaty with the king and his government and then in a public presentation relevant to all other members of the society.

The structured movement dimensions of the activities associated with *kātoanga* (pig pulling, enumeration of foodstuffs, kava mixing, group speeches with choreographed movements) visually emphasise the importance of rank and social solidarity, which pervade the society. The underlying principles of hierarchical ranking and the mutual interdependence of the various societal dimensions are transformed into visual surface manifestations. To separate the movement dimensions of these activities into dance and nondance would mask the underlying concept communicated to the observer and participant that formalised movement imparts information about social relationships — sometimes objectively, sometimes abstractly.

Tau'olunga — Tongan 'dance'

The movement dimension of the final activity to be dealt with here is known as *tau'olunga*, which is separated by Tongans from the activity it accompanies known as *hiva kakala*, sweet songs. Informal in style, *hiva kakala* are songs of a topical nature composed primarily to be sung. These songs appear to be an evolved form of *pō sipi*, short poems originally recited spontaneously by *matāpule* during informal kava gatherings. These poems consisted primarily of allusions to the female kava mixer on behalf of one of the young men in attendance. Allusions were phrased in terms of flowers, birds, and place names, which referred to the individual without naming her — a form of not-so-complex *heliaki*. During the 19th century, melodies usually in the form of Protestant hymn tunes in verse/chorus alternation were added. Movements, based on a Tongan prototype *ula*, were also added. These movements, now usually translated into English as 'dance', use many of the arm and hand movement motifs used in *lakalaka* and *mā'ulu'ulu* as well as motifs borrowed and adapted from Samoa. The main difference between Tongan and Samoan arm movements is that Tongan arm movements emphasise the rotation of the lower arm (while bending and flexing the wrists and curling the fingers) whereas Samoan arm movements emphasise bending at the elbows (while bending the wrists and curling the fingers). The leg movements are also adapted from Samoa and include small rotations of the lower legs, which move the heels in and out, used mainly to keep time, and a quick lift of the foot by a bend of the knee upward. These movements are not characteristic of other Tongan performing genres. The *fakateki* head tilt may punctuate the performance, but it is not an important element calculated to capture the attention of the observers and encourage them to explore the *heliaki* of the movement for hidden allusions.

Like its Tongan prototype, *ula*, the movements of the *tau'olunga* need not make reference to the poetry they accompany. Instead of alluding to poetry, the movements create beauty. In *ula* one or a few lines of text are repeated over and over and many movement motifs are used to accompany these verses. In *hiva kakala* the sentiment expressed verbally is often about an individual and specifically composed for one. *Tau'olunga* are often choreographed spontaneously, that is, not preset into a well-thought-out sequence. The movements are well-known motifs which in other performing genres are often used as fill-in motifs and need not attempt to go around (*heliaki*) the poetry. The *heliaki*, instead, alludes to the individual performing. The performer is judged on the execution of the motifs rather than on the interpretation of the poetry.

Hiva kakala with *tau'olunga* movement have a limited sphere of public or nonpublic appreciation, the movements being a showcase for the performer. For example, after the nonpublic presentation behind the palace of the *lakalaka* of the village of Kanokupolu preceding the 1975 *kātoanga*, the composer and leader of the *lakalaka*, Ve'ehala (who is also a high-ranking chief, noble, and cabinet minister) gave a marvellous speech that moved the audience to both laugh and cry. Following that he performed an improvised *tau'olunga* in which the movements had little to do with the poetry that was being sung. Ve'ehala is one of the most respected choreographers in Tonga and it is likely that allusion to the text was superfluous for this occasion. The beautiful movements alluded instead to the accomplishments of the performer — another kind of social metaphor. Such a showcase for an individual is enhanced by the addition of one or more *tulaufale* (supporting dancers), who perform movements that would be considered inappropriate if performed on their own. These movements allude to the proper movements through contrast. The *tulaufale* may do virile movements in opposition to the main performers' graceful ones, strike the ground, or even throw themselves on the ground. The cultural preference for allusion rather than statement can be conveyed by *heliaki* of beauty and nonbeauty as well as by *heliaki* of text.

Tau'olunga are only occasionally elevated to this semipublic venue. This *tau'olunga* was not part of the performance during the 1975 public *kātoanga* because choreographic and speech-making accomplishments of an individual were not relevant on that occasion. Instead it was the time to show publicly the support of Kanokupolu for the occasion, the king and his government, and the centennial celebration of the constitution. Kanokupolu's *lakalaka* was first to perform. The poetry concerned the aristocratic sport of snaring migrating pigeons. In addition to this historical allusion, the *heliaki* alluded to the high-ranking Samoan female who was 'snared' to Tonga as the female progenitor of the Tupou dynasty. The ranking female performer was Pilolevu, the king's eldest daughter — his descendant of highest rank, who, in time, would be snared to continue to elevate the dynasties of Tonga. The ranking male performer was Baron Vaea, and there was no immediately apparent reason why he should be performing with Kanokupolu. Vaea is the noble of the village of Houma and is of the highest personal or 'blood' rank although his title is not of the highest ranking. His performance as the central male performer of the village of Kanokupolu communicated visually, however, what it was not appropriate to state orally — that if other societal rules had been activated, he could have been king. By performing he also demonstrated that although he was of very high prestige, he was subservient politically — yet part of the power structure. Baron Vaea, noble and of elevated personal rank, also happens to be one of the best 'dancers' in the kingdom. Had he refused to perform, it would have been a personal affront to the king and his daughter. By performing, however, he demonstrated his support of the *status quo* and the sociopolitical system.

As a postlude on this public occasion a *tau'olunga* would have been appropriate if performed by the king's daughter. *Lakalaka* are occasionally followed with a *tau'olunga* performed by an important descendant of the village chief. This serves a similar function to the taking of the *fono* of a chief during a kava ceremony by an appropriate descendant of the title holder. Such a *tau'olunga* would be of relevance specifically to the village that was performing, and often occurs when the *lakalaka* is performed nonpublicly behind the palace before the day of the *kātoanga*. Usually *tau'olunga* are not permitted during the *kātoanga* itself, except for some publicly relevant reason. A *tau'olunga* performed by the king's daughter at this point would have served a similar function to the taking of the king's *fono* by Tu'i Soso — that is demonstrating that the genealogy of the king is relevant to all.

Tau'olunga performed on public or semipublic occasions are different in character from the original spontaneous performances that accompanied evolved forms of spontaneous poetry. Carefully composed poetry is given a melodic and rhythmic setting (based on European prototypes) and stringband accompaniment. Movements are choreographed to emphasise the beauty of the performer, to allude by *heliaki* to the text, and, in the best compositions, to have an overall *heliaki*. One such exceptional composition is *Manu 'o Palataise*

(Bird of Paradise). It was composed by the late Queen Sālote and the overall *heliaki* was conceived by her. Performed by two females and a male, the latter, as a bird of paradise in the Tongan role of a *tulaufale*, challenges others to stay away from his two females, who move about preening themselves. Wearing costumes of *kakā* (parrot) feathers, the different sets of movements illustrate appropriate movements for men and women, and by *heliaki* point out the proper role of men in regard to women. Women are elevated in rank within the *kāinga* (bilateral kindred) and while men have power, women have prestige. Women are to be pampered, elevated, and protected by specified kinsmen from threats to their dignity. A man will challenge anyone who might harm any of the women for whom he is responsible. *Tau'olunga* is the performing genre par excellence that can be used to instil attitudes and traditions dealing with the extended family and appropriate behaviour between individuals. Although superficially it might appear that the performance makes reference to male/female sexual relationships and advances, it does not. The *heliaki*, instead, alludes to nonsexual relationships and the female/male traditions that deal with prestige and power. In addition, the whole performance infers that Tonga is a paradise and is the proper place for Tongans.

Tau'olunga, thus, can vary from spontaneous 'dances' for nonprogrammed entertainment to elegant compositions on the most important occasions. Semiformal occasions such as a concert to raise money for a church or a floor show at the local hotel could be made up entirely of *tau'olunga* or might have the addition of a *mā'ulu'ulu* or other *faiva* with appropriate text. *Tau'olunga* are intended primarily to be light in spirit and are entertaining, while other performing genres, although they too can be entertaining and are performed in a festive atmosphere, have an underlying social message. Group speeches with choreographed movements are visual manifestations of social structure through movement and express political and social reality in a supportive form. *Tau'olunga*, when organised with an appropriate structure, can also express a social message, but that is really not their function.

Dance and Nondance — the Tongan View

The distinction between *'aho me'e* (day dance) and *pō me'e* (night dance) illustrates the Tongan view. *Pō* (literally 'night') adds informality to the word with which it is associated. For example, *pō talanoa* refers to informal conversation regardless of what time of day it takes place. *'Aho* (day), on the other hand, is when important things take place. Thus *'aho me'e* and *pō me'e* refer to occasions during which *me'e* are performed and not what kind of *me'e* are performed. *Me'e* is a now obsolete inclusive term for various performing genres. *Me'etu'upaki* (*me'e* standing with paddles) were separated from *me'elaufola* (*me'e* based on arm movements). The term *me'e* (the Tongan version of the Fijian term *meke*) fell into disuse when Protestant missionaries attempted to eradicate heathen dances. Instead of eradicating these important sociocultural forms based on formalised movement, Tongans 'invented' new ones and gave them new names. The newness resided in new combinations of old pieces of movement. It is apparent, however, from the existence of the term *me'e* that Tongans had a cultural conception of *me'e* as distinct from other ritualised movement and one which could be further categorised. *'Aho me'e* and its successors are preeminently social metaphors that can be used to convey information — some of which is best not conveyed orally — or can be used as a visual extension of oral literature.

The cultural preference for alluding to deep meaning in an indirect manner gives both composers and audience aesthetic pleasure. Structured movement that has its own *heliaki* transcends ritual movement, which functions primarily to 'make public'. Structured ritual movement is made ritual by a formal structure and often by the addition of *fakateki* head tilts. In the public rituals of pig pulling, food enumeration, and kava mixing, the formalised movements are (in spite of elaboration) real. That is, they do not say one thing and mean another, they do not involve allusion and *heliaki*. In short, structured movement in Tonga functions to make information public and to convey certain kinds of information as movement itself. When movement is given the additional dimension of *heliaki* it becomes something else. *Heliaki* makes movement aesthetic, in addition to public, and functions primarily as social metaphor. Movement, like language, serves different forms of communication, as well as entertainment. *Pō me'e*, and its modern successor *pō faiva*, like conversation, is to be taken lightly. Public structured movement such as pig pulling, enumeration, and kava mixing communicates important information as movement. Group speeches with choreographed movements have the additional dimension of movement *heliaki*. By the addition of *heliaki*, structured movements are transformed into dance.

Tongans who speak English translate 'dance' as *tau'olunga*. If pressed they might agree that *lakalaka* and other choreographed speeches can also be dance. But dance to a Tongan is entertainment and probably ephemeral and frivolous, while choreographed speeches are social metaphors to be remembered and passed on. The act of performing double *heliaki* and the information it conveys in poetry and movement is of primary importance, while the *product* dance is a form of entertainment that conveys joy. What choreographed speeches and *tau`olunga* have in common is that their products derive from performing double *heliaki*.

Various activity systems in Tonga have conspicuous structured movement dimensions, most importantly *pō faiva* (the successor of *pō me'e*) and *kātoanga* — the latter composed of several subactivities having formalised movement. A *tau'olunga* (dance in its narrow sense usually performed as *pō faiva*) can be elevated to a choreographed speech at a *kātoanga* by its inclusion as the end piece of a group's performance and the social metaphors that it reveals. It thereby becomes part of a group's speech, giving an additional *tau* (in the form of a *tau'olunga*, i.e., an elevated *tau*) to the per-

formance. Thus the Tongan cultural conception that might
be translated as 'dance' lies in the performance of a product
made up of structured recognisable movement sequences in
the form of double *heliaki*, that is, movement *heliaki* embedded in either text or beauty, which enhances poetic *heliaki*.
This cultural form based on double *heliaki* is but one of the
formalised structured movement dimensions of various activity systems in Tonga that are social metaphors, expressing the underlying principles and cultural philosophy of hierarchical rank and prestige.

[AK]

GLOSSARY OF TONGAN TERMS

- *'aho me'e* — day dance, formal dance
- *'āvanga* — sickness or infatuation believed to be caused by spirits
- *'eiki* — chief
- *faiva* — any kind of task, feat, craft, or performance requiring
  skill or ability, or anything at which an individual or group is
  clever
- *fakamuifonua* — style of wringing kava
- *fakatapu* — introductory section of a speech
- *fakateki* — side head tilt
- *fau* — fibre strainer used for mixing and straining kava
- *fono* — relish of pig and yams to be eaten with kava, but ritually
  taken away
- *haka* — to move the hands rhythmically, especially while singing
- *haka fakalongolongo* — *haka* performed without accompanying
  poetry
- *heliaki* — not going straight, to say one thing and mean another
- *hiva kakala* — sweet songs
- *kai fono* — one who ritually takes away the *fono* and eats it
- *kāinga* — ego-based kindred
- *kakā* — parrot
- *kātoanga* — festival, public festivity or celebration

- *kava* — an infusion of the root of the pepper plant, *Piper methysticum.*
- *kotone* — tree with fruit eaten by wild pigeons
- *lakalaka* — to advance or make progress (lit: 'to step it out')
- *maile* — a bush with small leaves (Alyria sp.)
- *matāpule* — ceremonial attendant
- *mā'ulu'ulu* — choreographed group speech, performed while seated
- *me'elaufola* — *faiva* emphasising outstretched arms
- *me'etu'upaki*—*faiva* performed standing with paddles
- *meke* — Fijian performance with formalised movements
- *milolua* — style of wringing kava
- *mokopuna 'eiki* — grandchild of high status
- *mo'onia* — way of stringing flowers
- *'otu haka* — seated section of a *fa'ahiula faiva*
- *pō faiva* — informal *faiva*
- *pō me'e* - a night dance; informal dance
- *pō sipi* — spontaneous love poems
- *puaka toho* —pig of the largest category
- *pulotu haka* — choreographer
- *siale* — flowering plant
- *sōkē,* — *faiva* using long sticks
- *tafi* — *faiva* similar to *mā'ulu'ulu,* often performed first in a group of *faiva*
- *tatau* — closing counterpart of the *fakatapu* or closing statement
- *tau* — section of sung poetry containing essence of the poem and during which performers do their best
- *tau'a'alo* — work songs
- *taumafa kava* — kava drinking in which the king partakes
- *tau'olunga* — a dance or *faiva* which often emphasises the performer rather than the poetry
- *tou'a*—persons whose duty it is to prepare kava for drinking, especially on ceremonial occasions
- *tulaufale* — supporting dancers who accompany the primary dancers in a *tau'olunga*
- *'ufi* — yams
- *ula*—*faiva* or dance which often emphasises the performer rather than the poetry.

PRECIS EXERCISE 5

[1]I propose that one of the tasks of an ethnographer is to study [2]all human movement that formalises the nonformal and to [3]elucidate what the movement dimensions of various activ- [4]ity systems are communicating and to whom. Such an [5]analysis could delineate similarities and differences in the [6]movement dimensions and their contexts as well as how [7]these are regarded and categorised and the components by [8]which they are grouped or separated. It might then be pos- [9]sible to illuminate cultural constructs that produce a cul- [10]tural conception of 'dance'. ... I will attempt to delineate [11]cultural constructs that might produce a cultural concep- [12]tion of dance for that society. In previous articles on Tongan [13]dance I have examined kinemic and morphokinemic struc- [14]ture, change in form and function of dance forms, aesthet- [15]ics, underlying principles, and the communication of so- [16]cial values ... I did not, however, really address the ab- [17]stract conceptualisation of what dance is or whether the [18] varied manifestations I described as 'dance' can be grouped [19]together in a way that implies that they have something in [20]common that separates them from nondance.

[21]Some activities in Tonga today that include structured [22]movement are the ceremonial presentation of pigs; the cer- [23]emonial enumeration of pigs, kava roots, and baskets of [24]food; the ceremonial mixing of kava; group speeches with [25]choreographed movements; and movements performed [26]in conjunction with *hiva kakala* (sweet songs), which may [27]have preset choreography or may be choreographed spon [28]taneously. The first four of these activities often occur as [29]part of a larger ceremonial occasion known as *kātoanga* [30]while the fifth is usually part of a less formal occasion. An [31]examination of each ... will illustrate some of the impor- [32]tant characteristics of the contexts and the movement.

[33]Ceremonial presentation of pigs today is usually part of [34]the prelude to an important kava ceremony, especially the [35]*taumafa kava*, kava drinking in which the king partakes. The

[36]drinking of kava, an infusion of the root of a pepper plant
[37](*Piper methysticum*), serves important functions in Tongan
[38]society ranging from informal get-togethers to an assem-
[39]bly of all the titled men of the kingdom. The *taumafa kava* is
[40]a representation of rank in action. It illustrates the relative
[41]ranking of titles and their proximity to the line of the indi-
[42]vidual holding the ceremony by the floor plan in which
[43]the title holders are seated and the order in which they are
served.
[44]Important ceremonial occasions for the drinking of kava
[45]are associated with weddings, funerals, and the bestowal
[46]of titles. The actual mixing of the kava is usually preceded
[47]by the ceremonial presentation and enumeration of pigs,
[48]kava roots, and baskets of food. The largest pigs are pulled
[49]on sledges into the ceremonial receiving area. Although
[50]these sledges can easily be pulled by a few strong men, a
[51]large number of men and women may ceremonially pull
[52]the pig. Ostensibly this performance illustrates that the pig
[53]is so large that a large group is required to pull it — cultur-
[54]ally, of course, it does much more than that. A number of
[55]persons dragging the pig distribute the burden and it is
[56]appropriate that the movements be coordinated. Some-
[57]times, however, a number of associated individuals make
[58]no pretence of pulling but simply move in consort with
[59]those who do. Such presentations are done in conjunction
[60]with the singing of *tau'a'alo*, work songs. The function of
[61]*tau'a'alo* is to lighten the heart and strengthen the muscles
[62]as well as to synchronise movements that need to be done
[63]together by a number of people, such as rowing a canoe,
[64]dragging a canoe, or dragging a pig for presentation. Ap-
[65]parently many *tau'a'alo* traditionally functioned in precisely
[66]this way ... This formalized pig presentation has become a
[67]*faiva* of Holonga. *Faiva* refers to any kind of task, feat, craft,
[68]or performance requiring skill or ability, or anything at
[69]which an individual or group is clever. *Faiva* is an impor-
[70]tant concept because of the cultural implication that some
[71]things require cleverness while others do not. ...The most

⁷²important element in this ceremonial pig presentation is ⁷³the poetic text. The poetry conveys information through ⁷⁴metaphor and allusion interwoven with the Tongan aes- ⁷⁵thetic principle *heliaki*. This concept, usually translated as ⁷⁶'not going straight' or 'to say one thing and mean another', ⁷⁷is characterised by never going straight to the point but ⁷⁸alluding to it indirectly. *Heliaki* is poetically realised through ⁷⁹the Tongan literary device of alluding to people and their ⁸⁰genealogical connections with place names, flowers, and ⁸¹birds, metaphorically making reference to the occasion and ⁸²those honoured by it. ...

Exercises

I. By now, you are aware of the importance of understanding key words in a text. Before going on, make a list of key words from the Kaeppler précis text and find out what they mean. The point is *honestly to assess what you need* in the way of vocabulary to ensure increased understanding.

II. Answer these questions:
1. What is the most important element in a ceremonial pig presentation [lines 72-73]? Why is the poetry so important? [lines 73-82].
2. What is the difference between *tau'a'olo* [lines 60, 61, 65], *taumafa kava* [line 35] and *faiva* [lines 67 and 69]?
3. In lines 75 and 76, you read that *heliaki* is a concept central to Tongan language and symbolic expression. **(A)** How would you explain what it is? **(B)** Why not just say that *heliaki* is 'lying' and let it go at that? **(C)** Can movement can be *heliaki*? [Item C is not answered in the précis text. You have to find the answer in the essay].
4. What does the author say is one of the tasks of the ethnographer [lines 1-4]?

III. Kaeppler's article is a good example of anthropological writing, including all the elements that, ideally, are meant to be there, i.e. good descriptive narration of events, clearly stated levels of explanation of the events and use of indigenous concepts and words to interpret and explain the meanings of the events.
(A) Would a novelist writing a fictional account of Tongan life be required to follow the same rules? Why?
(B) What would you say makes anthropological writing different from the letters a tourist might write home from Tonga?

READING VI

BIOGRAPHICAL NOTES: John Middleton is one of the best known Africanists of a senior generation of British social anthropologists. He received his D. Phil. from Oxford University in 1953. He taught anthropology at London, Capetown, Northwestern and New York Universities. He was then Professor of African Anthropology at the School of Oriental and African Studies, London, and later Professor of Anthropology and Religious Studies at Yale University, from which he retired in 1991.

He has done field research among the Lugbara between the years 1949 and 1953, the Igbo of Lagos, the Akan of Ghana, and the Swahili of East Africa. His main books have included *Lugbara Religion* (1960), *The Lugbara of Uganda* (1965) and *The World of the Swahili* (1992) and he has edited several books, in particular, *Tribes Without Rulers* with David Tait (1958).

The chapter reproduced below, retaining the original English spelling and punctuation, is taken from **Middleton, J. 1985.** The Dance Among the Lugbara of Uganda. *Society and the Dance* (Ed. P. Spencer). Cambridge University Press, Cambridge, U.K., Chapter 6, pp. 165-182. [N.B. The note acknowledging funding resources, etc. is omitted]. Reprinted by permission of Cambridge University Press.

Preliminary

In this chapter, I discuss certain aspects of the dances performed by the Lugbara people of northwestern Uganda. There are several ways in which one may consider the dance: as an aesthetic form of expression in which the key factor is movement, as an outlet for or expression of certain psychological states, as a form of drama for a watching audience, as a means of entering into communication with spirits by becoming possessed, as enjoying the sense of one's own physical movements irrespective of whether one is being watched or not; and there are others. Here I wish to see dances as parts of a totality of social behaviour, and to avoid any suggestion that the question 'what is the dance?' can simply be answered by stripping dances of their social aspects and functions so as to leave an irreducible basis of human activity. My aim is not to understand what 'dance' is in itself, partly because I am uncertain whether it is a separate and meaningful category, but also because it is its social context that gives it meaning. So I first ask what is that context and its significance for the people who are involved in it. I am concerned to study the Lugbara dance as a way of understanding Lugbara thought and the ways in which they order their experience. I am not primarily concerned with choreography, which is outside my professional competence.

One of the best-known statements about the dance is that reported of Isadora Duncan: "If I could tell you what it meant, there would be no point in dancing it". She was referring to inner psychological states and emotions that together made up the 'it' of her remark; they were beyond expression in words and could only be expressed by non-verbal means. Yet these states "existed" in her own experience and were meaningful both to herself and presumably to those to whom she communicated them by movement and gesture. Bateson notes that her statement "is a message about the interface between conscious and unconscious" (1973: 110). In this chapter I try to show that by their dancing the Lugbara are communicating messages about the structure of their society. These messages are that although they wish their society to be stable, in fact it is never so; that although they desire continuity, certainty, and knowledge about the social relations in which they are involved, in fact these relations are always uncertain and beyond their comprehension; that each lineage group regards its constellation of lineage ties that is part of the total social structure as unique and different from others, as a network that is centred upon itself [it is inextricably bound to all the others and in some aspects is the same]; and that they can never directly admit to or state these paradoxes in words. Like Isadora Duncan's 'it', Lugbara social structure, 'exists' in their experience as constraining it, but it is always ambiguous and conflict-ridden and its continuity is beyond their control. The interface here is not that between conscious and unconscious, at a psychological level, but is at a sociological level, between the idea of structure and the experience of its working and constraint. The Lugbara can express their knowledge about this interface in several ways: by fighting, by sacrificing to the dead and spirits, by verbal arguments about the proper behaviour associated with social roles, by playing games, by notions of pollution, and by dancing. They are all means — and there are others — of trying to comprehend and so control or resolve situations of structural ambiguity: here I consider only the last of them.

The Lugbara and Their View of the World

The Lugbara are an agricultural people of some quarter of a million, living on the high open plateau between the headwaters of the Nile and Congo rivers (see Middleton 1965). They lack traditional chiefs, although there have been administrative officials known as chiefs and headmen for the past eighty years. The population density is high, with more than two hundred persons to the square mile in much of the country. The basic social organisation is one of dispersed patrilineal clans; the largest jural communities are the sixty

or so subtribes, each based upon a subclan. These are seg-
mented into several levels of territorial sections, each based
on a lineage. The smallest is the family cluster formed around
a three- or four-generation lineage of which the genealogi-
cally senior man is the Elder or Head. Other than these many
Elders, each with domestic authority based on his control of
the lineage ancestral cult, the only other traditional holders
of authority are the rainmakers, one in each subclan, occasional prophets, and "men whose names are known" whose
authority is temporary and based on personal wealth and
influence. Thus there are few holders of formal authority
outside those at the level of the family cluster. This is a very
egalitarian society and one in which due largely to land pressure there is much competition for available resources and
perennial intergroup hostility.

The Lugbara believe that the Creator Divinity, *Adroa* or
Adronga, dwells in the sky and remote from men. *Adroa* has
an immanent aspect, *Adro*, which is said to be visible and to
dwell in the bushland outside the settlements. There are also
many kinds of spirits or divinities, generically known as *adro*,
that can harm and possess the living. The nature and powers of all these forces are beyond the understanding and control of ordinary people.

These live in their compounds, the centre for every family
cluster of order, authority, certainty and stability. Beyond are
various kinds of fields and beyond them the bushland, some
of it open and some of it forested. The dead are buried in
graves, some within the compounds and others in various
places outside them; most are in liminal areas between the
compounds and the surrounding bushland. Lugbara notions
about death are complex, but in the context of this chapter it
is enough to mention that the process of change from living
to dead is marked by the most important rites of transition
in Lugbara culture. At death the constituent elements of the
person separate and move from the social sphere to those
beyond it. The soul goes to Divinity in the sky, the spirit to
the wilderness with *Adro*; the soul is later redomesticated by

diviners and the spirit remains in the bushland. During this process the social status of the deceased is uncertain, beyond contact by the living, who cannot enter into any direct relationship with him or her: after the establishment of a shrine they may do so again (see Middleton 1960 and 1982).

The Lugbara hold certain views about time. It is thought generally to unroll season after season and generation after generation in an ordered and foreseeable manner. However, there are occasions when this process is disrupted and there are then disorder and confusion in social relations: these occasions include the end of an over-long dry season when people are waiting in desperation to plant crops; the end of an unusually wet growing season when too much rain will prevent ripening and harvesting of crops; and the period between a death and the redomestication of the soul as an ancestral ghost. The former two occasions are dealt with by rainmakers, who have the power to "control" time, the last by diviners; both are persons of ambiguous status who can mediate between men and Divinity.

Death Dances

All these factors are relevant to an understanding of the functions and meanings of the dance for the Lugbara. There are several kinds of dances. A dance is generally known as *ongo*, a word that also means 'song'. The verb 'to dance' is *ongo tozu*, 'to tread or step a dance or song'. Although there are songs without dancing there are no dances without song. More specifically the word *ongo* refers to those dances danced as integral parts of mortuary rites. There are also courtship dances known as *walangaa*, a word that has the connotation of 'to move sideways so as to form a circle'. There are also women's dances, harvest dances, and prophetic dances. I wish first to consider the death and courtship dances.

Properly speaking the dances called *ongo* are those dances after a death by groups of men and women related to the deceased by patrilineal lineage ties. Other *ongo* dances are specifically known as *abi*: these are danced by groups of

affines at various periods up to a year after the death. The
ongo proper are also referred to as *auwu-ongo*, "wailing
dances", and the *abi* as *avico-ongo*, "playing dances". Both
include some half-dozen distinct dances, each with different
names and slightly different musical patterns; but details are
not significant here.

The wailing dances are begun as soon after the death as
possible, in some cases even before the actual burial. They
are held mainly during the daytime, but may continue at
night if the deceased was an old and senior man. The dancers are his lineage kin: the more senior he was the wider the
span of lineage concerned and the longer the total period of
the dancing. The *abi* dances are danced later, properly a year
after the death. The dancers come from their own lineage
homes to that of the deceased, where they dance and are
given arrows as a sign that the affinal link is reaffirmed, even
though the person who originally linked the two groups is
dead. They come either as "sisters' sons", or as "sisters' husbands". The lineage members of the deceased come to dance
and wail; the affines come to 'play' and create and show joy,
aiiko. This word is used in many situations and refers essentially to the sense of joy and satisfaction that disrupted lineage and kinship ties have been reaffirmed. One wails for
the deceased but is joyful that the disruption caused by his
death has been repaired.

If the *ongo* is not performed, then the deceased is believed
to have been insulted by the lack of respect shown to him,
and may then send sickness or nightmares to his living kin
or appear to them as a spectre. In this case great care will be
taken to have *abi* dances performed about a year after his
death. Of course, a man who leaves no daughters or who
has only one or two sisters will have no affines or only a
handful of scattered ones who would not dance an *abi* dance
for him in any case. The dances for a young person, especially a young woman, or a child are small and may last for
only a few hours. On the other hand, those for a chief or a
very old and respected man may last for days on end, and

the *abi* dances may be spread over a year or even longer as various groups of affines come from far away to pay their respects to him. Death dances are not performed for infants, lepers, or those struck by lightning, all of whom are exposed in the bushland. Nor is the *ongo* danced for a rainmaker: his powers come to him directly from Divinity, and he is regarded as having 'died' symbolically at his initiation as rainmaker.

Both *ongo* and *abi* dances are performed in the open [at] a convenient flat piece of grassy land not far from the compound of the deceased. The site is chosen in relation both to the grave and to the shrines that will later be placed for the deceased. Most adult people are buried in a space in the homefields between the compound and the bushland; the grave is marked by stones but is soon hoed over and may be forgotten. The heads of minimal lineages are buried farther away and a fig tree is planted at the head of the grave, which stands there for many years and marks its site. Thus the dances are held in various places according to the status of the deceased, the higher the status the farther the arena being from the compound. Although to the casual observer the differences may not appear very noticeable, they are in fact symbolically highly significant.

Ongo and *abi* dances are at first sight similar, but there are significant differences between them, especially as regards personnel and the nature of the songs sung by the dancers. Both are danced by men in groups and by women as individuals, the men in the centre of the arena and the women at its periphery. As I have mentioned, the *ongo* proper are danced by members of lineages that are related patrilineally to that of the deceased. As the dancers dance they sing songs that praise the prowess of their own lineage segments and insultingly attack that of others whose members are present. They also praise the personal qualities of the deceased: they "bewail his name". Most of the dancers are youngish men, both married and unmarried, those known as *karule wara*, "big youths". The dancers have shaven their heads, often leaving small tufts of hair in which they put feathers, and the occasion is one of competition and hostility, both among themselves and more especially between the dance groups that succeed each other in the dance arena. Often there are fierce arguments which will be calmed by the elders present or which may lead to fist fights in which teeth are knocked out. A group will usually dance for about half an hour, to be followed by another group, which tries to oust its predecessors from the arena: there is frequent quarrelling between waiting groups as to which will dance first. The point here is that the order of dancing expresses the actual constellation of lineage ties which has been disrupted by the death and which must now be restructured and reaffirmed. It is similar in this regard to the pattern of seating for sharing meat at sacrifices to the dead. Women who are close patrilineal kin of the deceased shave their heads and cover their faces with white clay or white ashes, to show their close personal relationship to the deceased. But the aggressive and competitive elements in the men's behaviour are lacking in that of women, who do not enter the lines of dancers but stand outside it.

The group — perhaps two dozen men of a single lineage — dances as a single team, divided into two lines facing each other. The women dance outside, not in lines but in pairs or small groups and without the precision of the men. Every now and again a man will run out of the line or from the group of spectators and do a short individual dance, but one of the same movement as those in the lines are doing. He will also call his *cere* in honour of the deceased. The *cere* is a falsetto whooping cry which is "owned" by every adult, both male and female. The Lugbara language is tonal and the "melody" of the call refers to a sentence associated with its "owner". To utter the *cere* of another person is a deep insult, tantamount to trying to take over or possess their personality. A man calls his *cere* in warfare and at death dances, and when drunk, men often call them when lurching homewards as a sign that they are not enemies to be attacked. Now and again at a death dance a man will run out of the arena hand in hand with a related woman (at wailing dances a lineage sister, and at *abi* a sister-in-law), and at the edge of the bushland, facing it, he whoops his *cere* call and shoots arrows into the bush (or he may imitate doing so). The woman also gives her own *cere* call and imitates shooting an arrow. The pair then returns to the arena. This is an integral part of the dance and is done to show that the dancers wish both to avenge the deceased and also show the powers of the bushland, which are divine and dangerous, that they have no fear and will protect their homesteads from the terrors of the wilderness, which they are thus driving back to their proper domain — at death the powers of the bushland are thought to close in on a village. This also shows the *adro* or spirit of the deceased that it has no future place within the settlement.

A death dance for an important old man may be attended by well over a hundred people. Most of them are drinking, many are drunk and often hostile and aggressive. Most will dance now and again individually and in small groups even if not taking part in the main dance. All join in singing when they can although the main words are sung only by the dancers themselves. These dances are said to be times of confusion. People say that they are then "like children" not because they are behaving in a childlike way but because order and the recognition of legitimate authority have been destroyed by death. It is said that subclan and lineage siblings, normally separated by a rigidly observed incest taboo, may have intercourse in the bushland during the height of the dances, especially when these continue after darkness. A marked feature of these dances is the trancelike condition of the dancers after a long period of dancing and drinking, and usually with little food also; they also stagger about shouting incoherently and have often to be physically restrained by onlookers, who take their arms and hold them on the ground until the seizure wears off.

These dances attract onlookers from wide areas, especially younger men and women: *ongo* are considered to be public spectacles to a greater extent than are *abi*, which are rather the affairs of the respective groups of affines. The onlookers stand at the edge of the arena, often breaking into dance steps. This is not considered as "dancing", *tozu*, but as a sign of sympathy with the mourners. Their presence helps to define the arena: all are looking inwards to where the dancers and drummers are and their backs are turned towards the surrounding fields and bushland. They break ranks to allow through those who run out to call their *cere* and to shoot arrows, then close ranks again once these have returned.

Abi dances are essentially similar in that they are held in the daytime and are performed by members of lineages dancing in lines; in this case the lineages are affinally related to that of the deceased. However, their songs are not expressions of hostility but rather only of self-pride, and there is no running out of the arena to shoot arrows and call *cere*. The *abi* marks the closing of the full period of mourning and is complementary to the *ongo* proper in that together they make the restatement of proper lineage and affinal ties that is begun at the *ongo* and ended by the joy of the *abi*.

Dances of Courtship

The dance known as *walangaa* is different. This is a dance of younger men and women, held in the evenings when there is a moon, usually in a marketplace after the end of market day. The generally accepted purpose of the *walangaa* is to enable people from a wide area to meet and to make sexual assignations, as well as simply to have the pleasure of dancing in a crowd. It is not attended by married women or older widows, but by unmarried women and younger men; old men rarely attend. Children take part on the edges of the arena in the early part of the evening. There is not really an audience of onlookers but only of dancers who are taking a temporary break from the hurly-burly of the dance itself. Instead of watching and being clustered around the central arena, as in the *ongo*, the onlookers are themselves mainly engaged in flirting, talking, and taking and sending messages between lovers: couples are continually leaving the arena and newcomers entering it. Finally, in some places the licensee of the market-place itself may take a small fee from those wishing to dance, which would be unthinkable in the case of death dances.

The pattern of the dance is very different from that of the death dances. Whereas in the latter men enter the dance by lineage segment and the women stand at the edge of the arena, also more or less according to their lineage affiliation, in the *walangaa* men and women form dance lines that dance a foot or so opposite the other in a wide circle. Usually a group of brothers dances opposite a group of sisters, which is the pattern of visiting the girls' sleeping houses at night time. But often a single boy dances opposite a single girl, both in the main ring and also on the edges, where they dance surrounded by a few friends who admire their skill. There is great display of originality and agility in the dance movements, and pairs of dancers may give impromptu dance exhibitions while their neighbours in the ring stand back and applaud them. A man and girl dance opposite each other, their hands usually resting on each other's shoulders; if they are very skilful they may rest their foreheads together and leave their arms free for balance. In any case there is usually direct physical contact between them.

The Dances Compared

I wish here to make a brief comparison between the dances. Their various characteristics may be arranged in certain obvious categories: those to do with personnel, time, and place; gesture, music, and song; associated forms of individual and group behaviour; and the social relationships involved.

As regards personnel, the death dances are performed essentially by men. Women play a less important part as onlookers and they may run out to shoot arrows into the bushland; but these women are not otherwise dancing although they may join in some of the singing. In the *walangaa* the personnel comprise younger men and unmarried women,

that is, the socially less important members of the community. They do not dance or attend the dance as members of
lineage groups as such, although they may dance as groups
of siblings. And non-kin and even passers-by may attend if
they are known generally to the local people, whereas at
death dances, although neighbours may stand nearby and
watch, they stay on the edge of the arena, and passing strangers would be beaten if they tried to attend at all.

As for the occasion, the time and the place, *ongo* are mortuary dances, *walangaa* are for courtship: the former are for
"wailing" and for "joy", the latter for *o'buzu*, "cajoling" or
"seduction". *Ongo* are generally danced in the daytime,
walangaa in the late evening and night, although both may
spill over into other times on occasion. *Walangaa* are danced
throughout the year, whereas death dances are not danced
during the height of the planting or harvesting seasons but
mainly in the dry season (November to March) and the time
after the first harvest (May to September) when there is fresh
grain available for the beer making. As regards place, the
ongo are performed in the liminal area between the safe and
social centre of the homestead and the a-social and dangerous wilderness of spiritual power, where there are no social
boundaries at all. *Walangaa* are danced mostly in market-
places: these are in a sense liminal, because if near the centre
of a settlement they are not used for housing, and often they
are set between settlements on a road. They are places where
passing strangers may bring in foreign "medicines" to harm
people, and they are not attached to nor associated with any
particular local descent group. Both dances are danced in
liminal areas but these are of different kinds.

Death dances are characterised by permitted, indeed by
almost obligatory, near-trance and drunkenness (on beer);
walangaa are characterised by lack of trance or similar
behaviour and the disapproval of drunkenness (and if a man
is drunk it is typically on non-traditional local gin made from
sugar). Death dances are expected to be competitive and
aggressive: an individual nudge may lead to a fist fight and

even to one with weapons, and there is often fighting between groups to decide which will enter the arena first. Violence at *walangaa* is strongly disapproved and I have seen a dance stopped completely by the drummers in protest against loud and physical quarrelling between sets of brothers over the same girls.

The form of the dance itself is important. The male dancers in the death dances form two lines set within a circle of onlookers (who should really be regarded as participants in the sense that a theatre audience is composed of participants with the actors). This circle is set very close to the line of dancers and the whole forms a rigid pattern. On the other hand the *walangaa* is a circular dance without any straight or clearly defined linear pattern, and the edges of the dance are not clearly marked, people standing watching, resting, and talking, haphazardly without any pattern.

These dances are also occasions for music and singing. In death dances the music is played on various instruments: drums, horns, trumpets, rattles, and bells. There are three double-ended drums (the membranes being of skin from the ears of elephants), known as the daughter (treble), mother, and grandmother (bass). They play together, the mother supplying the main beat, the grandmother the steady bass supporting beat, and the daughter the high chattering that the Lugbara say makes the music exciting. They are accompanied by horns (cattle horns), by the small trumpets of wood with a finally attached gourd in which is the mouthpiece, and by the six-foot long wooden trumpets made of hollowed-out tree trunks, often shaped like a man and sounding a slow and majestic deep note that can be heard for many miles. In a dance there are always many false starts (often because a drum needs further tightening over a fire), but once the dance becomes "sweet", when the exciting and pervasive rhythm takes hold, then the drums may only rarely stop; new drummers take over from tired ones without breaking the rhythm and the music can continue for several hours without a break. There is also singing. Only the dancers sing, there being a soloist accompanied by the remainder chanting. Women join in often and punctuate the men's singing with ululations.

In *walangaa* the same three drums are used, but no horns, trumpets, or rattles. The rhythms are different from those used in death dances, and innovation in movement and beat is approved, whereas this is not so for the death dances. The songs, sung by women's and men's voices antiphonally, are topical and come and go in and out of fashion after a few months, whereas those for death dances remain year in and year out without change (although of course the details of lineage names change on every occasion). *Walangaa* songs are not sexually obscene, whereas those for *ongo* may often contain obscene insults directed at lineages other than those of the singers. In the *walangaa* a burst of singing and drumming may last for twenty or thirty minutes, followed by a break of a few minutes before the next dance as people catch their breath, think of new songs, or change drummers; *ongo* may continue for many hours without stop. Whereas in death dances there is a pattern or structure of dances and songs that fit into a programme, associated with the rivalry between dance groups that succeed one another, in the *walangaa* there is no programme of this kind: the dances and songs are similar throughout the evening, and although individuals come and go the general body of participants and observers does not change its identity or form itself into distinct groups.

There are also differences in the dance movements. The movements in both *ongo* and *abi* death dances are similar. Those of the men consist of leaping up and down. This is not the spectacular leaping of peoples such as the Maasai and Samburu but it has something of the same quality. It is a physically separate activity, with little variation in movement, with immense expenditure of energy that leads often (or indeed usually) to a condition of trance. Lugbara often refer to this condition as being *azazaa*, a word used also for prophets and for sexually promiscuous and 'wandering' women. The dance appears as an essentially inward-directed dance, in the sense that the dancer is intensely serious, unsmiling, intent on leaping up and down although also being conscious of fellow-dancers, because to nudge one of them while dancing in line can lead to quarrels and even wounding.

Men and women in the death dances make different movements, a distinction related by the Lugbara to their notions of the social characteristics and positions of men and women. In the *ongo* men dance from the feet, the legs being straight and together; the arms are either stretched out above their heads or holding weapons — spears, quivers, bows and arrows — or flywhisks made of cows' tails: all these objects represent masculinity and men's place in society. Women, in contrast, hop loosely, merely bending their knees, and the arms are held out in front of them at shoulder level and usually bent at the elbow; they hold their arms in a supple waving manner. In the *walangaa* there is no difference in the gestures of men and women. Whereas in the death dances the closest link between individual dancers is between those dancing side by side and of the same sex, in the *walangaa* it is between individual dancers of opposite sex who dance directly opposite one another and form a single unit. The gestures of both are identical and very free: if a man decides to lift his arms above his head in order to balance his body his partner will do the same. Much emphasis is placed on the agility of foot movements, and in the dancing of children on the edge of the crowd all their effort is put into using their feet gracefully and agilely so that they appear to be dancing several inches off the ground altogether. When I asked about these differences, I was told that men are heavier than women, with slower-moving limbs; they added that the real difference is that in death dances men dance in groups whereas women dance individually or as groups of sisters only: men are said always to act in groups and "therefore" to dance more rigidly than women who, being more individualistic, dance more freely as individuals. Women are also more liable to trance and so to act idiosyncratically: they are 'evil' and in touch more easily with spiritual power in the bushland rather than with the ancestors, who keep closer contact with men.

I turn now to what are in terms of symbolic meaning more basic differences. Death dances are elements in an important and elaborate rite of transition, virtually the only one among the Lugbara, who have no important rites at puberty. The funerary rites have certain main characteristics. One is the process from the physical death of a man, through the flight of his soul to the sky to be purified and strengthened by Divinity and that of his other spiritual elements to the bushland, and to the redomestication of the soul and its transformation into an ancestor or ghost with its own shrine. The other aspect is the process from the dissolution of the constellation of lineage, kin and neighbourhood ties centred on the status of the deceased to a new constellation of ties centred on the new status of ancestor and ghost. This is done by the distribution of arrows and the dancing of the *ongo* and *abi* dances. These have obvious characteristics of reversal and liminality (or marginality), both in space and time and in the behaviours of participants. Here the behaviour expected towards strangers — violence and sexuality — is reversed and carried out towards kin. They are associated with trance, the significance of which in this context is, I suggest, that the dancers become closely linked to the soul and other elements of the deceased in sky and wilderness. The wilderness is the seat of divine power and as such dangerous, and its forces are repulsed by the shooting of arrows and the demonstrations of personal identity in the face of otherwise overwhelming spiritual power by the calling of *cere*. Also by being in a state of trance the dancers forsake their customary relations with others within the lineage group and retreat into a form of total individuality, linked with Divinity and the dead.

The death dances are central elements in the most important rite of transition among the Lugbara and their characteristics represent that fact. The *walangaa* are quite different in this respect. There are fewer symbols of liminality and ambiguity attached to them. True, the space, that of the market, is outside ordinary social use and is associated with trade and non-kin, which represent the non-social. The night-time is a period of liminality, when the bushland is said to close in on the settlements. But the entire sense of ambiguity is much less clear than is the case with the death dances, mainly because the basic lineage organisation — ever-changing in fact although ideally unchanging — is not involved, nor the great and irremediable change of status from living to dead.

We may summarise the relationships between death and courtship dances by saying that they both make statements about the proper or ordered relations between men and women and between lineages. But there are differences that are complementary and that together add up to a single complex. Death dances take place in daytime, refer to situations of broken and then restored granting and control of women's fertility (by exchanges of arrows), and to relations of affinity. Wives take part, and dancers and movements are different, the difference representing their complementarity. Courtship dances take place at night, wives do not attend but only unmarried girls ('clan sisters' and 'lovers'), the emphasis is on sexuality and not on fertility, and the similarity of movement of men and women marks the lack of complementarity between men and women, whose roles only later become complementary with marriage.

Other Dances

These are not the only dances found among the Lugbara, and I wish here to consider three others. The first two are known as *nyambi* and are performed by women. The *nyambi* that is performed very frequently is a small dance by the women of a minimal or minor lineage group only, the sisters of a woman who has died or of a girl who is leaving her natal home to get married and who is thereby lost to her sisters, who mourn for her. The music is played on a special board of wood carved with charcoal and laid across a hole in the ground; on it are grated or rubbed two sticks that produce a harsh percussive sound, which is accompanied by gourd rattles (as are used by diviners to send themselves into trance). The songs refer to the occasion and are usually sexual in reference: men say that they are so obscene that they are shocked by them and cannot bring themselves to repeat them. The attendant women dance in a rather shuffling circle. It lasts a few hours only and is not of great importance even though frequently performed. It draws few spectators.

The other dance called *nyambi* is very much larger, the dancers properly being all the women of an entire subtribe. It is performed on two occasions, neither of which occur every year. The first is either immediately after an exceptionally good harvest or after a harvest that is very late due to too much rainfall during the ripening season; the second is at the very end of an exceptionally long dry season. These are both times when the orderly passing of everyday time is considered to have stopped, when there is likely to be much intergroup quarrelling and even fighting over scarce resources. The women come together in the bushland near the subclan raingrove and dance through the settlements, clapping their hands and shaking gourds and rattles, singing sexually obscene songs and abusing any man who may be rash enough to meet them. They may be led by a man wearing the antlers of a waterbuck or the horns of a buffalo, and sometimes women's pubic leaves worn over his male apparel. They dance finally up to the raingrove, where the rainmaker is waiting for them; he then enters to perform his rites. People say that this dance is a sign that the world has gone wrong and confused, that ordinary social hierarchies and relations are 'lost' or 'forgotten', and that the rainmaker must now "start" the new year and the orderly passing of time again. He reorders temporal and social categories, and thereby orders interlineage relations that have been threatened, weakened or even destroyed by quarrelling over resources whose scarcity and allocation have become all-important at these times (see Middleton 1978). Thus they have certain resemblances to death dances, in the sense that they are performed in times of categorical confusion and uncertainty and of temporal liminality. In this *nyambi* dance some features of the death dances are reversed and as it were parodied. I have been told by old men that although a dance, it is really the opposite of a dance, a kind of mirror reflection. Instead of men dancing in lines composed of patrilineal kin, it is danced by women of the subclan irrespective of their lineage and affinal affiliations; they have no organisation in the sense of dancing in groups but appear rather as a mob (I was told by men that they run like ants, in a fast-moving stream); and there are no dance steps or gestures, the women merely running and leaping while singing and shouting. The death dances resolve confusion and disorder in lineages and neighbourhood relations, the *nyambi* do the same in cosmic relations; the former are based, in Lugbara thought, on men, the latter on women. The distinctions between the dances are obvious and are hinged on the opposition between home and wilderness, marked especially by the *nyambi* being performed by women who come into the settlements from the outside, led by a transvestite hunter bearing the horns of the animals that he has killed in the bushland.

Both death and *nyambi* dances are concerned with the structuring of social and cosmological categories. There is a last case that is relevant here, although of course I have not witnessed it and details of the dance are sparse. This was a dance performed by the adherents of the great prophet Rembe in 1915 and 1916. Rembe was a Kakwa prophet who led the Yakan cult, which was based on the drinking of water in which was thought to be divine power. The aim of the cult was to remove a series of associated disasters that came to Lugbaraland at the time: meningitis, smallpox, rinderpest, Arab slavers, and Europeans. Rembe attempted to build a new form of society in which men and women, and old and young, were to be equal, and, by the encouragement of clan incest, ties of descent were to be ignored: he was trying to abandon the principles of sex, age, and descent on which traditional Lugbara society was based. He went into trance and spoke divine messages with glossolalia. The adherents marched up and down under a flagpole (to represent the new government) and then, after drinking the water, danced all day and night until totally exhausted. Songs were sung about the powers of Rembe and Divinity. I was told by old people who had taken part that they expected to awake later in the new Utopia. So here again we have a rite of transition, on a society-wide scale, and the restructuring of categories as part of the dance (see Middleton 1963).

Dances and the Resolution of Ambiguity

I wish now to argue back from these cases to my discussion of death dances. All are closely linked to notions of time, of external divine power, and of divine secrecy and truth. They are all elements of the processes of the cyclical development of lineage, neighbourhood, and the entire society.

Death dances, the *nyambi* dances, and the prophetic dances (the first mainly by men, the second by women, and the last by both men and women) are all associated with rites of transition and/or the changing of seasonal temporal rhythm; the *walangaa* is not so associated. The factor of ritual or formality is important. All the various features of behaviour, liminality, and reversal that mark the *ongo, nyambi*, and prophetic dances are formal and expected: they are items of ritualised behaviour. Whereas the *walangaa* is characterised by individual, free activity that lacks any content of authority, the other dances are characterised by formal activity and relations that contain and express authority (even when reversed, as in the *nyambi*). They contain movements that are clearly defined and proper, and behaviour by the participants is also defined and proper, even if sometimes absent (as with trance and drunkenness); movement is controlled and never free; and the occasions for them are all strictly defined — they are never performed *ad hoc*. They are all ritual performances, at times of social or cosmic uncertainty and confusion. All are associated with ambiguity in social relations, liminality in time and space, and the merging of the realms of the social and the Divine and so with the redefining and restructuring of social categories.

Other Lugbara institutions are (or have been traditionally) associated with such times and with the restructuring of relations (Middleton 1977). The most obvious is interlineage feud: this was also a formalised activity in which the participants were men grouped by lineage segment; it occurred mainly in the 'timeless' dry season; it was accompanied by the calling of *cere*; it took place in spatially liminal areas between lineage territories; the actual force was strictly controlled, and should men actually be killed or severely injured it was regarded as in a sense improper (even though both occured); it was an aspect of the working of a segmentary lineage system in which competition between segments lay at the heart of the activity whose aim was structurally to remove uncertainty as to the proper relationship between lineages and to restore an affirmed constellation of relations; like the death dances it resembled an organised game or sport.

The similarities between the feud and the dance should perhaps not be pressed too far. But consideration of them both brings us back to the original point of this paper: if Lugbara ritual dances are performed largely to mark, and thereby perhaps to effect, processes of restructuring social ties, why do they dance? *Why their dances are performed in liminal places and liminal periods, and marked often by reversal behaviour, is understandable and makes sense, but why not use other means?* (italics added). Sometimes they do, as in the feud and warfare, and these are in a sense reasonably final in deciding the new and effective constellations of lineage ties and authority relations. Let us return to the notion of 'joy', *aiiko*, which is a central part of the *abi* dances. This notion is also an ambiguous one: the affinally related groups come to dance, to mourn, and to rejoice. I was told by a friend watching affines coming to dance the *abi* for his elder brother: "Yes, it is good that they rejoice. Now we know that they did not cause my brother's death and that they respect us and are happy that we are still affines. Let them rejoice: you see, later they will die and then it will be our turn to go and rejoice there" (on the next occasion they will perhaps be sons-in-law themselves). I suggest that the death dances are performed as dances precisely because the situation is one of uncertainty and also of delicacy: verbal statements alone would — or might — be too crude. *There is no single motive for dancing* (italics added): it can be to rejoice in a Western sense (as in the *walangaa*), or to be glad that a difficult or ill-defined period is over, or even to insult in a subtle way. A similar ambivalence can be seen in the use of *cere* calls: it can be aggressive, protective, or insulting. In an ambiguous situation every participant can play as he pleases, and may if he wishes even retire altogether from his fellows by becoming in a state of trance and thereby being linked to the ancestors and Divinity; and also his actions and non-verbal statements may be interpreted by the onlookers as they please in their turn.

This notion of ambiguity needs more consideration than I can give to it here. Essentially it refers to the paradox that occurs in all Lugbara social relations. They hold that there is an ideally unchanging structure to their society, yet in actuality the constellation of relations that compose that structure is always changing in both form (the genealogical links between groups and persons) and in content (the distribution of legitimate authority among groups and persons). This paradox of disequilibrium comes about as a consequence of the structural and cosmic processes that have been mentioned earlier. In all these situations the Lugbara include dances as part of the rites that they perform in response to them. The dances are formalised ritual events in which the local groups and communities involved make certain statements, both to their own members and to the wider society and the ancestors. The central questions that I have asked in this chapter have been those of the content of these statements and the means used to make them. They contain two parts, details of which vary from one kind of dance situation to another. The first is that the group concerned shows that it has been thrown into temporary uncertainty and disarray by the confusion of social and cosmic categories, and they express this in terms of reversal and liminality. The second is that the group ends the dance, or sets of dances, by showing the re-formed and reordered social and cosmic categories, the means used being rejoicing, giving the rainmaker or prophet authority to perform their secret rites, and so on. In brief, they first demonstrate the existence of confusion or ambiguity in social relations, and thereby show that they comprehend it (as far as Divinity allows them to do so) and so intend to bring it under control. Then they act out this control and thereby bring about order and stability in society once again. We come here to a consideration not only of [the] dance but of drama and ritual, which lie outside the scope of this chapter. What I do wish to suggest is that at least in the case of Lugbara the dance is hardly a natural or haphazard pattern of movements performed by people because they find it agreeable to do so — although in the case of the *walangaa* this is to some extent true. To understand the Lugbara dance we must see it in its total context, as an expression of underlying structural contradictions and conflicts that cannot be expressed otherwise except by dogmatic or destructive statements.

[JM]

PRECIS EXERCISE 6

¹There are several kinds of dances. A dance is generally ²known as *ongo*, a word that also means 'song'. The verb 'to ³dance' is *ongo tozu*, 'to tread or step a dance or song'. Al-⁴though there are songs without dancing there are no dances ⁵without song. More specifically the word *ongo* refers to those ⁶dances danced as integral parts of mortuary rites. There are ⁷also courtship dances known as *walangaa*, a word that has ⁸the connotation of 'to move sideways so as to form a circle'. ⁹There are also women's dances, harvest dances, and proph-¹⁰etic dances. ...
¹¹Properly speaking the dances called *ongo* are those dances ¹²after a death by groups of men and women related to the ¹³deceased by patrilineal lineage ties. Other *ongo* dances are

[14]specifically known as *abi:* these are danced by groups of [15]affines at various periods up to a year after the death. The [16]*ongo* proper are also referred to as *auwu-ongo,* 'wailing [17]dances', and the *abi* as *avico-ongo,* 'playing dances'. Both [18]include some half-dozen distinct dances, each with differ-[19]ent names and slightly different musical patterns; but de-[20]tails are not significant here.

[21]The wailing dances are begun as soon after the death as [22]possible, in some cases even before the actual burial. They [23]are held mainly during the daytime, but may continue at [24]night if the deceased was an old and senior man. The danc-[25]ers are his lineage kin: the more senior he was the wider [26]the span of lineage concerned and the longer the total pe-[27]riod of the dancing. The *abi* dances are danced later, prop-[28]erly a year after the death. The dancers come from their [29]own lineage homes to that of the deceased, where they [30]dance and are given arrows as a sign that the affinal link is [31]reaffirmed, even though the person who originally linked [32]the two groups is dead. They come either as 'sisters' sons', [33]or as 'sisters' husbands'. The lineage members of the de-[34]ceased come to dance and wail; the affines come to 'play' [35]and create and show joy, *aiiko.* This word is used in many [36]situations and refers essentially to the sense of joy and sat-[37]isfaction that disrupted lineage and kinship ties have been [38]reaffirmed. One wails for the deceased but is joyful that [39]the disruption caused by his death has been repaired.

[40]If the *ongo* is not performed, then the deceased is believed [41]to have been insulted by the lack of respect shown to him, [42]and may then send sickness or nightmares to his living kin [43]or appear to them as a spectre. In this case great care will [44]be taken to have *abi* dances performed about a year after [45]his death. Of course, a man who leaves no daughters or [46]who has only one or two sisters will have no affines or [47]only a handful of scattered ones who would not dance an [48]*abi* dance for him in any case. The dances for a young per-[49]son, especially a young woman, or a child are small and [50]may last for only a few hours. On the other hand, those for

⁵¹a chief or a very old and respected man may last for days
⁵²on end, and the *abi* dances may be spread over a year or
⁵³even longer as various groups of affines come from far away
⁵⁴to pay their respects to him. Death dances are not per-
⁵⁵formed for infants, lepers, or those struck by lightning, all
⁵⁶of whom are exposed in the bushland. Nor is the *ongo*
⁵⁷danced for a rainmaker: his powers come to him directly
⁵⁸from Divinity, and he is regarded as having died symboli-
⁵⁹cally at his initiation as rain-maker.

⁶⁰Both *ongo* and *abi* dances are performed in the open [at] a
⁶¹convenient flat piece of grassy land not far from the com-
⁶²pound of the deceased. The site is chosen in relation both
⁶³to the grave and to the shrines that will later be placed for
⁶⁴the deceased. Most adult people are buried in a space in
⁶⁵the homefields between the compound and the bushland;
⁶⁶the grave is marked by stones but is soon hoed over and
⁶⁷may be forgotten. The heads of minimal lineages are bur-
⁶⁸ied farther away and a fig tree is planted at the head of the
⁶⁹grave, which stands there for many years and marks its
⁷⁰site. Thus the dances are held in various places according
⁷¹to the status of the deceased, the higher the status the far-
⁷²ther the arena being from the compound. Although to the
⁷³casual observer the differences may not appear very no-
⁷⁴ticeable, they are in fact symbolically highly significant.

⁷⁵*Ongo* and *abi* dances are at first sight similar, but there are
⁷⁶significant differences between them, especially as regards
⁷⁷personnel and the nature of the songs sung by the dancers.
⁷⁸Both are danced by men in groups and by women as indi-
⁷⁹viduals, the men in the centre of the arena and the women
⁸⁰at its periphery. ... As the dancers dance they sing songs
⁸¹that praise the prowess of their own lineage segments and
⁸²insultingly attack that of others whose members are
⁸³present. They also praise the personal qualities of the de-
⁸⁴ceased: they "bewail his name". Most of the dancers are
⁸⁵youngish men, both married and unmarried, those known
⁸⁶as *karule wara*, 'big youths'. The dancers have shaven their
⁸⁷heads, often leaving small tufts of hair in which they put

^{88}feathers, and the occasion is one of competition and hostil-
^{89}ity, both among themselves and more especially between
^{90}the dance groups that succeed each other in the dance arena.
^{91}Often there are fierce arguments which will be calmed by
^{92}the elders present or which may lead to fist fights in which
^{93}teeth are knocked out. A group will usually dance for about
^{94}half an hour, to be followed by another group, which tries
^{95}to oust its predecessors from the arena: there is frequent
^{96}quarrelling between waiting groups as to which will dance
^{97}first. The point here is that the order of dancing expresses
^{98}the actual constellation of lineage ties which has been dis-
^{99}rupted by the death and which must now be restructured
^{100}and reaffirmed. It is similar in this regard to the pattern of
^{101}seating for sharing meat at sacrifices to the dead. ...

[JM]

Exercises

I. Do you know what these words/phrases mean?
•lineage kin [25]; •lineage ties [13, 37, 88, 98]; •lineage homes [29];
•affine(s), (-al) [15, 30, 34, 46, 53]; •minimal lineages [67]; •patrilineal
[13]; •lineage segments [81]; •disrupted (-tion) [37, 39, 98-9]; •pe-
riphery [80]; •liminal (-ity) [pp. 138, 139, 141, 143 in essay];
•ululation(s) [p 136 in essay]; •glossolalia (p. 141 in essay].

II. On a separate sheet of paper, using your own words, answer these
questions:

1. The *ongo* dances [lines 5–7] are the "death dances" of the Lugbara.
Who are the chief participants in *which* dances? [lines 11-39].

2. [Lines 60-74] These dances are associated with specificplaces inside
and outside the compound. What is the significance of this?

3. [Lines 75-101]. **Summarize** the information the author gives about
ongo and *abi*. Be sure to cover all points.

III. If asked to **summarize the role of women** in the *ongo* dances, how
would you do it? What would you say? Use information from the entire
article, not just the précis passage.

ADDITIONAL THOUGHT EXERCISES

The sixth Reading marks slightly more than the halfway point of the course. By now, it is possible to see larger patterns emerge. For example, Keali'inohomoku, Royce and Williams all dealt with the definitional problem in somewhat different ways, but there were overlaps and divergences in their points of view. Kaeppler and Middleton also deal with the problem. Students should make their own evaluations of how each author deals with the issue, starting by asking themselves how they would compare or contrast, say, Kaeppler's and Middleton's handling with that of the first three authors. David Best dealt with the problem of definition in a different way. What connections are there, if any, between his philosophical analysis and the writings of the five anthropologists?

Although none of the authors of the first six Readings make a point of it, there are political considerations that clearly affect the dances. Tongan society, for example, is based on a monarchy, thus royalty and complicated ranking systems play significant roles in the formalized movement systems and dances that Kaeppler describes, especially in terms of spatial relationships.

On the other hand, Lugbara political identity is dominated by kinship ties, extended families and specific notions regarding 'lineage'. How and in what (differing) ways do these political structures (especially gender distinctions) seem to affect Lugbara dances?

How do students know (and if they don't know, how will they set about finding out?) what basis there is for Hopi social organization? For Zapotec social organization? These are important questions, because in each case (Lugbara, Zapotec, Tonga or Hopi), the dancers' bodies are not simply physical bodies. Royce's *fandango* dancers, Middleton's *walangaa* dancers, Keali'inohomoku's Hopi dancers, and Kaeppler's Tongan performers have physical bodies, to be sure, but these bodies are *selves defined with respect to other selves operating in spaces* that are more recondite than a physically measurable volume. Any dancer's 'here' and 'there'; 'then' and 'now' has a *social locus* because dancers carry their conceptual spaces with them. Alignment in space becomes a creative social alignment by its very nature.

The unfolding of space/time in a dance is linked to the unfolding of a person (or persons). Cosmological spaces, conceptual spaces of various kinds, and dramatic spaces all emerge *performatively* from the enactment of selves in a dance, whether those selves are roles assumed only for the duration of the dance or whether social selves and danced roles are the same.

Students should ask themselves, 'what influence do religious or theological ideas have upon the dances I'm reading about?'; 'Is it possible to identify something about Tongan or Lugbara *philosophy* from the ethnography?'; 'Do I know more about Tongan, Lugbaran, Hopi or Zapotec concepts of self from reading about the dances and other systems of formalized movements?' In other words, activity that may superficially appear to be mere relaxation or entertainment frequently yields more profound values, if we know how and where to look.

Finally, from a more technical point of view, could Royce, Kaeppler and Middleton write as they do if they couldn't understand the indigenous spoken languages of their people? What would be likely changes in their ethnographies if they were unable to speak the conventional languages of the people to whom the dances belong?

[The Editor]

READING VII

Notes On Comparative Method
[by the Editor]

In Chapter Six of her book on anthropology and the dance, Royce comments about the necessity of using comparative method in sociocultural anthropology and in the anthropological study of dances. She emphasizes the interplay of thought process and understanding required as ethnographers struggle to achieve a clear picture of a dance form different from their own:

> In the initial stages of observation we tend to see the unique aspects of all that is happening in the society around us. This is simply because we do not have enough information yet to fit all happenings into a larger scheme or pattern. At the same time, we are subject to the natural tendency to look for commonalities so that we can make the strange more familiar; so that we can say, "ritual X is not really so incomprehensible as it seems, for after all, it is very much like our own ritual Y"...

She goes on to say,

> This search for links between a foreign culture and one's own is accompanied by a tendency to look for similarities between events as a way of handling data that would be unwieldy if they were treated as unique occurrences. We may, for example, recognize the fact that each wedding is unique in a variety of ways, but still we recognize aspects common to all weddings. In addition to allowing us to organize a great deal of information, this kind of categorizing enables us to anticipate events, one of the basic criteria of the adequacy of our description. ... Observation, description, and analysis are steps that must characterize the study of one culture or society, but, in order to achieve the goals of anthropology, they must be repeated in the comparative study of several cultures or societies. Edgerton and Langness state this quite clearly in their book on anthropological method:
>
>> However well anthropologists may call attention to patterns of cultural behavior in one society, anthropology's ultimate goal is the understanding of [humanity] in all societies, a goal which can only be accomplished by making cross-cultural comparisons. Cross-cultural comparison involves a search for regularities in [people's] cultural behavior. But even more important, it is a

search for wider theories of human behavior which bind these regularities together and provide an understanding of how and why cultures take the forms they do (cited in Royce 1977: 133).

The statements that begin Royce's Chapter Three (1977: 38-39) are also relevant:

One of the major reasons that the anthropological study of dances lags behind the discipline of anthropology itself must surely be the attitude of most anthropologists. They have defended their neglect of dances by shrouding them in mystery, by relegating them to the category of esoterica (about which it is nice to know something but which is not really essential compared to the more important categories of ethnographic research), and finally by referring to the "difficulty" of observing and collecting information about the dance in the first place, and of analyzing and storing it in the second place. The purpose of this chapter is to remove at least some of the veils of mystery surrounding the dance and to suggest practical means for lessening the difficulties of collecting data about dances.

As Juana de Laban noted in 1954, "movement is one of the least explored of all forms of communication when it comes to making a permanent record of its manifestations" (1954: 291, cited in Royce, 1977). We have made some progress since 1954 in our ability to produce permanent records of danced phenomena although the recording of dances is still not a commonplace procedure like, say, the recording of music.

Although dancing is commonly thought to be one of the oldest of the arts, it has had one of the shortest histories in terms of permanent records. An adequate system of dance notation, which is one kind of permanent record, must deal successfully with three different elements: movement through space, movement through time, and the stylistic variations and idiosyncrasies that comprise what we may call "performance" (Royce 1977: 38-39).

Anthropology of the dance and human movement studies has come a long way since 1977 when Royce wrote her book. It has achieved far greater sophistication in the intervening twenty years of its existence, especially with regard to the recording, not only of dances and other forms of structured human actions, but in terms of newer theoretical underpinnings pertaining to its use of comparative method.

The difficulty with comparative method, when the ethnographer gets down to the brass tacks of what Evans-Pritchard called "the writing-up side" of his or her work (1951: 88) is this: *what does one compare?* If someone is going to look for, then state with confidence, that there are "commonalities" in the dances of X , Y and Z societies, what are these commonalities and how do they operate? For example, "[I]n the jazz idiom there is a step called "rubber-legs"[1] and in Wanam dancing, a step called "shake-a-leg". These steps, *illustrated by Laban texts, carry many visual and physical similarities that could be mistaken one for the other,* but on closer examination it can clearly be seen that the two moves are quite different. ... While I was in western Cape York working with Arbui Peter on some of the *Wanam* dances, he tried to teach me shake-a-leg. Through my frustration at not being able to master the step I tried performing rubberlegs, which has many variations, all of which I demonstrated. "Can you do things like this in shake-a-leg", I asked. He shook his head, smiled and said "... that's not the right step". The point is that steps may have superficial similarities but they are in fact not the same. Other considerations must be taken into account; language, meaning, purpose, intent. A great deal of confusion arises when such inaccurate and misguided assumptions are made" (Arnold, Fieldnotes, 1988 - italics added).

Arnold represents an emerging, relatively new breed of movement ethnographer; one who can *write movement,* who uses such writing (and resulting texts) as an essential part of field methodology. As Juana de Laban so rightly pointed out, one of the biggest difficulties with human movement studies in the past has been "making a permanent record of its manifestations" but the notion of recording is only a bare beginning:

> We know as much as we do about the speech component of discursive practices because we remove them temporarily from the flow of "real time" by writing them down for the purpose of analysis. We are able to do this because of the invention of the alphabet and because we are literate in relation to speech. The production of written movement texts using the Laban script supplies the same conditions for the analysis of the bodily, spatial, and dynamic components of actions. (Farnell 1995b: 23-4).

It is only fairly recently that movement writing has begun
to come into its own in anthropological circles (see Farnell
and Williams 1990).

The Literacy of Movement

Learning movement-writing increases the ability to visualise movement. Notators are able to construct a visual impression of a movement event from a movement text and can actually see more than
from a film screen. This is because the text describes in three dimensions and with a 360° perspective of the movement. Regardless of
familiarity with an action system, a skilled reader can establish a personal relationship to the actions of a text, and thus to an event. This
occurs in a much more direct way through performing the actions
from the text. Viewers of a living event establish a personal relationship to the spatial patterning of an event as they are part of that event.
This differs from the false distancing that occurs between a viewer of
a screen and the filmed event. No comparable personal relationship
can occur from the non-involvement of a detached audience.

Like the literate musician, what a literate movement-writer sees
through reading a movement text are the essential elements and parameters of performance to which actors can then add their personal
qualities and interpretations. Apart from their entertainment and
personal history value, analytically, films can be extremely useful to
a notator as a memory aid and as an example of a possible interpretation of an event. However, it is the notation score that indicates the
criteria of identity of behaviour … in an action system. These criteria
rely on adequate and relevant classifications, and such abstract thinking is a product of literacy.

Movement-writing, as with other literate methods, provides a
highly developed framework for viewing and thinking about movement *through categories that derive from that medium* (Page 1990: 84 —
italics added).

There are some, however, who would say that movement-
writing merely *artifactualizes* dances, reducing their rich, live-
performance appeal to incomprehensible squiggles and
marks on a page. They tend to regard making records a misguided venture from the outset, but we think that's because
they see the issues involved in oversimplified terms.

In our eagerness to be aware of the limitations of scripts, it is important to remember that literacy also provides tremendous possibilities

for the imagination. Poets and novelists as well as anthropologists cannot do their work without writing. Musicologists and (most) Western composers require their musical notation systems — indeed, the revolt against the rationalism of traditional Western tonal music was facilitated through the invention of new notation systems, not without or in spite of them. Movement literacy too provides that kind of possibility for the imagination, the creation of alternative cartographics (Farnell 1995b: 26).

Rather than being recognized as an exciting methodological breakthrough, Farnell remarks that movement writing appears to arouse negative responses on the part of many social scientists:

> Not all of this has to do with an anticipated tedium of having to spend time and energy learning to become literate. There are deeper cultural reasons. For example, perhaps the overall advocacy of a *publicly visible acting self* so deeply challenges Western individualism that writing actions appears to threaten the solipsistic Cartesian conviction that one's "real" self is essentially private and unavailable to inspection by others ... (Farnell 1995a: 26 - italics added).

Given that we accept movement literacy as a "good thing", even if we see no other function of Laban's script than that of "making records", we haven't yet addressed the issue with which we began: what (and why) does one compare?

Fairbank's treatment of minority dances in China (1985) deals with this issue, and with the dilemmas that confront communities, especially of traditional dancers and movement-writers, in the face of relentless political pressures to create a unitary 'Culture' out of an existing diversity of subordinate minority traditions regardless of moral or ethical costs. She says,

> This chapter deals with the Han [Chinese] cultural traditions which inform the national cultural campaign and various policies towards China's ethnic cultures. Although China has a longer recorded history than any other nation, historical records have suffered damage and loss through purge, neglect, and natural demise. In recent years, particularly during the Cultural Revolution (1966-1976), thousands of documents and artifacts were destroyed. The lineage of great artists who had passed their traditions down through the generations

was nearly broken. These artists, including stage actors, storytellers, dancers and calligraphers were persecuted for their artistry and forbidden to practise or to pass on their skills. This was true for the minority peoples as well as the Han themselves, although it would be a misnomer to classify minority traditions as 'art' The recent resurrection of these cultural traditions and arts brings into question the degree of awareness and accuracy the administrators actually possess with regard to this material. ... The process of nationalization and modernization has resulted in the mixing of a multitude of separate source materials, hence the creation of a new movement form entirely ... Inevitably a situation of pidginization has been created.[2] PRC [People's Republic of China] dance art, such as staged versions of the minority dance forms, present western researchers with numerous complex issues. Political considerations and questions of ethnic identity are inextricably entangled with this subject (Fairbank 1983: 32-3).

The Chinese case provides an example of comparative method used in a highly suspect manner from the point of view of those who want to see all of the diverse forms of Chinese dancing preserved as closely to their original structures and meanings as possible. This isn't happening. When searching for commonalities in dances, for example, many Chinese processors of dances look for, *and then teach and use,* what they believe to be "most representative" in a particular style — especially what they conceive to have the "best appeal". In other words, the minority dances of China aren't being recorded or passed on in their original forms. The movement texts are interpretations.

This approach to comparative method is based on the notion that the so-called "folk traditions" must be "developed" for the stage and turned into "art". To be acceptable politically and otherwise, the minority dance style must be "beautified". Fairbank says, "In this way",

minority dances are *stereotyped* and broadcast widely under the auspices of the top political leadership. The minority peoples are represented by a *processed facsimile* of their dress, song styles, work habits (1983: 111 - italics added).

Clearly, there are different *levels* of comparison and different *levels* of perceptions of events; levels which, if they are not taken into account, place ethnographers in serious danger of creating distortions and misconceptions of all kinds.

One could say that Chinese political authorities compared the minority dances with Han dances, and found the minority dances wanting. They weren't pleasing to their eyes because they weren't sufficiently similar to Han dances. They were not "smooth" but "rough". They were not "acceptable", therefore, they had to be "developed", as Fairbank tells us. In fact, the Chinese minority dances have been changed. It is important for readers of this book to note that *they were changed through an initial idea of using comparative method, thus we see that the method itself isn't infallible, nor does the method ensure uniform results.* How the method is conceived of and used is what counts.

Furthermore, the initial ideas about comparison held by the Chinese which were applied in their methods of recording minority dances weren't what anthropologists refer to when they speak of "comparative method". Conflation of the two notions leads to serious misconception. Even if Chinese minority dances *hadn't* been changed through unfavorable comparisons with Han dances, the *concept of comparison* would be different.

In considering cross-cultural (or intra-cultural) comparison, anthropologists of human movement have to take many more things into consideration than a superficial resemblance to events with which he or she may be familiar. Nor is it enough for an investigator in this discipline to reconstruct a dance or to reach some general descriptive formula meant to demonstrate a pet thesis about dancing or dances in general. That is, dancing as a vehicle for leisure and entertainment; dances as precursors to spoken language; dances as repositories of emotion; any of the explanations enumerated by Williams (see above, pp. 56-7). Nor is it enough for the ethnographer to say (in effect), "Mexicans dance *this* way", but, "Africans dance *that* way", "Aborigines dance *this* way", etc. The relevant anthropological question is, "so what?"

Good ethnographies take us towards *a more comprehensive*

understanding of what the similarities and / or differences consist. That is, an anthropologist who has made a study of formalized and non-formalized systems of movement in a culture (*cf.* Kaeppler's work in Tonga), has reached certain conclusions about the role of these systems in social life because of the research process — including the task of ethnographers. It is necessary for investigators to offer conclusions about their work that have wider validity.

A good ethnography *includes, but goes beyond* description. For example, Middleton concludes,

> They are all ritual performances, at times of social or cosmic uncertainty and confusion. All are associated with ambiguity in social relations, liminality in time and space, and the merging of the realms of the social and the Divine and so with the redefining and restructuring of social categories (see p. 142-43 above).

Here are some theoretical ideas worth consideration: social ambiguity, liminality and the "merging of the realms of the social and the Divine" *to the purpose of re-structuring social categories.*

However, having identified a theoretical concept, where do we go from there? We start by asking, "are there other dances elsewhere in the world that also do (have or illustrate) this?" If there are, then how and in what ways do they do *so*? We ask, "how *widespread* is the claim that dances resolve ambiguities?"

What would it take to prove the claim stemming from Kaeppler's work that non-formalized movements have to be considered before we gain a clear understanding of what 'dance' is? Obviously, these questions and their answers must be based on more than superficial resemblance.

Following Royce's suggestions, it may be the case that Mexican, Israeli, Norwegian and Egyptian cultures all have wedding dances, but, what are the common elements among them? Are these elements related to any other social facts in the societies to which they belong — or to those with which they are being compared? To say that the wedding itself *is* the common element (which is true in a limited sense), simply isn't enough, for it merely tells us that four cultures have marriage customs, but we already knew that, didn't we? However,

> [W]e are subject to the natural tendency to look for commonalities so that we can make the strange more familiar ... ritual X is not really so incomprehensible as it seems, for after all, it is very much like our own ritual Y (Royce, see p. 152 above).

Few would argue the point Royce makes, yet, as we have seen, our tendencies to make the world comprehensible are often grossly misleading. Human desires to see the strange and alien as common and familiar can lead to false interpretation and outright distortion.

Social Reality and Personal Experience

On the whole, some of the difficulty lies in the fact that anthropologists who write about dances and dancing are preaching to the converted. Those who know and accept the reality of concepts and ideas in dances do not feel the need for explanations of those concepts and ideas. Those who think that dances are living, moving systems of human sociocultural realities *rarely feel the need for an explanation of the realities of 'person', 'agency' and the language-based nature of human actions.*

But, there are those to whom dances consist of gross physical movements (which are no more than the raw behaviors of 'organisms', minus their social, cultural, linguistic and historical properties). For these people, biological reality takes precedence over the sociocultural realities in human realms. In other words, the two points of view entail different conceptions of human 'be-ing' - see Prost (1996), Farnell (1996), Varela (1996), Urciuoli (1996) and Williams (1996) for discussion of these issues. New generations of students must make *informed theoretical choices* between, for example,

> [The] semasiological perspective, grounded as it is in a conception of persons and agency arising from the new realist philosophy of sci-

ence [offering] a cogent alternative to the pendulum that has been swinging between Cartesian intellectualism and phenomenological, existentialist subjectivism for several decades (Farnell 1995b: 10).

Forty-five years ago, Evans-Pritchard observed that

> There has always been a popular, though not unhealthy, prejudice against theory as contrasted with experience. However, an established theory is only a generalization from experience which has been again confirmed by it, and a hypothesis is merely an unconfirmed opinion that, judging by what is already known, it is reasonable to assume that further facts will be found by research to be of a certain kind. Without theories and hypotheses anthropological research could not be carried out, for one only finds things, or does not find them, if one is looking for them. Often one finds something other than what one is looking for. The whole history of scholarship, whether in the natural sciences or in the humanities, tells us that the mere collection of what are called facts unguided by theory in observation and selection is of little value (Evans-Pritchard 1951: 64).

The popular bias *towards* experience frequently finds strong expression among dancers, dance educators, critics and apologists, recalling Keali'inohomoku's preoccupations with the world of dance scholarship and Best's section on experience and observation (pp. 77-81). While it is true that anthropologists can be theoretically biased or myopic with reference to human movement studies, it doesn't follow that dance practitioners, with nothing more to guide them than their *experience* of dancing, will give unbiased, more honest accounts of dances — which is the implicit claim.

The difference between the written accounts of anthropologists of human movement and their theoretically unschooled counterparts begins at a student level. That is, trained investigators make their observations and carry out research based upon generalizations that have been made by their predecessors and themselves in a specialized intellectual discipline. Their generalizations may be coterminous with — or counter to — those which exist in the discipline. In either case, field research, knowledge of the language of the people concerned and much else is required before the generalizations, whatever they may be, are permissible. By that, I mean that anthropologists of human movement are *accountable* to their colleagues for the veracity of what they write.

In contrast, lay people make generalizations that usually arise out of nothing more profound than popular opinion, which is frequently (though not always) dead wrong, and, the layperson isn't ultimately accountable to anyone. He or she merely claims the right to their opinions, whatever they may be, regardless of the presence or absence of supporting evidence. The point is this: *both the anthropologist of human movement and the layperson have theories.* The former are systematic, reflective, and subject to criticism. The latter are often unsystematic and frequently unreflective. Criticism or accountability aren't major issues.

Unfortunately, popular notions about movement, posture, gesture, dances and signing are inadequate guides, not only to informed evaluations of dances (and dancing), but to personal understanding and experience. That is,

> I thought I could always rely on hand gestures and signs when the going got rough ... But I quickly learned that they never worked as well as I had hoped. None of my hosts knew my sign language. One time when I pointed to my chest with my forefinger to indicate 'me', I was shown to the bathroom because to the Japanese that same gesture means 'I want a bath'. The Japanese point their fingers to their noses to mean 'me' (Simmons 1983: 107, cited in Williams 1991: 196).

Simmons's belief that she could rely on hand gestures and signs emerged from the popular belief that 'body language' and the semantics of hand gestures are universal. But, naive theories of universality like this are among the first to be jettisoned by aspiring anthropologists of human movement studies because of well-known, well-documented counterexamples. Simmons's beliefs let her down when she tried them out, because they were based on a serious misconception about the universality of movement in the first instance. While the results are amusing and entertaining, they have a more serious side.

The relatively brief history of the anthropology of human

movement can usefully be regarded as a slow, but persistent substitution of *informed opinion* about dancing and dances (signing, the martial arts and other structured systems of human actions) which replaces *uninformed opinion*, definitions, classifications, etc. Starting from the late 'sixties, a prodigious amount of work has been done in this field, and the progress that has been made is, we think, roughly relative to the amount of disciplined, informed knowledge that is available. In the end, *the only thing that counts* is the variety, the accuracy and volume of well authenticated fact that is available. It is the sole function of theories (and their accompanying methods) both to stimulate and guide the collection of data, which in turn provides the facts that result from research.

THOUGHT EXERCISES

The most important question with regard to comparative method is, 'What does one compare?' It is essential for students to begin to understand that a morphological problem exists and why it is important.

So often, what passes for comparison of dance steps isn't real comparison but a mere cataloging of resemblance, as the example provided by Arnold (p. 153) illustrates. Saying that one dance step *looks like* another doesn't amount to using comparative method. There are many spoken and written words *which sound* alike, i.e. 'soul' and 'sole', but the fact that they *sound* alike doesn't make them *mean* alike, does it? Likewise, if two dance steps *look alike*, does the visual similarity make them *mean alike*?

Questions like these call to mind an old East Indian tale about a man who was badly frightened on his way home at dusk because of a coiled snake lying in his path. When he told his wife about his experience, she nodded, but asked if he was sure it was a snake, saying that she had noticed an old piece of coiled rope on the path when she went to gather vegetables for their evening meal. The man went outside to the path again. This time he realized there was no snake. The object was only a piece of old rope that to him, had looked like one. Comparisons between superficially similar gestures and action signs can be more confusing than coiled ropes and snakes, unless we are equipped with the kinds of conceptual insights made possible by movement literacy.

Page draws a comparison, saying, "Like the literate musician, what a literate movement-writer sees through reading a movement text are the essential elements and parameters of performance ..."(p. 154). They don't see in the same ways that non-movement-literate observers do. Not only that, there are great practical advantages to be had by using movement texts because they provide excellent *evidence*.

Marjorie Franken used movement texts to provide evidence for the claims she makes about several forms of Swahili dancing (see pp. 236 *ff*). Franken's dancers embody significant social moments in a Kiswahili universe in Mombasa (Kenya) *that are made more visible in the texts* than they otherwise might be. Why?

Because what people see depends to a large extent upon what they consciously or unconsciously look for. If the observers of *wangwauna* and *watwana* dances know how to read the social iconography of the dances (which is based on the social originals of Swahili-speaking, urban Muslim society), then the portrayal in the dances makes perfect sense to the observers. For the dancers, the dancing re-affirms who and what they are. If, however, the observers do not know how to read the dances ('read', that is, while they actually watch, or read Franken's movement texts and their accompanying explanations) it is highly likely they *will not understand* what is going on.

Apart from the use of movement texts as evidence and reference (but preserving the theme of observers and the observed), on pp. 155-56, Fairbank points out that minority dances in China are *stereotyped*. That's to say present-day audiences in Beijing see "processed facsimiles" of the original

Chinese minority dances in theaters because they have been changed to suit the tastes of the dominant culture.

Politics thus enters into the consideration of dances in different ways, and, what was said on p. 157 bears repeating: *it is important for readers to note that [the dances] were changed through an initial idea of using comparative method, thus we see that the method itself isn't infallible, nor does the method ensure uniform results.* As with any methodology in any discipline, it is how the method is conceived of and used by individual investigators that counts.

Finally, a somewhat more technical question: when, on p. 160, Farnell talks about "the pendulum that has been swinging between Cartesian intellectualism and phenomenological existentialist subjectivism for several decades", students should examine what it is they think she's talking about — or if they have any idea what she is talking about. If the subject is a mystery, it should be cleared up before going on.

The essay from which the quotation regarding Cartesianism is taken (Farnell 1995b) provides an excellent accompanying text for this section.

READING VIII

BIOGRAPHICAL NOTES: Edward ("Buck") Schieffelin received his B.A. in physics and philosophy from Yale University in 1960 and then went to the West Coast of the United States to become a carpenter. After two years he entered the University of Chicago, where he received a Ph.D. in anthropology in 1972. His dissertation and book on the Gisaro ceremony were based on 26 months of fieldwork in Papua New Guinea in 1966-1968. After a period of teaching at Fordham University in New York, Dr. Shieffelin returned to Papua New Guinea in 1975-76 to study the performance of seances by spirit mediums. This and subsequent fieldwork in 1984-85, 1989 and 1992 has provided the basis for further published work on ethnography and theory in ritual performance. He is at present living in the United Kingdom where he teaches anthropology at University College London.

The following are extracts from **Schieffelin, E. 1976.** *The Sorrow of the Lonely and the Burning of the Dancers*. St. Martin's Press, New York. Reprinted by permission of St. Martin's Press.

Extract # 1

The Kaluli people live in the tropical forest of the Great Papuan Plateau on the island of New Guinea. The Papuan Plateau stretches from the Kikori River (or Hegigio, as it is called locally) westward toward the Strickland River. The area with which we are concerned is bordered to the north by the escarpment of the Karius Range, which forms the edge of the New Guinea Highlands. To the south, the region is bordered by the collapsed cone of an extinct volcano, Mt. Bosavi. This region, which covers roughly 525 square miles between the Sioa and Hegigio rivers, is sparsely populated by about 2,100 people (1966 government census), who speak at least five different languages (1976: 5) . ...

The Kaluli people with whom I stayed are one of a number of local groups who characterize themselves collectively as Bosavi *kalu,* or "men of Bosavi", as distinct from the Onabasulu and Etoro groups nearby to the north and west.

The Bosavi *kalu* live in about twenty isolated longhouses around the base of the northern flanks of Mt. Bosavi. They make up the largest single language group and more than half of the population north of the mountain, numbering about 1,200 in 1966. Most of their longhouses are located between the altitudes of 900 and 1,100 meters on land drained by the Isawa and Bifo rivers. The northern edge of this drainage provides their boundary and may be located roughly by a line arching westward from the Hegigio River via the Bifo and Kulu and then along the Isawa where it turns toward the Strickland (1976: 7) ...

The Bosavi people distinguish four different groups among themselves, on the basis of what they claimed to be linguistic and ethnic differences. The group among whom we spent most of our time called themselves Kaluli *kalu,* or Kaluli men. The name is possibly derived from a conjunction of the word *kalu,* which means 'man' or 'men', and the suffix *-li,* which connotes validation: 'actual' or 'real'; thus it might be approximately glossed as "the real men". ... Although I speak primarily of the Kaluli group throughout this ethnography, what I say may be taken to apply to [the Orogo and Walulu] groups as well. (1976: 9)

The origin of the Bosavi people is obscure. Despite their close geographical proximity to the heavily populated highlands and fairly extensive trading contact with the Huli people north of the Karius Range, they are neither physically nor culturally very similar to [other] highlands groups. The Bosavi are rather part of the broadly lowland Papuan series of cultures that range from the Daribi of Mt. Karimui … through the inhabitants of the Lake Kutubu area … westward to the Strickland River and south to the coast. According to the Bosavi people, they have always inhabited the plateau, and their mythology and traditions do not point to an origin elsewhere. There is some evidence to suggest that they may have originated on the plateau somewhat to the west of their present location (1976: 9-10). …

Extract # 2
The Gisaro Ceremony

The most elaborate and characteristic ceremony in Bosavi is called Gisaro. Like all Kaluli ceremonies, Gisaro takes place at night in the longhouse. It is performed by the guests at a formal social occasion for the benefit of their hosts and lasts until dawn. The first Gisaro I saw was held to celebrate the gathering of pigs for a forthcoming pork distribution. Preparations at the host longhouse at Wasu took two days. The Wasu people cooked large quantities of pandanus, a tropical fruit, and painted and decked themselves in their shell and feather ornaments.

The dark interior of the longhouse was packed with spectators sitting on the sleeping platforms behind the row of house posts that lined each side of the central hall. Light was provided by five or six resin-burning torches held by young men at the sidelines. Everyone was turned expectantly toward the front doorway for the dancers and chorus to enter.

A group of about twenty-five men came in, their faces

downcast. They moved in a body quietly up the hall to the middle of the house. There they drew apart to reveal the resplendent figures of the four Gisaro dancers in their midst. After a moment, all whispered "shhhh" and sat down, leaving one dancer standing alone.

His body was painted in red ocher with black markings, his head crowned with feathery black cassowary plumes tipped with white cockatoo feathers. His chest was hung with shell necklaces; his wrists, arms, and legs decorated with bracelets and bands. His whole figure was outlined against waving streamers of stripped yellow palm leaf, which shot up to shoulder height from behind his belt and fell away to his feet: "break like a waterfall", as the Kaluli say. The dancer was slowly bounding up and down in place, his eyes downcast, his manner withdrawn. A rattle suspended from his hand was clashing softly on the floor in time with his motion. As the house became quieter, his voice became audible, singing softly in a minor key.

The ceremony had a simple form. Throughout the night, one by one the four dancers took turns dancing in place or moving up and down the small space in the middle of the hall, singing songs in company with the choruses seated at each end. The songs concerned familiar places in the surrounding countryside known to most of those who were present. As dancer followed dancer, the songs began to refer to specific places on the host's clan lands and recalled to the listeners former houses and gardens and close relatives, now dead, who lived there.

One dancer sang a song that alluded to the dead son of a senior man of the host clan. The youth had died at a small house near a creek called Abo, and his soul was believed to have gone to the treetops in the form of a bird. The dancer sang:

There is a Kalo bird calling by the Abo waterfall,
juu-juu-juu.
Do I hear my son's voice near the Abo spring?
Perched, singing in a *dona* tree, is that bird my son?

The senior man, who was sitting with the crowd at the side-lines, brooding and withdrawn, suddenly became overcome with grief and burst into loud wails of anguish. Enraged, he jumped up, grabbed a torch from a bystander and jammed the burning end forcefully into the dancer's bare shoulder. With a tremendous noise, all the youths and young men of the host community jumped into the dancing space, stamping and yelling and brandishing axes. The dancer was momentarily lost in a frightening pandemonium of shadowy figures, torches, and showers of sparks. Showing no sign of pain, he moved slowly across the dancing space; the chorus burst into song. The senior man broke away from the crowd and ran out the back door of the house to wail on the veranda. This scene was repeated over and over from dancer to dancer during the course of the night.

Finally, at dawn, when the first birds began to sing, the dancers, the chorus, and the visitors suddenly rose to their feet with a shout, "*Buuwɔɔɔ!*"[1] breaking the spell of their performance, and bringing it abruptly to an end. The dancers, whose shoulders were quite badly burned, then paid compensation to those they had made weep, and all the visitors trooped out of the house to go home. Since many people wept, the ceremony was felt to have been a good one. Some of the visitors left wailing out of sympathy with their grief-stricken relatives among the hosts. The rest were exhilarated, and hosts and visitors shouted to each other that they would surely live long.

For several days afterward, the performance loomed large as a topic of conversation. Men remarked on how well so-and-so had danced, how much they themselves had cried, and what they had received in compensation (or complained that they had not received enough). Young people and children sang the songs and played at dancing in off moments, while others responded with mock crying and mimed the plunging of the torch.

The Kaluli regard Gisaro with enthusiasm and affection. They find it exciting, beautiful, and deeply moving. The dancer in full regalia is a figure of splendor and pathos. This is not because of the ordeal of burning he must face; rather, it is the very beauty and sadness that he projects that causes people to burn him. From the Kaluli point of view, the main object of Gisaro is not the burning of the dancers. On the contrary, the point is for the dancers to make the hosts burst into tears. The hosts then burn the dancers in angry revenge for the suffering they have been made to feel. To the dancer and the chorus, this reflects rather well on their songs. Moreover, a well-decorated and graceful dancer may project such magnificence as to cause a girl among the hosts to lose her heart and elope by following him home after the performance—a significant social coup for the visitors.

The dancers are always volunteers. When it is decided to perform Gisaro, several men immediately step forward. For ceremonies involving less severe ordeal, I have seen boys of ten or twelve proudly and excitedly announce that they were going to participate.

Gisaro is the most widely known ceremony among the people of the plateau and seems to be historically the oldest. The Kaluli and their neighbors also perform five other kinds of ceremonies,[2] which differ in the number of dancers, the nature of the songs, the appearance of the regalia. However, most of them have the same basic themes: they are staged in the communal house at night; the dancers are elaborately costumed; the songs concern people's lands and evoke grief, crying, and burning from the hosts for which the dancers offer compensation. They seem to be alternative ways of expressing the same things.

Kaluli ceremonies are not connected with any particular season or time of year, so long as there is sufficient food available to feed the guests. Any ceremony may be performed in connection with any important occasion that people wish to mark. The one exception is that ceremonies are not held at funerals, for Kaluli feel it is improper to jiggle a dead person with dancing. Besides, after a death people are grief-stricken, somber, and angry and are more in the mood for murder than for ceremonial dances. Which ceremonies will be performed depends largely on practical considerations, such as how elaborate the occasion is going to be, how long a time there is to prepare for it, and what people wish to do.

Ceremonies such as Gisaro are striking to an outsider at first because of their dramatic qualities; but, more important, one perceives that the people are deeply moved, in their grief and violence, and for that moment one glimpses something fundamentally important about their lives. Gisaro fascinated me while I was in Bosavi because I felt that, if I could grasp what is was about, it would provide a way to understand the people who performed it .

This kind of social giving and exchanging is basic to the Kaluli way of life. Friends and relatives in the same longhouse community normally expect to be able to borrow food and tools or request gifts of wealth from each other if the need arises. Among people in different longhouses, this sort of reciprocity is even more visible because it tends to be carried out in a formal and conspicuous way. The exchange of women and wealth in marriage provides the basis for the provision of hospitality for visiting, support in conflict, invitations to hunt and fish, mutual assistance in garden labor, and occasional ceremonial prestations, which are formal, customary gifts of food, especially meat. ... It is difficult to give an adequate impression of the pervasiveness of this sort of social reciprocity in Kaluli life. A man's relations with, interactions with, and affection for his affines, for example, are so bound up with situations of reciprocal gift-giving and mutual help that he tends to think of his life with his wife, on reflection, in terms of the situations in which he worked cooperatively with her and reciprocally with her relatives and exchanged countless minor gifts of food. ...

Kaluli celebrate their relationships with others formally in large-scale ceremonial prestations, when most of the people of one longhouse community distribute pork or smoked game to people in other communities. It is to celebrate these big occasions of food giving, or important stages in their preparation, that Kaluli most often stage ceremonies such as Gisaro.

Indeed, while celebrating occasions of reciprocity, Gisaro embodies some of its characteristics. Compensation (*su*) must be paid for feelings deeply moved, and one ceremony is explicitly given in return (*wel*) for another. A performance that has caused a lot of grief motivates the hosts to return an equally affecting one to their guests. Gisaro is itself, therefore, a reciprocal transaction in the esthetic domain. All this suggests that social reciprocity is not merely punctuated by ceremonies such as Gisaro but is deeply bound up with what they express. Gisaro clearly involves emotional or ideological matters of wider cultural significance than only the giving of the food. It points to ways that reciprocity may be bound up with other realms of cultural symbolism and social experience.

At the same time, ceremonies retain a character independent of the events they usually celebrate. Kaluli sometimes perform them in the absence of important social transactions,[3] in times of fearful portents, such as when the first airplane flew over the plateau, or at the approach of epidemic disease. In the latter case, the community may perform sickness-warding magic and invite another community to perform a ceremony that night. If sickness is already in the longhouse and there have been several deaths, magic is dispensed with, and, in a mood of panicky anxiety, people announce their imminent arrival to another community and go there to dance.

If Kaluli social life takes much of its form through processes of reciprocity, it is not surprising that reciprocity should be celebrated by ceremonies that express important human concerns in deeply moving ways. It is in ceremonies such as Gisaro that these wider concerns are focused and made visible. If we are to appreciate them, and what they mean for Kaluli people, we must learn what Gisaro is about. And for Gisaro to yield insight into Kaluli experience, we must learn how to interpret it (1976: 21-28).

Extract # 3
Gisaro and the Opposition Scenario

What, then, is Gisaro all about? The songs project the members of the audience back along their lives, through images of places they have known in the past. As a visiting government interpreter once remarked to me, "It is their memory". Tragic situations are renewed, allowing people to take account of them once more and settle them in their hearts and minds. It is not the nostalgic content of the songs, however, but the angered and anguished *taking of account* in Gisaro that is most striking to an outsider, and it is the taking of account, I believe, that to the Kaluli gives the ceremony its special character. The listeners' feelings and reactions are not merely a response to the performance; they are integral to its structure and significance. The dancing and singing by the performers and the weeping and burning by the audience stimulate and aggravate one another. If the *aa bisɔ* (hosts, defenders) fail to respond to the songs, even enthusiastic performers soon lose interest, and the ceremony falls apart before the night is over. On the other hand, if the *aa bisɔ* weep and burn the dancers even desultory performers rapidly pull themselves together and assert a determined momentum. The movement of Gisaro is ultimately to be understood in terms of the opposition scenario.

A Drama of Opposition

Gisaro is a drama of opposition initiated by the dancers but played out by everyone. Within a structure of reciprocity, the action of the performers and the feelings of the audience are brought into a relation with each other that allows intelligibility and resolution. But at the same time, *aa bisɔ* and *miyɔwɔ* (longhouse visitors, raiders) confront each other in an interaction of such tension that it not infrequently blows the performance apart. If an enraged host treats a dancer too harshly, or a minor dispute among the gathering escalates, or some other event occurs, people may jump angrily to their feet shouting recriminations, and the ceremony ends abruptly.

On one occasion described to me, an *aa bisɔ* youth began banging on a drum. This was probably part of the clowning the hosts perform during the first part of the ceremony, but it had the effect of drowning out the songs. Unfortunately, the dancer at the time was a man of strong temperament, who became enraged, left the dancing space, smashed the drum, and threw the youth bodily out of the *aa* longhouse. With that, the *miyɔwɔ* jumped to their feet, grabbed axes, and wrecked the interior of the *aa*. A few *aa bisɔ* squared off in token defense, but most fled outside appalled at what was happening and how their young man had behaved.

In social anthropology, when violence and antagonism are expressed ceremonially between two groups, it is customary to assume that they represent underlying stresses between the groups and thus to search for a deeper content to the opposition in the underlying tensions of social relationships. The *aa bisɔ* and *miyɔwɔ* involved in any occasion of celebration (or dispute) are not opposed as residential or descent units but as action groups, of temporary and heterogeneous composition, in which members of the same lineage or residential unit may be on either side. There are no clearcut or lasting lines across which *structurally* engendered tensions might develop. The oppositions invoked on ceremonial occasions are circumstantial and pertain to the particular *issues* involved.

The question then is: are the particular issues of the occasion the basis for an antagonism expressed in the ceremony? Kaluli ceremonies are usually connected with weddings and prestations. At a wedding, when a woman is brought to her husband's *aa*, the *aa bisɔ/miyɔwɔ* opposition is roughly between those who are giving bridewealth (the hosts) and those who are to receive it (the guests). For a prestation, the division is roughly between those who are making the prestation and those who are receiving it. Since about 60 percent of the meat on these occasions is given to people classed as affines, we might suppose that the *aa bisɔ* and *miyɔwɔ* on ceremonial occasions are opposed principally across lines of affinal connection.

While the principal donors are often *aa bisɔ* for celebrations of preparation, some future recipients act together with them as hosts for one ceremony and come as guests for the next, or vice-versa. Often this is done in a kind of rotation, so that, in effect, everyone gets a chance to be *aa bisɔ* and *miyɔwɔ*. The only time when the line between *aa bisɔ* and *miyɔwɔ* really approximates that between donors and recipients is on the day of the distribution itself, when hosts and guests dance together and there is no weeping or burning. Because *aa bisɔ* and *miyɔwɔ* divide and switch around in this manner, it is difficult to say exactly what these oppositions really mean for a Gisaro in terms of the opposing groups and affinal exchange.

A wedding presents a more clear-cut opposition. The social division is drawn between those who support the groom and those who come with the bride. The question is whether the Gisaro ceremony performed for the occasion can be taken as fundamentally expressive of a temporary antagonism between the two sides. The issue is difficult to resolve clearly. The locus of tension is associated with the bridewealth negotiations and focuses on those people involved in them. However, the principal figures in the Gisaro ceremony—for example, the dancers—are more often than not peripheral to the bridewealth issues (if they are involved at all) and bear no close network relation to the negotiators.

[The attached chart in the book] outlines the relationships between dancers and those receiving the major bridewealth payments in a representative wedding. Although everyone on the list knew all the others, none of the dancers volunteered out of close kin or affinal connection with the bride's family or important participation in the bridewealth. Similarly, those who composed the songs for the ceremony (not shown) did so because they had some knowledge of the groom's clan lands and those of other *aa bisɔ* not because of network connections to the family of the bride. In other words, the principal figures in the Gisaro performance are not themselves set up in opposition to the *aa bisɔ* on the same basis as those involved in the bride-wealth negotiations. In any case, the grief and violence involved in the ceremony seem far out of proportion to whatever actual tension and difficulties are involved in the particular occasion. The antagonism evoked in the ceremony may indeed parallel, and perhaps dramatize, those concrete social tensions that do underlie the occasion, but it is not primarily founded on them.

Now undoubtedly a certain amount of personal pique between particular individuals on the *aa bisɔ* and *miyɔwɔ* may be worked off through the medium of the songs and the torch. However, only once did I hear someone speak of using ceremonial violence to express outside grievances. In a heated conversation in the longhouse, I overheard a man complain about a dispute with his brother-in-law over rights to a fishing spot. "Just wait until they Gisaro", he yelled. "I will really plunge the torch on that man!" Those who have serious grievances against someone at a ceremony either settle them publicly before the ceremony or refuse to attend. If hostility exists between two groups who show up at a ceremonial occasion, it will usually erupt before the ceremony begins. Kaluli are not good at masking their anger or keeping their feelings to themselves. On one occasion that is well remembered, some members of the *aa bisɔ* and *miyɔwɔ* who had only recently reached a settlement over a murder become enraged with each other over a trivial incident during the afternoon. Men leaped up, bows were drawn, and those not involved had to rush between the groups and push them apart. They were then segregated in separate houses near the *aa*, and the ceremony was held without them.

From the Kaluli point of view, the fear that people will fight, attack the dancers too severely, or refuse to pay compensation is not the reason why they do not Gisaro when they are on bad terms. Rather, the reason is that the *aa bisɔ* would be "hard", no one would weep, and the ceremony would go off badly.

Thus, though there is room in Gisaro for expression of displaced antagonism between people, it would be a mistake to emphasize this kind of factor in the significance of the ceremony. Whatever social tensions may be present on a Gisaro occasion, they are better understood in terms of a displacement of antagonism into a violence that already exists in the ceremony, rather than as the hidden basis for violence …

Kaluli social processes proceed through the formation of oppositions and these have implications of their own apart from the particular circumstances that bring them about. Whenever two groups, however temporary in composition, stand against one another in opposition over a transaction, there is a certain awkwardness to the situation. This is reflected in the formal message customarily conveyed in the fact that *aa bisɔ* and *miyɔwɔ* do not share food. If a ceremony is to be performed, especially if withdrawn dancers and chorus are present, the atmosphere of tension is thereby increased. *Aa bisɔ* and *miyɔwɔ* are placed implicitly in a posture of assertion against each other.

Kaluli do not regard their ceremonies as expressing hostility. They see them as grand and exciting, deeply affecting, beautiful and sad, but not antagonistic. The songs are presented, not as taunts or mockery of the listeners, but in the same spirit of sympathy with which the guests themselves weep at the end of the ceremony for their friends and relatives among the hosts who have suffered. Indeed, composers and dancers sometimes share with their listeners the sorrows their songs are about … The ceremony is much too moving to be accepted in an atmosphere of animosity. It is for this reason that hostile listeners would not let themselves be open to it — would be "hard" — and instead of the dancers being attacked with increased savagery, the ceremony would fail altogether. The anger expressed in Gisaro thus has more to do with mutual understanding between friends than hostility between enemies.

We have already spoken of the assertiveness, the posture of independence, the pride in physical endurance that are traits of Kaluli character and style. This is intensified in the image of the Gisaro dancer: beautiful and strong but sorrowful; self-sufficient but lonely. He is at once desirable and touching, magnificent and enraging. His song is a gentle but relentless imposition on the *aa bisɔ*—calling to them, appealing to them, inflicting on them their own grief and pain. At the same time that the songs provoke anger in the listeners, they are a resolute source of strength to the dancer. As a man sings out against his own pain or fatigue or fear, so do the dancer and chorus assert themselves resolutely against the attacks of the *aa bisɔ*.

An outsider gets the impression that the more the hosts attack the dancers, the more the dancers dare them to do their worst. The more anger is generated and energy expended, the more intense and powerful the performance becomes. The music drones and swells, filling the house and permeating everything with a resolute and majestic order.

The hosts, for their part, respond to the evocation of loss and sorrow by retaliation. The swift and decisive reaction in the ceremony has a dramatic magnificence that inspires the Kaluli imagination. It asserts and embodies a person's inviolability and integrity, the fundamental aspect of a person that we call human dignity. There are recognized limits to which the violence can go in the ceremony, but to deny a person permission to attack the dancer is an assault on his fundamental self-image and the intelligibility of his life (Schieffelin 1976: 197-204).

A Sense of Proportion

While I was in the field, the local administrative officer decided to prohibit the burning of dancers in Kaluli ceremonies because of the dangers that he felt would result from infection of burn injuries. Kaluli could still hold ceremonies, he said, but they were not to burn anyone. This edict was received with general consternation. It was widely feared that, if people could not retaliate for their grief, they would refuse to grieve. There would be no weeping and the ceremonies would come to nothing. To preserve the ceremonies, the Kaluli hit upon the idea that the *aa bisɔ* could attack the dancers, but only thrust the torch into the *mise æsu* (protective coverings), so as not to actually hurt them. They also adjusted the mode of compensation so that, instead of paying a single item of wealth to a host who had cried (but retaliated), the *miyɔwɔ* would pay each host an item of wealth for each time he had wept. The local village constables put on their uniforms to supervise the proceedings.

The result was that the violence, rather than being more controlled, got completely out of hand. In two Gisaros that I saw, the pattern was the same. At first, the *aa bisɔ* thrust their torches into the *mise æsu*, but later, as they became increasingly furious, their frustration at not being able to give real retaliation to the dancers led them to seek new ways to attack them.

Men began throwing huge ember logs at the backs of the dancers; they showered them with burning coals and pounded them on the *mise æsu* with their fists. The torches were painful, but blows with ember logs and fists promised to be dangerous. The first Gisaro under the new regime broke up early in the night when a dancer was burned with a misdirected torch. The second broke up when a furious member of the *aa bisɔ* clubbed a dancer on the head with a log. On that occasion, a brawl was only narrowly averted.

To move a person deeply with the songs and then deny him the right to retaliate is to make him suffer helplessly, unable to return his pain. Kaluli reactions are immediate. The grief and anger generate a tension between dancers and audience during the performance that requires some sort of periodic release if the ceremony is not to blow up. This cannot be accomplished by stamping a torch out on the *mise æsu* no matter how forcefully. "If one plunges the torch only into the *mise æsu*" one informant told me, "he comes away [still] angry. But after burning the dancer on the skin, he is only a little angry". For listeners to wait until the end of the ceremony was more than the urgency of their grief and rage could sustain. In the ceremony that followed these two Gisaros, the Kaluli went back to burning the dancers.[4]

This does not reflect a Kaluli inability to control their violence but rather a return to their proper sense of proportion. The burning of the dancers allows a balance to be maintained between the audience, whose feelings are anguished, and the performance, which continually aggravates them. The prohibition of the burning by the government officer interfered directly with the way this balance was maintained, with results both disastrous to the ceremony and producing ill feeling in the community (Schieffelin 1976: 204-206).

Payment of Compensation

The sorrow and the violence coming to terms with each other show that people may suffer grief and loss without being helpless. As the listeners strive against the dancers, they return pain for anguish, transform their sorrow by releasing it in anger, and turn their vulnerability into strength and positive action.

However, retaliation on the dancers releases only the listeners' anguish of the moment and allows them to assume a posture of strength. It does not finally reconcile their feelings or give satisfactory closure to the event. This comes with payment of compensation (*su*) at the end of the ceremony, which completes Gisaro dramatically and emotionally by asserting that one will receive return for the things in his life he has lost, as sympathy and/or conciliation from those who are responsible. Without *su* one suffers in lonely, angry humiliation, deprived of acknowledgment or release from the pain of his situation. "A person is not unwilling to weep", one man said in reference to Gisaro, "since he knows he will receive compensation. If he thought he were not going to receive it, then he would be unwilling". If people are not compensated at the end of the performance, they feel hurt, insulted, and angry. It is this that animates the discussion in the longhouse after every ceremony when the dancers have left. Those who feel slighted in compensation go off to ask for more. If no compensation is forthcoming, as sometimes happens, bad feeling arises, which is then carried over for expression and resolution into the context of the next ceremony... .

Acts of compensation at the end of a ceremony formally convey a certain intimacy of feeling. The dancers, chorus members, and other guests make an effort to see that everyone who wept receives something but also tend to pass it out to those who are the most important or beloved figures in their networks of personal relationships (1976: 206-7).

The Significance of Gisaro

Kaluli social occasions are characterized by exuberant fellowship and conversation among familiar friends and relatives; people turn outward toward each other. Gisaro is marked by agonized intimacy forced on one by an attractive but oblivious stranger (the dancer); people turn inward and confront themselves and their sorrows. Prestation celebrates closeness achieved between friends through gifts of food or a marriage. Gisaro represents the closeness achieved between reconciled enemies through (sometimes) mutual sorrow, retaliation, and payment of compensation. Both affirm faith in the reciprocity of human relationships, though in different ways, and both assume a continued relationship through predication of a return of the occasion (whether it be prestation, bride, or ceremony). In the end, the two are complementary but inverse statements of the same reality. Appropriately enough, therefore, weddings and prestations take place in the day, whereas Gisaro is performed at night.

From the point of view of traditional social functional analysis, the songs make present to the *aa bisɔ* the most deeply unmanageable concerns of their lives. In this Gisaro can serve as a vehicle for the expression of social ambivalences and minor hostilities between *aa bisɔ* and *miyɔwɔ*, and it certainly evokes those centrifugal forces of antagonism that would seem frequently to threaten to tear Kaluli society apart. The ceremony, then, attempts to weave these back into sociality by symbolically allowing their resolution and reiterating the orderly form of social processes.

The intelligibility and indeed practicability of human life depends precisely on well-understood, even beloved, processes in which the values of the society are actualized to bring about those results in life that every person desires and in some sense stands for. As action and value are adjusted in events, esthetic considerations of form and proportion play a prominent part. For Kaluli to view the opposition process esthetically is not merely to celebrate or embellish it but to render it into more perfect form, hence increasing its acceptability, its intelligibility, and its efficiency. Though the tensions of Gisaro derive from sorrow for the dead and times past, the songs and response are cast in a processual framework generic to the way all losses and conflicts are handled in Kaluli society. In doing this, the ceremony generates, in the abstract, the movement of Kaluli social life itself. For it is the formation of oppositions and the progression toward their resolution, whether over death and dispute or weddings and prestations, that provides the motion of social and political events.

However, to anyone who has seen Gisaro, the ceremony is clearly more than a continually reiterated statement about the nature of life and social relationships. It is a way of constantly reflecting on and reworking these things. Gisaro is not really concerned with how conflicts are resolved but rather with how conflict resolution is integral to human relationships and life. It does not state the problems Kaluli society has, with its centrifugal tendencies; it embodies the way these centrifugal tendencies energize the human actions Oppositions and their resolutions are seen, not as problems or strategies for affecting life, but the very stuff of it. An outsider is tempted in these circumstances to endow the opposition scenario with a metaphysical significance.

Kaluli do not come to understand their lives by explicating them in a rationalized system of ideas. Rather, they play out and resolve the issues of their lives in a passionate and

dramatic ceremonial performance that shakes the participants profoundly and calls upon their deepest emotional
resources. Gisaro puts events of life, death, and the passing
of time into intelligible relationship without at the same time
putting them at a reflective distance. Thus, they may be resolved emotionally and accepted concretely in committed
real action. Gisaro is therefore more than a statement concerning life. It is a thrusting oneself on it. It is not so much a
reflection on death as it is an assertion against it.

This assertion to the Kaluli is quite real. We recall that Kaluli
ceremonies, and particularly Gisaro, are felt to have a death-
averting or sickness-halting power. My informants were not
able to explain why this was so, beyond saying that one
danced during times of sickness to "keep back the dying out"
(*danili*). In other contexts, they would remark that a *sei* (witch)
usually will not attack people at a ceremony. This was not
because everyone was noisy and wakeful but because even
the *sei* himself is charmed by the performance. He loses his
rage on seeing the dancers and is caught up in the prevailing
mood of pathos and nostalgia. At the same time, Kaluli do
not seem to connect the charming of *seis* with the sickness-
averting power of the ceremony (though that might seem to
us a contributing factor). Rather they feel that both of these
are the result of the generally life-enhancing power of the
performance itself that derives from something they cannot
easily articulate about its significance.

There is, then, apparently a dimension of significance to
Gisaro that we have not yet been able to reach. To look for it,
we may turn, as Kaluli often do in times of puzzlement, to
see how Gisaro appears in relation to the unseen (Schieffelin
1976: 210-212).

Gisaro and the Unseen

At first sight, Gisaro performances would seem to have
very little to do with the invisible side of reality. Ceremonies
are not performed in relation to invisible people or for their
special benefit. *Ane mama* (spirits) are believed to sometimes
come and watch ceremonies invisibly from the rafters of the

aa. (They are said to be called by the *miyɔwɔ* before they leave
their longhouse for the ceremony, though I never saw this
done). A moth or other insect flying around the dancer is an
indication of their presence. Occasionally an *ane* person will
contribute a song or a bit of magic to a dancer through a
medium, and these things are supposed to have special po-
tency to move the *aa bisɔ*. But the actual concern about the
presence or participation of *ane* people at the Kaluli ceremonies I witnessed was at best a very minor one.

However, other contexts and traditional lore reveal that
Gisaro provides an important link between the two aspects
of reality. During a seance, when an *ane mama* enters the body
of a medium in the fully darkened *aa*, he first addresses the
assembled audience by singing a Gisaro song. The listeners
answer him in chorus. Soon, singing of river pools and forested hills, they attain a unity of melodic purpose and attention and settle into an intimate, expectant, nostalgic mood
that provides the atmosphere in which dead and living may
converse. Here Gisaro not only recalls to Kaluli their sorrows
and their dead but establishes a solidarity between them.
Singing Gisaro with one's dead brother at a seance is one
way, for a short while, of being with him again.

Kaluli informants generally agree that Gisaro was originally given to men by the *ane* people, though they differ about
exactly how. Some say that *ane mama* originally taught people
Gisaro by coming up and singing through a medium. One
version describes how a medium went out into the invisible
to investigate the origin of a thunderstorm and discovered
ane mama coming together for Gisaro. He attended the ceremony and found it good. Later, the *ane* invited him to dance
himself. *Ane mama* came up through his body and sang Gisaro
songs to the people of his *aa* all night. When morning came
and lit the *aa*, he was seen to be decorated as a dancer. Then
he showed everyone how to do Gisaro. A quite different version comes across rather like a myth:

> A man went hunting and was going through the forest when he heard
> Gisaro singing. "What's this?" he said. He searched and searched the

ground, the trees. "What is this?" Then lo! by a waterfall there was a man: a beautiful headdress, *mise æsu*, bird of paradise plumes, woven black and yellow armbands, a beautiful *olɔ sæsælɔ* (striped cane), a beautiful shell rattle! The man was dancing by the waterfall. The man who had come to see him stayed hidden and watched and listened to the songs, learning them. When the Gisaro man was finished singing and started to leave the waterfall, the other man grabbed him and asked for the magic of this thing he was doing. The Gisaro man told him, whereupon the other man threw him into the river pool and shot him with his bow when he emerged to the surface. Then he grabbed the *olɔ sæsælɔ* and the rattle, and took off the armbands and the bird of paradise feathers and the bark belt and the fiber streamers and the headdress, and took them back to his *aa* (Field notes).

The story continues to the effect that the man returned to his *aa* and taught other people to do Gisaro. They first sang and wept among themselves (as today with practice singing); then they decided to perform it at another *aa* when they brought a bride to be married. To their astonishment and gratification, a woman was so moved that she followed a dancer home; ever since, people have performed Gisaro at other *aas*.

There are various differences of opinion about the first part of the story. Some people say the man at the waterfall was not killed but merely passed on his knowledge and costume. Some say he was a *kalu hungɔ* or an *ane* person; others insist he was an ordinary man who lived alone. His appearance in full regalia singing alone by a waterfall (often the home of *ane* or *hungɔ* people) has a definite preter-natural quality.

It was from this man by the waterfall that the hunter obtained the first *olɔ sæsælɔ*—the key contribution of the *ane mama* to the Gisaro ceremony. The *olɔ sæsælɔ* is a piece of arrow-making cane about one-quarter inch in diameter and about three inches long, carefully decorated with incised lines (one of the few decorated objects I saw in Bosavi) and containing a piece of rock crystal (*Gisaro i*, "Gisaro wood"). This object can come only as a gift from a soul of the dead to one of his relatives who is living. It is presented to a chosen person from the chest of a medium. The *olɔ sæsælɔ* is the magical object that rivets the attention of the *aa bisɔ* and enables

the dancers (who suck on their *olͻ sæsælͻ* when they are prac-
ticing) to be graceful and remember all their songs. In performance, dancers use it as the handle by which to hold the
string to the mussel-shell rattle. Thus, it performs the mediating juncture between the dancing motion and the music.
Olͻ sæsælͻ are carefully preserved and passed from father to
son or brother to brother, and everyone who dances must
obtain one somehow, or no one will weep for his singing.

The relation between Gisaro and the unseen is crucial.
People of the unseen are responsible not only for the origin
of Gisaro among men but also (through infrequent gifts of
olͻ sæsælͻ) for its continued efficacy. What part, then, does
Gisaro play in the unseen itself? Is there something important about the ceremony that has its manifestation in the visible world but whose true significance is invisible?

Descriptions of the invisible by knowledgeable men always
characterize what are rivers in this world as broad roads leading to the west (downstream), which people pass up and
down on their way to Gisaro ceremonies. My friends remarked that they themselves performed Gisaro infrequently
and only on the celebration of big occasions, whereas *ane
mama* went from house to house to Gisaro all the time, without need of special reason. This was a situation Kaluli clearly
found enviable by comparison with their own. The full significance of these invisible Gisaro ceremonies, however, was
known only to mediums and perhaps to a very few senior
men.

Most people know that when a person dies his soul goes
to the treetops in the form of a bird; they don't know the
process by which this happens. According to a medium who
has seen it:

> When a man dies, his soul doesn't go out the door of the *aa* and down
> the entrance ladder. Rather he finds himself suddenly under the house
> as if he had fallen there. As he picks himself up and takes his small
> bag of possessions, dogs of the house gather round him barking (be-
> cause he didn't give them much food in life) and chase him off to the
> Isawa River. The Isawa appears not as a river but as a wide, white

road. The dogs chase the soul far downstream. As he gets toward the end, they call out, "Blow on the fire!" and the *ane mama* gathered there blow on the dormant embers of a huge fire called *Imɔl*, which is built in the water, and it bursts into enormous flame. The dogs chase the soul into the fire, where it is burned to a crisp.

Meanwhile, among the *ane* people who have been watching is a young woman, who, seeing the man running, has taken a fancy to him and wants him for a husband. *Ane* people may enter the fire without harm, and so she takes the burnt remains of the soul, wraps them in soft yellow leaves, and puts them in a little net bag. Then she carries him back up the Isawa, stopping at each (spirit) *aa* on the way to attend a Gisaro. At each performance *ane* men dance while those *ane* women who have dead souls' ashes in their net bags sit among the chorus near the front of the house and chorus the dancer (something that is never done in a real ceremony).

These Gisaro ceremonies are intended to make the burnt remains of the souls grow up into a man again. Finally, after attending many Gisaros they reach the man's homeland and say: "Enough. This is your home. Be here". And the *aa bisɔ* of the place say: "All right. Now go as a wild pig. Come back. Go as a cassowary. Come back. Go as a *kalo* (pigeon)", and so on. And so forth for all of the various manifestations a dead soul can assume. The soul is then washed with water drawn from the Sili, so that he cannot be seen by living men, and his tongue is cut so that he cannot speak with human voice but only as a *kalo*, *hi* (another kind of pigeon), or some other bird. He is then married to the woman who brought him in the net bag and lives thereafter in the *ane* house (Field notes).

In this account, Gisaro appears in a new light. It clearly plays an important part on a whole other (though hidden) level of Kaluli experience—in an invisible journey of the dead. There seems to be no clear counterpart to the events in the visible realm; thus, to understand what they mean, it seems reasonable to examine them in relation to other events that we know take place in the unseen. The most conspicuous of these are those involved in the curing process. ... A medium cures illness by restoring the missing pieces of a man's invisible body, which have been dismembered by a *sei*. He does this by first locating the missing parts, cleansing them of decay in the invisible river Sili, and then warming them back to life in the *Imɔl* fire before sticking them back on the body. The journey of the dead involves the opposite transformation (to death, not health). A man is first chased from his home and destroyed by the *Imɔl* fire; then he is rescued by an *ane* woman who carries his remains in a net bag (like an infant) back to (near) his original home, where he is finally washed in water from the Sili to complete his transformation into an *ane mama* and is married to the woman who saved him.[5] The figure of a woman here appears to have the significance of both mother and bride. My informant (a medium), however, spoke of her entirely as "wife" or "woman" (*ga*), not as "mother" (*nɔ*), and seemed to see her recovery of the soul from the fire as analogous to the recovery of invisible body parts in the cure. (Certainly, rescue of the soul from the fire is motivated by conjugal rather than maternal sentiments). Such a curative rescue by a spirit sweetheart had its counterpart in my informant's own curing experience. Once when he was very ill, he heard a noise and, looking up expecting to see a *sei* approach, he found instead his *ane* wife beside him with a net bag full of his dismembered body parts, which she had brought back to put together. What mediums do for ordinary people—returning the invisible body parts of the sick—is sometimes done for the medium himself by his spirit wife.

If we examine these two sets of events closely, we see that the differences between them match the opposite significance of the events themselves: cure and return to life versus death and permanent removal from life. The major symbolic elements of water and fire are reversed: the fire that warms the body parts back to life in the last stages of the cure destroys the soul at the first stage of death. The water of the Sili that cleanses the body parts of death (decay) in the first part of the cure irrevocably separates the soul from life (confers final invisibility) in the final stages of death. Moreover, the treatments by fire and water no longer occur between the "recovery" of the damaged body and their "return", as they do in the cure, but precede and follow them, respectively. This, in turn, changes the significance of the mediating figure (the medium for the cure, the spirit fiancée for death). The medium restores a situation to what it was before (health to health); the spirit woman transforms it into something quite different (transition to permanent spirit condition).

The narrative "gap" left in the journey of the dead—where, in the curing scenario, fire and water are used to heal and revitalize—is filled by Gisaro ceremonies. The woman carrying her destroyed love from Gisaro to Gisaro to grow him back to manhood corresponds to both of the crucial transitions treatments performed by the medium in the cure: cleansing of decay and revitalization to life. This is consistent with the Kaluli feeling that Gisaro has a death-averting, healing power.

If we examine the Gisaro ceremony itself in relation to the curing sequence ... we find the same symbolism present in both. Fire and water in Gisaro are manifested not in the Sili and *Imɔl* but in the weeping and the torches. The *aa bisɔ* plays the role analogous to the broken spirit body. A complicating difference between the ceremony and the cure is that there are two figures of mediation in the latter but only one in the former. In illness a *sei* opens the scenario by dismembering the invisible body. A medium then treats it with water and fire and returns it to wholeness. In Gisaro the mediating figure is the dancer, but he corresponds to neither the *sei* nor the medium alone but to both at once. He causes sorrow and distress, not by acting like a *sei*, but by acting rather like a medium, not by taking apart and hiding a person's invisible pieces, but by revealing and putting together scattered images of a person's past life. In Gisaro the *aa bisɔ* understandably retaliate for the pain they suffer. But as the dancer acted like a medium in order to cause pain, so, in a matching reversal, the sufferers apply the fire and water to him in the passage toward catharsis. The dancer, like the medium, brings back wholeness to the proceedings but by paying compensation rather than by returning exactly what was lost. Here clearly Kaluli express their awareness of reciprocity as a healing, life-restoring process.

We have called the scheme in which reciprocity takes place an "opposition scenario" because the original gift (or loss, or whatever) sets up an opposition, a certain tension, between the two sides—defining them against each other. The "healing" aspect of reciprocity comes at the point where reciprocation of *su* or *wel* is completed and this opposition is resolved (just as the return of the rejuvenated body parts effects the cure). But what about the nature of the opposition itself before reciprocity is completed?

In real life the awareness of a live opposition provides an urgency, a kind of energizing tension to the activities of the participants that motivates their preparations for resolution. At the same time, resolution through reciprocation embodies a certain element of transformation. The object given or taken as *wel* must be different from, though equivalent to, the original one; otherwise resolution does not take place and there is no social movement. The meaning of *wel* here is revealed metaphorically in the scenario of the cure: the "same" body parts are returned, but they have been rejuvenated. Here rejuvenation is analogous to "differentness". The change takes place while the opposition is in force and is absolutely necessary for its resolution.

Gisaro clearly emphasizes this aspect of the opposition process. Between the time the first dancer starts to sing and the final compensation is paid, the opposition consists of continually aggravated pain, tension, and violence, with dancers and audience striving against each other to a tremendous pitch of intensity. But the tension of the opposition, though aggravating and painful, is like the stinging nettle applied to a sore arm: the vitalization and the energization of living processes.

Looking at Gisaro from this perspective, we can see more clearly the meaning of the particular transformations its symbolism represents from that of the curing sequence. The dancer, like the medium, ultimately provides healing (through paying *su*); but, unlike the medium, he is an exasperating figure, evoking and intensifying the pain while being beautiful and desirable.

Correspondingly, the *aa biso* do not submit passively to the treatment, as the patient does to the medium, but are aggravated and aroused by it. The tears caused by the ceremony release sorrow, but painfully; the fire revivifies, but in retaliatory violence. Gisaro emphasizes the process of strengthening and vitalization that comes from the tension of oppositions.

We can now make sense of the presence of Gisaro in the journey of the dead. The most striking difference between the journey of the dead and the curing sequence is that the journey of the dead is not an opposition scenario (though it retains the ghost of its form). This is, first, because the dead is not really returned visibly from whence he came and, second, because the process of transformation to full social status (as *ane mama*) is not completed until after the "return" through the washing in the Sili water and the marriage to the spirit woman.

If the journey of the dead is not an opposition scenario, however, it cannot by itself transform or revitalize anything. In order for the dead to be transformed, there must be an opposition scenario. Hence the presence of Gisaro. The particular vitalizing emphasis of the ceremony is appropriate to the radical treatment required to transform the soul of the dead to full, adult *ane* status. While the transformation is analogous to a cure, the "body" requires more than cleansing and reanimating; it must be entirely regrown. Here Gisaro's vitalizing value reveals its final symbolic analog. While the spirit fiancée plays a mother role to her future husband in her net bag, Gisaro plays the role analogous to homosexual intercourse, which stimulates a boy to attain full manhood. Here the notions of stimulative male energy and the opposition scenario finally come together, symbolically—matching their obvious association in reality. It may be the feeling for this connection, on some level (by people who cannot know it explicitly), that underlies the marked homosexual reference in the way *aa bisɔ* wags tease the dancers before the ceremony.

We are now in a position to sum up the significance of all this for Kaluli experience. From our look at the invisible side of Kaluli reality, it is not surprising that the Kaluli should feel that Gisaro has a death-averting power for the community and perform it or similar ceremonies when they are threatened with epidemic or disaster. In performing Gisaro, people are participating in the same process that reinvigorates their dead, not to mention their social relationships. Few Kaluli actually know how Gisaro is related to this rejuvenation process. Indeed, hardly anyone knows the significance of Gisaro in the journey of the dead. Yet, on some level, everyone is aware of it and feels that those who participate in the ceremony become stronger: "You have spirit; you won't be dying quickly!" The medium's description of the invisible Gisaro articulates not what ordinary people know but what is common in feeling to their experience of the ceremony. The curative value of Gisaro that Kaluli feel is not connected with invisible events; rather, the curative value is fundamentally implicit in the symbolic way that they organize and understand their experience. It is a fundamental, though implicit, aspect of the opposition scenario on whatever level of awareness it appears.

The Kaluli belief that the key to understanding their own experience lies basically in the invisible side of reality is in this regard quite correct.

Gisaro provides the Kaluli with a continuing tangible link with the invisible, as they remember their dead in the ceremony and sing with them in seance. The invisible dead themselves provide their visible sons with the means (in the *olɔ sæsælɔ*) of continuing the performance.

The ceremony reveals the symbolic, metaphysical significance for Kaluli experience of the fundamental processes of opposition and reciprocity that animate the life of their society. Within its confines, during performance, Kaluli generate and mobilize their strongest qualities and values and intensify their own awareness of themselves as people who think and feel in their particular ways. It is a process of energizing and coming to understand themselves and the world through the very processes that make them both work.

Viewed from a social perspective, the ceremony expresses, not the structural aspects of Kaluli society, but its forms of social process, through which Kaluli social relationships and experience are continually reworked in the course of events. The focus on social process is of a piece with those individualistic values of personal initiative, equality, and vitality that give the Kaluli their particular character and style. It represents an acute and relevant perspective on their own society.

In a society where it is not groups that produce oppositions so much as oppositions that crystallize groups, it is not surprising that social life should be perceived more in terms of the processes that give it shape than in terms of structures that may emerge when those processes take place. It is this perception that is revealed in the Kaluli feeling that the forces of growth and life are generated in oppositions, and it is with this, as a life condition, with all its beauty, exuberance, tragedy, and violence, that they try to come to terms in Gisaro (Schieffelin 1976: 212-223).

[ES]

APPENDIX
Dances and Ceremonies Performed by Bosavi People

Aside from Gisaro, the people of Bosavi perform five other types of dances and ceremonies ...
Ilib Kuwɔ

Ilib Kuwɔ is not a full-scale ceremony but a kind of celebratory dance performed in the longhouse during the day by one to four men to project an exciting atmosphere for some significant event. The dancers are costumed as in *Heyalo* and *Kɔluba* with characteristic arched-frame headdresses of white cockatoo feathers with palm-leaf streamers (*fasela*), and they wear springing rattles of crayfish claws in their waistbands at the back.

Dancers usually position themselves two at each end of the longhouse facing the interior and bounce back and forth in short hops across the hall from side to side beating hand drums (*ilib*). There is no singing, and the dancers make no effort to coordinate their motion or drumming. As in all Bosavi ceremonies, each performer is withdrawn and does not address or relate to his audience. When a dancer tires, he turns around to face the end of the hall and rests for a while.

Members of a longhouse community may perform *Ilib Kuwɔ* among themselves to mark a noteworthy occasion such as a successful raid or the preparations to receive a ceremonial party of guests. In the latter case, the dancers customarily move into the houseyard to greet the arrival procession, and the arrivals in turn lead out of the forest with their own *Ilib Kuwɔ* entertainment until evening, when a major ceremony may be performed.

Kaluli say that *Ilib Kuwɔ* originally came up from the southeast side of the mountain at the same time that drums were introduced. *Ilib Kuwɔ* is now familiar to every longhouse north of the mountain.

Sæbio

Sæbio is also a minor dance, though it occasionally may be performed for a whole night in the absence of another ceremony. It is usually performed from about dusk to ten o'clock at night by the youths and young men of a group visiting another longhouse (for example, as carriers for a government patrol) and seems aimed at catching the attention of the local girls. Alternately, if the occasion for the visit is an important one at which an all-night ceremony is to be performed, people may perform *Sæbio* in the late afternoon amid the *Ilib Kuwɔ* dancing until shortly before the other major ceremony is to begin.

In performing *Sæbio*, the youths stand in two lines facing each other across the head of the hall, wearing no special costume beyond the usual finery of visitors. The singing is led by those at the ends of the lines, who tap the rhythm with ax handles or sticks on the floor, while the others jiggle rapidly up and down in place. The song (usually no more than two lines), is passed from one youth to another up and down the two lines in a call-response manner. After about three songs, the youths trot to the center of the hall, where they sing for a while in the same manner. From there they move to the women's end of the hall to sing, then back to the center, and finally return to the head where they may take a short break before forming up again and continuing the performance.

Sæbio songs consist of conventional two-line formulae into which new words (food names, wealth objects) may be inserted. Place names do not usually appear in *Sæbio* songs, but without them the performance is not moving.

Kaluli say that *Sæbio* originated in the area southeast of Bosavi and that only those with connections to clans Wasu and Swabesi know how to do it. It appears, however, that the knowledge of the dance is more widespread among Bosavi people than this.

Kɔluba

Kɔluba is a major all-night ceremony performed at the usual occasions for such things. The performers do not arrive with the rest of the visitors but remain in the forest to prepare for the ceremony. At dark, eighteen to twenty-four young men (costumed as in *Ilib Kuwɔ* and *Heyalo*) emerge from the forest in procession three abreast and enter the longhouse. They move with little bounding steps once up and down the hall singing a procession song. Then all but two dancers sit down in a semi-circle along the edges of the sleeping platforms at the head of the hall. The two remaining dancers face each other at the head of the hall and, hopping up and down, tap time with sticks on the floor and sing. At the end of the song, they move with little hopping steps to the middle of the hall, where they sing the song again. Then they proceed in the same way to the women's end, the middle, and back to the head, where they finally sit down and another pair of dancers stands up. After all have danced up and down the hall in this manner, they wind up with a procession around the hall. Then they sit down in the semi-circle again and pairs of men dance as before with a new set of songs. Songs are made up for each occasion; they concern place names and evoke sorrow and burning of the dancers. *Kɔluba* is said to have originated with clans Wasu and Swabesi to the southeast of the mountain and was still moving westward into the Kaluli area in 1967.

Heyalo

Heyalo (or *Feyalo*) is a major all-night ceremony. As with *Kɔluba*, the male performers do not appear until dark, when they emerge

in procession from the forest and enter the longhouse. The eighteen to twenty dancers (costumed as in *Ilib Kuwɔ* or *Kɔluba*) are
joined by five or six women in *sosomaya* (woman's dance) regalia.
With their backs to the audience, the male dancers sidle up one
side of the hall and down the other with a hopping step while
singing and beating drums. The women precede and follow the
line as it moves around the hall and shout "Aeo! Aeo!" in high-
pitched voices. After singing one song several times, which takes
about twenty minutes, the dancers all sit down for a five minute
break before starting up again with a new song. The songs, which
are made up anew for each occasion, mention places in the local
territory and evoke weeping in the audience and burning of the
dancers.

Heyalo is said to have originated among the westward Bosavi
neighbors of the Kaluli, and the origin myth of the ceremony associates it with Lake Campbell. *Heyalo* is as familiar and widely practiced north of the mountain as Gisaro. It evidently has changed in
form since the 1930s, when it was danced without drums, with a
different song style, and with male and female dancers alternating
in the line around the hall.

Iwɔ

Iwɔ is danced only on the night before pigs are killed, making it
the one ceremony in Bosavi that relates to a specific type of event.
The performers (both hosts and guests) decorate themselves openly
amid the afternoon gathering of people in front of the pigs "so that
the pigs will see them and turn out fat". The performance begins
after dark when two men burst through the door of the longhouse,
shouting and banging axes on the floor in the middle of the hall.
They are immediately followed by the dancers, who are arranged
in order of height, the tallest first and the shortest last. In *Iwɔ*, boys
from the age of about five to men well into their fifties may dance.

Singing is led by a man (host or guest) who knows the traditional one-, or two-line songs. The songs are picked up and repeated by the dancers for about fifteen minutes as they shuffle
around the hall in single file. After each song, the dancers rest for a
minute until two men burst through the door as before and bang
axes on the floor, following which a new song is introduced.

The songs are supposed to be traditional and known only to men
who have connections to the southwest of the mountain among

the "Aibalisɔ" people (Kokonesi longhouse), who are said to be the originators of the songs. Unless there are a few men present who know the songs, the ceremony cannot be performed. Song lines mention rivers and place names framed in references to pigs. However, the places mentioned are all on "Aibalisɔ" ground unfamiliar to Kaluli and hence are not moving. Iwɔ seems to have been performed among the Bosavi people for at least thirty years (Schieffelin 1976: 225-229).

PRECIS EXERCISE 7

¹This kind of social giving and exchanging is basic to the ²Kaluli way of life. Friends and relatives in the same ³longhouse community normally expect to be able to bor- ⁴row food and tools or request gifts of wealth from each other ⁵if the need arises. Among people in different longhouses, ⁶this sort of reciprocity is even more visible because it tends ⁷to be carried out in a formal and conspicuous way. The ex- ⁸change of women and wealth in marriage provides the ba- ⁹sis for the provision of hospitality for visiting, support in ¹⁰conflict, invitations to hunt and fish, mutual assistance in ¹¹garden labor, and occasional ceremonial prestations, which ¹²are formal, customary gifts of food, especially meat … It is ¹³difficult to give an adequate impression of the pervasive- ¹⁴ness of this sort of social reciprocity in Kaluli life. A man's ¹⁵relations with, interactions with, and affection for his ¹⁶affines, for example, are so bound up with situations of ¹⁷reciprocal gift-giving and mutual help that he tends to think ¹⁸of his life with his wife, on reflection, in terms of the situa- ¹⁹tions in which he worked cooperatively with her and re- ²⁰ciprocally with her relatives and exchanged countless mi- ²¹nor gifts of food. …
²²Kaluli celebrate their relationships with others formally in ²³large-scale ceremonial prestations, when most of the people ²⁴of one longhouse community distribute pork or smoked ²⁵game to people in other communities. It is to celebrate these ²⁶big occasions of food giving, or important stages in their ²⁷preparation, that Kaluli most often stage ceremonies such

[28]as Gisaro.

[29]Indeed, while celebrating occasions of reciprocity, Gisaro [30]embodies some of its characteristics. Compensation (*su*) [31]must be paid for feelings deeply moved, and one ceremony [32]is explicitly given in return (*wel*) for another. A performance [33]that has caused a lot of grief motivates the hosts to return [34]an equally affecting one to their guests. Gisaro is itself, [35]therefore, a reciprocal transaction in the esthetic domain. [36]All this suggests that social reciprocity is not merely punc-[37]tuated by ceremonies such as Gisaro but is deeply bound [38]up with what they express. Gisaro clearly involves emo-[39]tional or ideological matters of wider cultural significance [40]than only the giving of the food. It points to ways that reci-[41]procity may be bound up with other realms of cultural sym-[42]bolism and social experience.

[43]At the same time, ceremonies retain a character indepen-[44]dent of the events they usually celebrate. Kaluli sometimes [45]perform them in the absence of important social transac-[46]tions, in times of fearful portents, such as when the first [47]airplane flew over the plateau, or at the approach of epi-[48]demic disease. In the latter case, the community may per-[49]form sickness-warding magic and invite another commu-[50]nity to perform a ceremony that night. If sickness is already [51]in the longhouse and there have been several deaths, magic [52]is dispensed with, and, in a mood of panicky anxiety, people [53]announce their imminent arrival to another community and [54]go there to dance.

[55]If Kaluli social life takes much of its form through processes [56]of reciprocity, it is not surprising that reciprocity should be [57]celebrated by ceremonies that express important human [58]concerns in deeply moving ways. It is in ceremonies such [59]as Gisaro that these wider concerns are focused and made [60]visible. If we are to appreciate them, and what they mean [61]for Kaluli people, we must learn what Gisaro is about. And [62]for Gisaro to yield insight into Kaluli experience, we must [63]learn how to interpret it.

[64]What, then, is Gisaro all about? ... The movement of Gisaro

65is ultimately to be understood in terms of the opposition
66scenario … Gisaro is a drama of opposition initiated by
67the dancers but played out by everyone. Within a struc-
68ture of reciprocity, the action of the performers and the feel-
69ings of the audience are brought into a relation with each
70other that allows intelligibility and resolution. But at the
71same time, *aa bisɔ* and *miyɔwɔ* (visitors, raiders) confront
72each other in an interaction of such tension that it not in-
73frequently blows the performance apart. If an enraged host
74treats a dancer too harshly, or a minor dispute among the
75gathering escalates, or some other even occurs, people may
76jump angrily to their feet shouting recriminations, and the
77ceremony ends abruptly.

Exercises

I. Please answer these questions, in your own words, on a separate sheet
of paper.

1. What is a 'prestation'? [lines 11, 23].

2. The author talks about reciprocity, using the word 'reciprocity' (and
'reciprocal') repeatedly [6, 14, 17, 19-20, 29, 35-6, 40-41, 56, 68]. We find
the phase "structure of reciprocity" [68-9]. What does it mean?

3. Another important word is "opposition" [65-66]. In Extract #3 (p.
173), we find a section about the drama of opposition, and in lines 65-6,
the author says *our ultimate understanding* of Gisaro must be in terms of
an opposition scenario.
    (A) What is the dictionary definition of the word, 'opposition'?
    (B) Does the author use the word in that strict sense, or is there some-
thing else indicated?
    (C) In your own words, describe what you think the author means by
an *opposition scenario.*

4. The word 'affines' is used only once in the précis passage [line 16],
but it, and the word 'affinal', have been used many times in the 3 Extracts. Remember, too, that *affines* and *affinal relations* played an important part in Lugbara dances. *Summarize* how the author of Gisaro uses
these terms, then summarize how the author of *ongo* dances uses the
terms. Briefly comment on these relationships as you understand them.

II. Check back to **pp. 56 through 59**, and the précis exercise on p. **67**, then *re-think* the questions following the précis for Reading III, using this 3-step outline:

(A) What do you think of common definitions of dancing now, after discovering more about what dances mean, looked at from a global perspective?

(B) Do *you* think the popular definitions and reasons for dancing that Williams lists are adequate for *Ongo* dances, Hopi or Tongan dances, or the Gisaro?

(C) Does this provide you with insights about how and why the dances of other peoples (and many of our own) are so often misrepresented by writers who don't know much about anything beyond local practices and their own experience?

READING IX

BIOGRAPHICAL NOTES: Marjorie Franken was born in Kansas. She has taught anthropology at Arkansas State University and several colleges and universities in California, including University of California at Riverside and Whittier College. Dr. Franken became acquainted with the Swahili people while she was a Peace Corps volunteer in Kenya in 1974, when she began to learn the Swahili language. She returned to Kenya in 1983 to study the history and forms of Swahili dances, completing her Ph.D. in anthropology at University of California, Riverside, in 1986.

Her current research projects focus upon the formation of nationalism, post-colonial national culture and gender roles through the study of dancing in Egypt. She is currently completing a book on Egyptian dancing. An essay, 'Egyptian Cinema and Television: Dancing and the Female Image' appears in *Visual Anthropology* (Vol 8: 267-285). Her research on Egyptian dancing was facilitated by travel grants both from the National Endowment for the Humanities and Arkansas State. Franken met Williams at an American Anthropology Conference in Phoenix, Arizona in 1988, and Kaeppler at an A.A.A. conference in Atlanta, November, 1994. She presently resides in California.

This Reading reproduces **Franken, M. 1992.** The Dance and Status in Swahili Society. *JASHM*, 7(2): 77-93. Reprinted by permission of the *Journal for the Anthropological Study of Human Movement* [JASHM].

ABSTRACT

In this paper I illustrate how dancing, as one aspect of ngoma, *is one of many status-laden activities in Swahili society. Through a brief introductory analysis of distinctive structured movement patterns, the reader can see exactly how understanding of the uses of the body itself and the space around it contributes significantly to our understanding of the nuances of social roles and the differentiation of Swahili social status on the coast of post-independent Kenya.*

The Swahili are a Muslim African people characterized by a stratified town culture of many centuries duration. Their society illustrates the integration of Islamic cultural codes into indigenous Swahili urban culture, providing a synthesis that has been incorporated into a particular set of performances known as ngoma. *Swahili* ngoma, *as a category of activities that includes music, poetry and dancing, is one of many activities in Swahili urban society that mark social class.*

This paper will examine some of the ways in which the most elite class, the aristocrats of Swahili towns usually referred to as waungwana, *strove to establish and maintain this distinctive, recognizable, important place in town life through* ngoma. *As a category of activities* ngoma *has frequently been overlooked in the literature, yet it can be shown to shed considerable light upon social roles and class distinctions in Swahili society.*

•

Text of Journal Article

The Kiswahili word, *ngoma*, means 'drum', or 'dance' or 'music'. The verb form is *kiatezea ngoma*, "to play a dance", and I will use it throughout this essay instead of the phrase "music and dance event". I wish to avoid the word 'dance' because I don't want to limit readers' conceptions of these performances to western notions of "steps" or "step patterns" and to the notion of movements performed only while standing on the feet. Some of the performances I will describe take place while the participants are seated, but in spite of that, they fit into the Swahili category *ngoma*.

The status markers that were most obvious were tall white-washed stone houses. These were so distinctive, set amidst the small brown mud and thatch houses of a town that they were mistaken by Europeans as part of a foreign cultural heritage. Inside those houses were still more material goods and also activities that marked the inhabitants as upper class. The familiar description of imported porcelain from China and Persia comes immediately to mind.

The stone houses can be thought of as showcases for a wide assortment and great variety of status-marking objects and activities. One activity possible in a large house with an enclosed courtyard is the complete seclusion of women. Devotion to religious observance and study were perhaps second only to pedigree in marking *waungwana* status, and seclusion of women is a highly noticeable act signifying religious purity and wealth. A separate room into which women retreat when male guests are present (a 'harem' or *ndani*), and an enclosed area for domestic tasks were only affordable for wealthy upper class people.

Another function of large houses was their use as a framework for *waungwana* rituals and ceremonies. Indeed, it has even been suggested that the *zidaka* on the back wall of the *ndani* (women's quarters) were used primarily as a backdrop for the most lavish ceremonies of all — those done for a new bride (Allen 1979). In the more public rooms at the front of the house, and in the courtyard *ngoma*, (music and dancing events) could be held. Poetry composition was another activity that required time and tutelage to study and perfect, which was another marker of high status.

The poetry competitions between a women's team and a men's team were possible in such a house, when a purdah curtain across the first great room could separate the competing teams. What better way to display all one's status-markers at once than in a stone house, richly appointed, surrounded by one's elite friends, performing in poetry and dance recitations? We will now focus on these *ngoma* occasions and their forms of activity as another kind of status-marker in Swahili culture.

We begin by discovering two *ngoma* that in the past were done in this setting of a stone house as exclusive *waungwana* affairs. The first was *ngoma la hazua,* a men's dance done for weddings and circumcisions. The dancers were adult men dressed in their best *kanzu* (a spotless white and freshly pressed prayer robe), and their best *kofia* (a richly embroidered prayer cap). In addition to drums and music, a singer intoned poetry, recounting the noble deeds or distinguished ancestors of the sponsoring family.

The men moved in unison, in a line formation; they stepped at a diagonal forward on the right foot, thrust the sword they carried to a fully extended arm position to the upper right. They fell back on the left foot while lowering the sword, stepped to the side right while moving the sword across the body and wiping it with a handkerchief held in the left hand, after which they stepped left while lowering the sword, point to the ground (see Figure 1, p. 236). This pattern was repeated as long as the performers wished to keep on. After the performance, a feast was served.

Foregoing analysis for a moment, I will describe a second dance that was also done in private homes at the turn of the century. This dance is called *lelemama,* an "adult" (that is, married women's) dance done usually as a rite of passage.

The *lelemama* costume in those times was *suruali ya njiwa,* so named because the fitted leg ended in a ruffle like the fluffy feathers above a dove's foot. The body and sometimes the head were covered by a pair of *leso* which were bright rectangles of printed cloth. On the fingers the dancers wore *mbiu,* little gazelle horns tipped in silver, with the hollow end fitted over the fingertips, perhaps as finger cymbals are worn. Sometimes a single *mbiu* was struck with a small stick. The dancers stood in a line, or in ranks and followed a leader in a sort of drill. The motions were arm extensions and finger flexions done in a smooth, slow, graceful manner (see Figure 2, p. 237). A singer also intoned poetry to the musical accompaniment. Again the dancing was followed by feasting.

These two *ngoma* are still performed today, but there have been some alterations over the last 80 or 90 years. *Ngoma la hazua* is most often now seen outdoors in the town of Lamu, performed for weddings or during *Maulidi* week.

Maulidi is a name derived from the Arabic term *mawlid* or *mulid,* meaning a poetic recitation of the events surrounding the birthday of the Prophet. *Maulidis* are recited on any important occasion, but most frequently on the anniversary of the Prophet's birthday. This recitation form is pan-Islamic, but the Swahili have added some variations and adaptations of their own. *Maulidi* can be sung for small family occasions as a devotional exercise or can be public events as parts of weddings. Characteristic movement patterns frequently form an integral part of the performances (Franken 1987).

The largest *maulidi* performed today is held in Lamu, one of the most traditional Swahili towns and distinguished for both religious learning and famous poets. *Maulidi* week on the coast is somewhat like Christmas week in America, in the sense of being a time for parties, traveling, visiting, fun, and some serious religious activities. The centerpiece of the week is a *maulidi* recitation at the biggest mosque in Lamu on Thursday night. Hundreds of people attend, traveling from all over East Africa (Franken 1986).

In this context, men use *bokora*, thin wooden canes instead of swords. *Lelemama* is still sometimes performed in Mombasa for weddings, and the popular dress is a military uniform style, such as sailor-collared dresses. The *mbiu* are gone.

We can now ask, what are the *waungwana* status emblems in these two historical performances as I have described them? First (and indispensable) was the setting of a stone house. Next were the guests — one's family and friends, also from the upper-class. Fine clothing is a familiar status-symbol. Men used both quality materials and a religious style of clothing to signify high status. Women displayed affluence by having special dancing clothes and paraphernalia. Poetry singing was a mandatory part of the *ngoma* and finally, food was offered. These are the familiar emblems of high status; wealth, as shown in houses, clothes, food, fine friends and refined pastimes. It is easy to see counterparts in our own and many other societies.

What is not so obvious is that the actual danced movements are also valued as *waungwana* kinds of movement. By way of contrast, we will now look at two *ngoma* of very humble classes of people in Swahili culture in order to make the contrasting movement styles clear.

The contrasting dance I will describe is called *uta*. This is another men's dance that is one of the showpieces of *Maulidi* week in Lamu. It is known as the "coconut-cutters dance" and it has always been performed out of doors in a *kiwanja*, a cleared sand-lot area between houses. The name *uta* means 'bow' as in 'bow and arrow', pointing to the principal instrument plucked while the player also intones the *uta* song.

More vital for dancing purposes are the leg rattles worn by the dancers. These are called *msewe* and are woven on a strip of palm fiber rope, about every 6 inches. The rope is wrapped around the dancer's legs from ankle to knee. The dancers thus make their own music, for no drums or other instruments are used. They wear typical Swahili men's work clothing; a *kikoy* (like a sarong), a shirt and sandals and a prayer cap (*kofia*), perhaps.

The dancers form a rough circle and leaning on canes placed before their feet, stamp the *uta* rhythm in unison, producing a percussive rustling sound of the fiber rattles (see Figure 3, p. 238). Occasionally, a dancer breaks out of the circle, raises his cane over his head and twirls through the center to take a new place on the opposite side of the circle.

Another men's dance, *mwaribe*, can also be seen in Lamu during Maulidi week, and it is then done out-of-doors by young men. The instruments are *msondo* (also an alternate name for the dance) which is a long narrow drum somewhat similar to a conga drum. The dancers wear smart street clothes — trousers and new shirts — "western wear".

The dance begins with one person inviting a partner into

the dance space by hopping onto one foot to a position directly in front of the partner, who then responds by hopping forward in unison as the first person hops backwards.

The sequence continues: hop forward on the right, put feet together, hop back on the left, (again, feet together), step in place and step in place again. The arms and hands are held chest high and the hopping motion gives them the appearance of flapping like birds' wings (see Figure 4, p. 239). This dance is the only one I ever heard of that is sometimes performed by mixed-gender groups.

My informant told me that forty years ago, on Kiunga island (north of Lamu), mixed groups of men, women and children did this dance together, even single and married women dancing with the men. This dance is also said to be especially liked by the Pokomo, a people who live adjacent to the Swahili area on the coast. They and other related inland groups, the Miji-Kenda people, for example, are said to have other, similar dances. In larger Swahili towns, however, *mwaribe* is never performed by mixed groups. Young girls dance *mwaribe* indoors, at strictly secluded girls' parties and young men perform it outdoors, as described here.

These dances, the *mwaribe* and the *uta*, may be said to be characteristic of the *watwana* class in Swahili society. The *watwana* are the lowest class. In fact, one meaning of the word is "slaves". These people are said to lack all *waungwana* attributes. That is, they are recent arrivals in town life, they have no pedigree or distinguished ancestors, they practise a slack sort of Islamic religion and, of course, they are economically poor. *Uta* is a dance of a very humble occupational group: coconut cutters. As a type of work, it is dirty and hard, therefore only for poor and unrefined men.

Mwaribe betrays its humble status by its similarity to Miji-Kenda dances which are done by non-believers and, in relation to town-dwellers, lower class people. It is low in status because of the tendency to perform it in violation of purdah strictures.

It is interesting to compare the two pairs of dances: *ngoma la hazua* and *lelemama*, which exemplify *waungwana ngoma*, on the one hand, and *uta* and *mwaribe*, which are *watwana* dances, on the other. What are the contrasting attributes of each pair? Before answering that question, a clarifying point must be made. The reason that *watwana* dances are "low status" in Swahili society is simply because lower-class Swahili people dance them. From the point of view of the outside observer, there is nothing intrinsically better or worse about the movements themselves, but Swahili society *assigns* class meanings to these dances, therefore, they are talked about as if there were something in the nature of the dances themselves that was "lower" or "poorer" than the *ngoma la hazua* dances.[1]

The relatively "easy-to-see" contrasts between the two types of dancing can be thought of in this way: the *waungwana* dances are distinguished by place, music, poetry, dress and feasting. They are not mixed-gender dances. Groups of men and women are kept strictly separated. Only *ngoma la hazua* dances can be performed in the *waungwana* context described in detail earlier, notably, the great stone houses. Men have an option also to perform these dances out-of-doors, but women must maintain their elite seclusion standards. If they do dance outdoors (as I saw in Mombasa in 1984), they do so inside a tent that conceals both dancers and audience.

Waungwana styles of dress also distinguishes aristocratic dances from all others. Men display their religious status by dancing in their finest prayer dress, and women show conspicuous consumption by making special costumes and paraphernalia. *Waungwana* music is relatively complex and refined. It uses a full complement of Swahili percussion instruments: drums and *utasa* (a metal tray played with brushes); a melodic instrument, either a *zumari ya mtapa* (like the Arabic *mizmar*), or a western trumpet. Both mark the players as sophisticated cosmopolitan people. The lyrics of the songs consist of poetry composed especially for the occasion by the best poets of the town, who are members of the performing class.

The *watwana* dances are marked by being held out of doors, even in mixed gender groups. People dance in clothes that do not advertise piety or wealth. Their musical accompaniment is confined to percussion only; their singing is identifiable mainly by its volume, rather than refined or witty poetry composed especially for the event. These contrasts are tabulated below as Fig. 5.

WAUNGWANA

Dance Name	Move/Place	Music/Dress
Ngoma la Hazua [Men]	arm extensions with sword and danced in or out of doors.	zumari drums religious dress
Lelemama [Women]	arm extensions with hand-finger actions, only performed indoors.	zumari drums special costumes

WATWANA

| Uta [Men only] | stamp feet and danced outdoors | msewe, uta work clothes |
| Mwaribe [Men and Women] | leap, foot to foot danced outdoors | drums street clothes |

ALL WOMEN OF ALL CLASSES

| Chakacha or Ngomi ya Ndomi [Women only] | hip drops, danced in tent or outdoors. | drums, zumani utasa and best clothes. |

Figure 5

The first column (which remains to be discussed), contrasts the movement patterns of the dances of the two extremes of Swahili class structure. The elements in this column show that the Swahili identify their status by moving differently in dances and by using different body parts. Specifically (in a rather oversimplified manner), *waungwana* danced forms can be characterized as "arm dances". *Watwana* dances can be characterized as "foot dances".

Waungwana forms use the feet only to support and give spatial direction to the dance and to the important features of the dance — the arm extensions and hands, adorned with swords or *mbiu*. Movements are up and away from the torso. *Watwana* forms use the feet as part of the percussion and as a focus of the danced movements. The dance takes place primarily in a vertically defined space, the dancers' weight moving in an up-and-down pattern.

If the reader finds this contrast surprising, so too, I think, would the Swahili. I did not ask them about these things during the research period because I didn't notice them myself until I had returned to the United States and was in the process of analyzing my data. I think this aspect of dancing is largely out of awareness, just as the differences in upper class and lower class speech in many societies are salient defining features of class, but they are not attended to much of the time. I do not think that the dance movements that differentiate classes are deliberate inventions, any more than class speech differences are deliberate inventions. I *do*, however, think that they are a result of a process of participation, feedback and observation that a dance community, like a speech community, takes part in as it sees itself dancing.

Dancing, Status and Role

Dancing communicates. It can communicate a narrative plot, as in many classical ballets, or emotional and ideational affects, as in much early American modern dance. In a society such as that of the Swahili, where there are no professional choreographers or ballet masters, dancing is intended to communicate something entirely different and it is not the result of a single individual's creative endeavor.

Dancing in Swahili society reiterates to the society at large (the extended audience) something about the dancers' status and role. For example, this dancer is a young working class male; that dancer is a high status bride. These positions in society are usually indicated by many other forms as well, i.e. dress, housing, paraphernalia and so on. If the danced action itself has anything to add to this picture of status and role, it will have to utilize the medium of movement itself to formulate the message.

Phrased in another way, dancing for the Swahili (and many other societies) is an important part of class differentiated behavior because it uses another medium — another form of social actions — to designate different social groups. Dances are at once redundant in actually defining groups, but they are unique in isolating movements of different parts of the body as markers of contrasting categories of people.

I must add here that there are no *formal* rules for Swahili dance participation or sponsorship, nor are there fines for doing the "wrong" dance. Anyone is free to dance in any way they like, to sponsor dance types of any kind they like. The trick is to get all the right people to attend. Assuming one's pocketbook can stand the strain, one can only ask, not command, the best musicians and poets to perform. Likewise, one can only invite the best people, or the traditional performers of a certain dance form. One can even join a dancing group of a different social category and no one will forcefully object. They may cut you dead, but they will not call a "bouncer".[2] The "rules" are unwritten and consensual. The movements are prescribed and recognized and the dances are advertisements for, and re-affirmations of, the dancers' social position.

To conclude, I want to look at another dance, probably the most well-known of all and perhaps the most ambiguous — but not, I hope, confusing. This dance is *chakacha* the women's hip dance that all women, regardless of class, participate in. *Chakacha* appears to be a new name for a very old dance, formerly called *ngoma ya ndani*, meaning 'dance of the private women's quarters'; that is, a harem dance.

Because it is intentionally erotic and celebrates female sexuality, it fits the western stereotype of a harem dance. *Chakacha* could be and still is done at any time when a group of women are relaxing together at home. It was also done as sexual instruction for a bride during wedding festivities. The new name seems to denote its outdoor version, still maintaining purdah, however, by the use of gunny sack tent walls with a fancy ruffled awning above.

When the dance is held indoors, women wear their most glittering finery: jewelry, flowers, hair-dos and make-up. Out of doors, most of this opulence is partly concealed by black *bui-bui* veils. The instruments for the dance include a full range of drums and percussion, a *zumari*, usually a western trumpet and sometimes an electric organ. So far, this dance — this *ngoma* form — has attributes that make it seem like a *waungwana* display of status. But, what of the movements? Do they fit the pattern of differentiated movements by social rank in the same way as the other dances we have examined? Here is the anomalous part of *chakacha* (*ngoma ya ndani*).

The focus of body movements for *chakacha* are neither with the arms/hands extended horizontally in space, (like the *lelemama* and *ngoma la hazua*), nor are they with the feet in the vertical, under-the-body space, (like the *uta* and *mwaribe* of *watwana*). *Chakacha* focal moves consist of two forward hip drops to the right followed by two on the left, repeated throughout the dance (see Figure 6, p. 240).

A meter-length cloth (*leso*) is tied tightly around the dancer's hips to accentuate the movements. The arms are relaxed, flexed at the elbow, hands horizontal, perhaps consciously framing the movement of one hip. The feet do very little, perhaps shuffle forward in tiny steps as alternate hips drop.

There is no necessary spatial formation. Sometimes the dancers move about following one another as in the familiar 'conga' line.[3] Sometimes the dancers perform solo, sometimes they pair off and dance towards each other in a friendly competition. If we were to diagram *chakacha* movement, it would look like the bottom entry in the first column of Figure 5, putting it midway between the others, in terms of the body space utilized. The movements do not require the arms in extended spaces. They are vertical, but there are no percussive elements — no impacts of feet to the ground. Can we explain the median position and movement of this dance by other contextual clues?

One is tempted to think of other female dances involving hip drops and hip sashes — middle Eastern 'belly dances' come to mind immediately. However, this genre as an origin is probably not likely for several reasons. First, the most similar movements are from the Saidi region of Egypt, which is an area with far less contact with the Swahili than other middle Eastern areas. Second, the most recent (and most intense) contact was with Oman, but women in these areas do *not* dance primarily with hip movements, as they wear voluminous dresses when dancing that conceal everything but the head, the neck and lower arms, and most of their characteristic dance movements involve these body parts.

It seems reasonable to assume that *chakacha* indicates something else about Swahili society because it was (and is) danced by *all women* regardless of class. *Chakacha* danced movements represent women's special role (and rank) in Swahili society. Their role was reproduction. Their rank was in one sense ambiguous. In another sense, their rank was high, although tightly limited, contained and controlled.

That all women, regardless of social class, could perform *chakacha* is not surprising because all women in Swahili society could (and do) produce legitimate offspring. Female household slaves often achieved manumission by producing a child fathered by the head of a household. A woman's occupation, then, no matter what her pedigree, was primarily child-rearing and domestic work. Unlike men who were divided into occupational statuses of high or low prestige and who indicated rank by dance types, women were united in the kind of labor they performed. They also danced their occupation, so to speak, with their hips.

The tension between Islamic ideas and African heritage also affected women's position in the Swahili context. As many authors have noted, Swahili women — as part of their African heritage — have more rights and higher status than their Arab sisters. Property ownership and management, and independence after divorce are two important rights Swahili women enjoy. But the Islamic ideal puts women in a totally dependent and subservient condition. Swahili women had more latitude in their society, with the option to act either as autonomous African women and/or subservient Muslim women. Swahili women danced a dance that was all their own, that celebrated their clear and vital role in society as child-producers and bearers, which left behind the high status dance of the upper body and the low-status dances of foot movements. Women were squarely *in between*, in religion and rank — and in their danced movements.

[MAF]

PRECIS EXERCISE 8

[1]We can now ask, what are the *waungwana* status emblems [2]in these two historical performances as I have described [3]them? First (and indispensable) was the setting of a stone [4]house. Next were the guests — one's family and friends, [5]also from the upper-class. Fine clothing is a familiar status-[6]symbol. Men used both quality materials and a religious [7]style of clothing to signify high status. Women displayed [8]affluence by having special dancing clothes and parapher-[9]nalia. Poetry singing was a mandatory part of the *ngoma* [10]and finally, food was offered. These are the familiar em-[11]blems of high status; wealth, as shown in houses, clothes, [12]food, fine friends and refined pastimes. It is easy to see [13]counterparts in our own and many other societies.
[14]What is not so obvious is that the actual danced move-[15]ments are also valued as *waungwana* kinds of movement. [16]By way of contrast, we will now look at two *ngoma* of very [17]humble classes of people in Swahili culture in order to make [18]the contrasting movement styles clear.

19The contrasting dance I will describe is called *uta*. This is 20another men's dance that is one of the showpieces of 21*Maulidi* week in Lamu. It is known as the "coconut-cutters 22dance" and it has always been performed out of doors in a 23*kiwanja* a cleared sand-lot area between houses. The name 24*uta* means 'bow' as in 'bow and arrow', pointing to the 25principal instrument plucked while the player also intones 26the *uta* song.

27More vital for dancing purposes are the leg rattles worn 28by the dancers. These are called *msewe* and are woven on a 29strip of palm fiber rope, about every 6 inches. The rope is 30wrapped around the dancer's legs from ankle to knee. The 31dancers thus make their own music, for no drums or other 32instruments are used. They wear typical Swahili men's 33work clothing; a *kikoy* (like a sarong), a shirt and sandals 34and a prayer cap (*kofia*), perhaps.

35The dancers form a rough circle and leaning on canes placed 36before their feet, stamp the *uta* rhythm in unison, produc-37ing a percussive rustling sound of the fiber rattles. Occa-38sionally, a dancer breaks out of the circle, raises his cane 39over his head and twirls through the center to take a new 40place on the opposite side of the circle.

41Another men's dance, *mwaribe*, can also be seen in Lamu 42during *Maulidi* week, and it is then done out-of-doors by 43young men. The instruments are *msondo* (also an alternate 44name for the dance) which is a long narrow drum some-45what similar to a conga drum. The dancers wear smart 46street clothes — trousers and new shirts, i.e. "western wear".

47The dance begins with one person inviting a partner into 48the dance space by hopping onto one foot to a position 49directly in front of the partner, who then responds by hop-50ping forward in unison as the first person hops backwards. 51The sequence continues: hop forward on the right, put 52feet together, hop back on the left, (again, feet together), 53step in place and step in place again. The arms and hands 54are held chest high and the hopping motion gives them

[55]the appearance of flapping like birds' wings. This dance is
[56]the only one I ever heard of that is sometimes performed
[57]by mixed-gender groups.

[58]My informant told me that 40 years ago, on Kiunga island
[59](north of Lamu), mixed groups of men, women and chil-
[60]dren did this dance together, even single and married
[61]women dancing with the men. This dance is also said to be
[62]especially liked by the Pokomo, a people who live adja-
[63]cent to the Swahili area on the coast. They and other re-
[64]lated inland groups, the Miji-Kenda people, for example,
[65]are said to have other, similar dances. In larger Swahili
[66]towns, however, *mwaribe* is never performed by mixed
[67]groups. Young girls dance *mwaribe* indoors, at strictly se-
[68]cluded girls' parties and young men perform it outdoors,
[69]as described here.

[70]These dances, the *mwaribe* and the *uta*, may be said to be
[71]characteristic of the *watwana* class in Swahili society. The
[72]*watwana* are the lowest class. In fact, one meaning of the
[73]word, is 'slaves'. These people are said to lack all *waungwana*
[74]attributes. That is, they are recent arrivals in town life, they
[75]have no pedigree or distinguished ancestors, they practise
[76]a slack sort of Islamic religion and, of course, they are eco-
[77]nomically poor. *Uta* is a dance of a very humble occupa-
[78]tional group: coconut cutters. As a type of work, it is dirty
[79]and hard, therefore only for poor and unrefined men.

[80]*Mwaribe* betrays its humble status by its similarity to Miji-
[81]Kenda dances which are done by non-believers and, in re-
[82]lation to town-dwellers, lower class people. It is low in sta-
[83]tus because of the tendency to perform it in violation of
[84]purdah strictures.

[85]It is interesting to compare the two pairs of dances: *ngoma*
[86]*la hazua* and *lelemama* which exemplify *waungwana ngoma*,
[87]on the one hand, and *uta* and *mwaribe*, which are *watwana*
[88]dances, on the other. What are the contrasting attributes
[89]of each pair? Before answering that question, a clarifying
[90]point must be made. The reason that *watwana* dances are
[91]"low status" in Swahili society is simply because lower-

⁹²class Swahili people dance them. ... There is nothing in-
⁹³trinsically better or worse about the movements them-
⁹⁴selves, but Swahili society *assigns* class meanings to these
⁹⁵dances, therefore, they are talked about as if there were
⁹⁶something in the nature of the dances themselves that was
⁹⁷"lower" or "poorer" than the *ngoma la hazua* dances.

Exercises

I. Find definitions for these words, making sure you know what they mean in the context.

•status [1, 5, 7, 11, 82-3, 91]; •mandatory [9]; •emblems [1, 10-11]; •humble [17, 77, 80]; •attributes [74, 88]; •*Maulidi* [21, 42]; •gender [57]; •purdah [84]; •intrinsically [92-3]; •*waungwana* [1, 15, 73, 86]; •*watwana* [71, 72, 86, 90].

II. On a separate sheet of paper, answer these questions:

a. Franken uses the word 'status' at least seven times in 97 lines of writing. Does the word mean the same thing every time she uses it?

b. Upon what would you say "class" is based in Swahili society?

c. In lines 92-94, Franken says, "there is nothing intrinsically better or worse about the movements themselves". First, state whether you agree or disagree with her, then give reasons why you agree or disagree. Are there comparable examples in your own society / culture?

III. How would you compare (show similarities between) and contrast (show differences between) Swahili dances and Lugbara dances? After you have explored the comparisons and the contrasts, answer this question: Is it *useful* to anyone to carry out this kind of comparison? Regardless of how you answer, explain why you have chosen to answer as you have.

The Abstract at the beginning of Franken's article is actually a *précis* of her paper. An abstract *is* a précis.

A. Do you think this author did a good job of summarizing her paper?

B. Again, regardless of your answer, give reasons why.

C. From this list: 1. Keali'inohomoku, 2. Best, 3. Kaeppler, and 4. Middleton, choose *one* essay, then **write an abstract** for the essay **using no more than 300 words**.

IV. What does 'manumission' mean (p. 213)?

Signs and Symbols
[by The Editor]

There is no *necessary* or *causal* relation between symbols and that which is symbolized whether the symbol is painted, danced, sculpted, carved or written, as are the symbols that compose the Roman alphabet. Saussure said signs and symbols are 'arbitrary' (1966: 67*ff*). We say signs and symbols *are also conventionally agreed upon* for three reasons: (1) humans make their own meanings; (2) these meanings work for us (that is, they consistently operate in human societies), and (3) human beings engage in activities that, without exception, are signal or symbolic or both.

The color red in a traffic light, for example, *means* stop, but there is no *natural* or *causal* reason why another color couldn't have done just as well. *That red means stop* in the United States, Europe and elsewhere *is a socio-linguistically derived concept.* There are hundreds, thousands, perhaps millions of other examples: many Chinese wear white as a symbol of mourning, but black is the conventionally accepted color in European countries. The *emu* is one of the national symbols of Australia, but the bald eagle is the national symbol of the United States; the bear of Russia. Roses were kingly symbols in mediæval England, but squash blossoms are favored among the Hopi. Readers can doubtless think of many similar examples from their own knowledge and experience.

On the other hand, if we say that smoke is a *sign* of fire, there is a different kind of relationship involved between signifier (the smoke) and signified (the fire), because fire *causes* smoke. Fire happens to be red as well (or that is how we name it in our conceptual scheme of colors), but there are obvious differences between the redness of fire, the redness of a traffic light or the redness of a Spanish matador's cape.

Redness itself does not *cause* motorcars to stop at a traffic light. The redness itself doesn't *cause* a bull to charge at the matador's cape. The bull would charge if the cape were yellow, blue or white. Use of the word, 'cause' is too strong. In the case of the traffic light, instead of saying, "red *causes* stop", we say, "red *means* stop" referring to the intrinsically *conventional* nature of the relationship between symbol and symbolized. This relationship between signifier and signified works for us in everyday life only because drivers have tacitly agreed to use a conventional system of traffic rules including the colors red, green and yellow (or amber).

Some symbols are found in all cultures: the symbols for the male phallus (*lingam*) and female sexual organs (*yoni*), as they are known in India, or the *mandala* figures based on the cardinal directions of north, south, east and west. These are often regarded as universal and in one rather limited way of looking at them, they are. Even in these cases, however, we have to say that although all human beings possess sexual organs and all human societies exist within the cardinal directions in geographically defined spaces, these features of human life are *structurally* universal, but *they are not semantically universal*, because, for example, each of the directions may be 'weighted', that is, each direction may have different *assigned values* from culture to culture (see Williams 1995).

The spatial dimensions of up/down, front/back, right/left and inside/outside — even sexual symbols and the cardinal directions — are assigned different *semantic* value. They frequently have quite dissimilar meaning across cultures, although *structurally*, they are the same.

The structural nature of human symbolic expressions of the opposition right/left, for instance, are to be found all over the world, but their conventional usages and semantic applications within different ethnicities aren't universal; *they require translation*. Not only that, they often require prodigious efforts of understanding, because human beings tend to think their particular sets of categories and classifications are natural and right but those of others are alien and 'strange', therefore less desirable. As universal structures, however, the spatial dimensions and the cardinal directions are referred to by semasiologists as "semantic primitives" (see Williams 1995 for thorough discussion).

About the use of signs and symbols in sociocultural anthropology, Schieffelin has this to say:

> Symbols are usually conceived as "meaning" or "standing for" something else. At the same time, they exist in various logico-meaningful relationships with other symbols in a larger system. A traditional view [in social anthropology] holds that meanings are primarily stored in symbols and brought out for use when they are required. Though symbols undoubtedly have this storage capacity, I would like to emphasize their more creative aspect. Symbols do not just "stand for" something else. They constantly and actively "bring things into meaning". This happens because symbolic activity brings objects and concepts into new and different kinds of relationships in a larger system of meaning, formulating and organizing them in new ways according to a few simple procedures. This "rendering into meaning" is the symbolic process by which human consciousness continually works reality into intelligible forms.
>
> As a practical matter for ethnography, we are interested in examining the way meanings develop over a series of events to which they give form. I deal with this issue primarily by examining sequences of events that I call "cultural scenarios". A cultural scenario is a series of events embodying a typical sequence of phases or episodes, which between its commencement and resolution effects a certain amount of social progress or change in the situation to which it pertains. The concept of cultural scenario differs from that of a ritual (which may, however, express or dramatize a cultural scenario) in that the cultural scenario is embodied in everyday, informal courses of action. It is empirically recognizable in the general procedure by which a people repeatedly approach and interpret diverse situations and carry them to similar types of resolution. The situations themselves need not be similar; it is the similar manner in which they are interpreted, carried forward, and resolved that is important.
>
> The structure of the cultural scenario must be not only analytically visible to the observer but also in some way present in the awareness of the participants. This is sometimes a difficult matter to specify. In general, a people may be said to be aware of a cultural scenario when they feel that a given situation admits of a certain kind of resolution and implicitly direct their actions and expectations toward attaining that resolution. The implication is that people orient themselves and interpret events in terms of the culturally familiar implications of a larger, well-known course of action.
>
> A cultural scenario, as a typical event sequence, has a structure of its own that may be dealt with apart from the social organization of the society in which it takes place. On the other hand, however, many of the normative principles of the society may pertain to behavior in

particular cultural scenarios, and the organization of the society may be to a large degree maintained by the processes entailed in them. This would more or less be the case for those scenarios related to exchange and reciprocity in New Guinea societies.

The thrust of this book [i.e. *The Sorrow of the Lonely and the Burning of the Dancers*] is basically processual. I am interested in the theme of reciprocity less for what it contributes to the structure and coherence of the social organization than for what it implies about the way Kaluli approach and conceive situations and understand their lives (Schieffelin 1976: 2-4).

Fourteen years earlier, Ross pointed out that

Communication is always social. It contains three elements, one of which has an important corollary: (1) a person who communicates, (2) the signs by which he communicates, and (3) a person who interprets the signs. The communicator need not be present, or even alive. Dead authors and artists communicate. The signs must be present to the interpreting mind, although they need not be present in fact. They may *be* only remembered, as the first chapter of a book is when one is in the middle, or the first movement as a symphony nears its close.

The corollary is implied by the third element. To be able to interpret a sign one must know the conventional system with-in which the signs have their meaning. One must know English in order to understand an English sentence. To an Eskimo visiting one of our cities for the first time, a green light at an intersection may have no meaning, or it may not have the meaning intended by the highway commission; one must understand the system of traffic signals in order to interpret a green light successfully...

'Community' and 'communication' are words which show an immediate similarity. They emphasize commonness, togetherness. People gather or live together for certain purposes, and they share meanings and attitudes; the first presupposes the second, for without communication there is no community. Community depends on shared experience and emotion, and communication enters into and clarifies the sharing. Forms of communication like art and religion and language are themselves shared by a community, and each of them contains and conveys ideas, attitudes, perspectives, and evaluations which are deeply rooted in the history of the community (Ross 1962: 157*ff*).

Symbols and Signs are Shared

The shared nature of symbols is part of their conventionality, because *if they are to provide the means of communication, there has to be agreement between senders and receivers* regarding their meaning. Symbols (whether words, gestures or entire ceremonials), couldn't be as basic to human life as they are if they were entirely private. They *are* social, conventional and shared. This is an important idea, because the study of signs, symbolism and meaning, in virtue of the shared, public nature of languages, symbols and meanings, frees us from criticisms of looking at some hidden, mysterious realm inside some individual's head. In other words, we aren't mentalists, nor are all of our conclusions 'subjective'. Symbols, language, body languages and culture are *shared*. They are thus potentially 'objective' in that they are publicly used and expressed in a common public domain.

Signs and symbols allow for the transmission of culture over time. Infants *become human* through acquiring systems of signs and symbols. Helen Keller (1954) told the world that *she became human only when she discovered the connection between symbols and reality* — when she experienced the *relationship* between signs, symbols and raw sensory stimuli, starting with water flowing out of a pump onto her hand. The stimulus by itself wasn't enough, as we all know. Her teacher *signed* the word 'water' into her hand, and finally, she understood.

Signs and symbols hold human societies together. They are the 'glue', the 'binding material' of a society, so to speak. The primary symbol sets used by human beings belong to their languages — spoken languages and body languages alike. Unlike animals, human beings live in more dimensions of reality because they have *conceptions of* living. Therefore, the social life of humans is not best understood through references to other forms of life, even chimpanzees (see Baynton 1996 for apposite discussion). Many anthropologists postulate a difference in *kind* between human beings and other sensate life forms, thus they provide different explanations for human systems of movement communication than theories which start from the premise that animal communication and human communication are separated, not by *kind*, but by *degree*. Several years ago, Ross made these important points:

> Only [human beings have] a developed, or verbal, language, so it is only man who can learn things precisely and store them in memory in all their essentials. Language is a necessary condition for the existence of culture, for what is learned by one man is transmitted to others; and what is wanted for cooperative undertakings of any complexity can be expressed in words. Then the organization of a society and the things it has learned can be transmitted to the next generation, thus continuing the culture that has been created. Language manages what nature cannot: the transmission of acquired characteristics. Each generation adds to the store of culture, or changes what it has inherited, making culture cumulative. Growth and change give [human beings] a history, and, properly speaking, [they are] the only creature[s] who [have] a history. ... Socialization not only makes a person a member of the culture, but it also makes him fully a human being. Apart from society, man does not even exhibit potentiality for living in the most rudimentary culture. We cannot be sure precisely how much the humanness of [people] depends on language, but there is a good deal of evidence that without it [people are] scarcely recognizable as human, and that language is probably necessary for all higher cultural accomplishments. ... Social symbols bind us to one another in society and allow us to share the attitudes, emotions, and values that make social groups cohesive. Such symbols may be objects like the flag, the cross or crescent, the eagle, the hammer and sickle; or they may be formalized action of the sort we call ritual (Ross 1962: 155-156).[1]

So What's the Point?

After all, why shouldn't everyone bury their dead quickly and hygienically, and marry or separate merely by recording intentions — if that? Why shouldn't everyone try to live as rationally (or as irrationally) as possible? Why not simply look out for Number One? The answer is that, apart from their purely religious significance, mortuary ceremonies, weddings, art festivals, pig presentations, *fandangos, mwaribe, Gisaro, walangaa* and rituals of all kinds re-affirm each person's place in society, in families, in friendship, and in love. They commemorate his or her existence; the *particulars* of life, and the gap the deceased leaves in the lives of others.

A person isn't meant to be nothing but an information processing machine. In fact, no human being is replaceable in every detail by any other. Each human being is unique and this uniqueness, too, is commemorated. In the existence of funerals, members of human societies express their interest in the deceased, but they also express interest in the continuance of its surviving members. Funerals both affirm the death of a man or woman and his or her continuance in memory and influence to family, friends and society itself.

The so-called 'bonds' of society are the shared symbols, signs, rituals, values, and beliefs of its members. It is in these bonds that essential meanings of the society or the group are to be found. *Bonds may restrain,* like the chains on prisoners, *or they may sustain,* like the ropes mountain climbers use. Social bonds do both.

They contain people within the limits of social approval, yet they also provide the ways in which we develop our lives and our culture, providing the means to be creative and innovative. There is an analogy here to forms of art: the sonnet form in poetry on the one hand limits its author severely, yet those limitations can give the work scope, incisiveness and power. The restrictions of a danced idiom limit a choreographer, but (as we have recently seen through the attempts by the Judson Church group in the 1980s in New York to call all movement "dance" and all performance "art"), *no limitations* on human worlds merely results in vacuity.

Personal freedom, so highly valued by people in western cultures, yields many varieties of social order and tradition. *Personal freedom within the context of a social order is valuable,* not only to the individual, but to the group. In fact, personal freedom can only be guaranteed in a political and social order, and the value of individual differences — of choice and free intelligence (and the humanities, arts and sciences they nurture), depend upon shared rituals, symbols, intellectual constructs and emotions. Our social roots are often forgotten or neglected because they are so firmly embedded, hence they seem to raise no practical problems. However, if we forget them too long, we may uproot them, and with them, our Selves.

Two authors whose words are as relevant today as they were when they were written are those of the anthropologist, Leslie White, and the semanticist, S. I. Hayakawa. The following are relevant extracts from their work.

White (1940)

That there are numerous and impressive similarities between the behavior of [human beings] and that of ape is fairly obvious; it is quite possible that even chimpanzees in zoos have noted and appreciated them. Fairly apparent, too, are [people's] behavioral similarities to many other kinds of animals. Almost as obvious, but not easy to define, is a difference in behavior which distinguishes [human beings] from all other living creatures. I say "obvious" because it is quite apparent to the common [person] that the nonhuman animals with which he is familiar do not and cannot enter, and participate in, the world in which he [or she], as a human being, lives. It is impossible for a dog, horse, bird, or even an ape ever to have any understanding of the meaning of the sign of the cross to a Christian, or of the fact that black (white among the Chinese) is the color of mourning. But when the scholar attempts to define the mental difference between animal and man he sometimes encounters difficulties which he cannot surmount and, therefore, ends up by saying that the difference is merely one of degree; [people have] bigger mind[s], larger power[s] of association, wider range[s] of activities, etc.

There is a fundamental difference between the mind[s] of [humans] and the mind of non-[humans]. This difference is one of a kind, not one of degree. And the gap between the two types is of the greatest importance—at least to the science of comparative behavior. [Humanity] uses symbols; *no other creature does*. A creature either uses symbols or ... they do not: *there are no intermediate stages*.

A symbol is a thing the value or meaning of which is bestowed upon it by those who use it. I say 'thing' because a symbol may have any kind of physical form: it may have the form of a material object, a color, a sound, an odor, a motion or an object, a taste.

The meaning, or value, of a symbol is in no instance derived from or determined by properties intrinsic in its physical form: the color appropriate to mourning may be yellow, green, or any other color: purple need not be the color of royalty; among the Manchu rulers of China it was yellow. The meaning of the word 'see' is not intrinsic in its phonetic (or pictorial) properties. "Biting one's thumb at" someone might mean anything. The meanings of symbols are derived from and determined by the [people] who use them; meaning is bestowed by human beings upon physical forms which ... become symbols.

All symbols must have a physical form otherwise they could not enter our experience. But the meaning of a symbol cannot be perceived by the senses. One cannot tell by looking at an 'x' in an algebraic equation what it stands for; one cannot ascertain with the ears alone the symbolic value of the phonetic compound /si/; one cannot tell merely by weighing a pig how much gold [it] will exchange for; one cannot tell from the wave length of a color whether it stands for courage or cowardice, "stop" or "go"; nor can one discover the spirit in a fetish by any amount of physical or chemical examination. The meaning of a symbol can be communicated only by symbolic means, usually by articulate speech ... All culture (civilization) depends upon the symbol. It was the exercise of the symbolic faculty that brought culture into existence, and it is the use of symbols that makes the perpetuation of culture possible. Without the symbol there would be no culture, and [people] would be merely [animals], not human being[s].

Articulate speech is the most important form of symbolic expression. Remove speech from culture and what would remain? Let us see. Without articulate speech we would have no *human* social organization. Families we might have, but this form of organization is not peculiar to man; it is not *per se* human. But we would have no prohibitions of incest, no rules prescribing exogamy and endogamy, polygamy or monogamy. How could marriage with a cross cousin be prescribed, marriage with a parallel cousin proscribed, without articulate speech? How could rules which prohibit plural mates possessed simultaneously but permit them if possessed one at a time, exist without speech?

Without speech we would have no political, economic, ecclesiastic, or military organization; no codes of etiquette or ethics; no laws; no science, theology, or literature; no games or music, except on an ape level. Rituals and ceremonial paraphernalia would be meaningless without articulate speech. Indeed, without articulate speech we would be all but tool-less: we would have only the occasional and insignificant use of the tool such as we find today among the higher apes, for it was articulate speech that transformed the nonprogressive tool-using of the ape into the progressive, cumulative tool-using of man, the human being.

In short, without symbolic communication in some form, we would have no culture. "In the Word was the beginning" of culture—and its perpetuation also.

To be sure, with all his culture man is still an animal and strives for the same ends that all other living creatures strive for; the preservation of the individual and the perpetuation of the race. In concrete terms these ends are food, shelter from the elements, defense from enemies, health, and offspring. The fact that man strives for these ends just as all other animals do has, no doubt led many to declare that there is "no fundamental difference between the behavior of man and of other creatures." *But [humanity] does differ, not in ends but in means.* [Humanity's] means are cultural means ... And, since these means ... are dependent upon a faculty possessed by man alone, the ability to use symbols, the difference between the behavior of [people] and of all other creatures is not merely great, but basic and fundamental.

The behavior of [people] is of two distinct kinds: symbolic and non-symbolic. [Humans] yawn, stretch, cough, and scratch [themselves]. [They cry] out in pain, shrink with fear, "bristle" with anger, and so on. Non-symbolic behavior of this sort is not peculiar to [humankind]; it [is shared] not only with the other primates but with many other animal species as well. But [people] communicate with [their] fellows with articulate speech, [they use] amulets, confess sins, make laws, observe codes of etiquette, explain dreams, classify relatives in designated categories, and so on. This kind of behavior is unique; only [human beings are] capable of it; it is peculiar to [them] because it consists of, or is dependent upon, the use of symbols. ... It is the symbol which has transformed [people] from mere animal[s] to human animal[s] ...

A baby is not a human being so far as his [or her] behavior is concerned. Until the infant acquires speech there is nothing to distinguish his [or her] behaviour qualitatively from that of the young ape. The baby becomes a human being when and as he learns to use symbols. Only by means of speech can the baby enter and take part in the human affairs of [humankind]. ... The most important form of symbolic expression is articulate speech. Articulate speech means communication of ideas; communication means preservation—tradition—and preservation means accumulation and progress. (White 1940: pages 219-221; 223-224, condensed and footnotes deleted).

Hayakawa (1964)

Animals struggle with each other for food or for leadership, but they do not, like human beings, struggle with each other for things that *stand for* food or leadership: such things as our paper symbols of wealth (money, bonds, titles), badges of rank to wear on our clothes, or low-number license plates, supposed by some people to stand for social precedence. For animals, the relationship in which one thing stands for something else does not appear to exist except in very rudimentary form.

The process by means of which human beings can arbitrarily make certain things stand for other things may be called the symbolic process. Whenever two or more human beings can communicate with each other, they can, by agreement, make anything stand for anything. For example, here are two symbols: X   Y

We can agree to let X stand for [rice] and Y stand for [bread]; then we can freely change our agreement and let X stand for the [the basketball team] and Y for [the football team]; or let X stand for [Jomo Kenyatta] and Y for [Babe Ruth], X for [Socrates], Y for [Queen Elizabeth II], X for [South America], and Y for [Indonesia] and so on. We are, as human beings, uniquely free to manufacture and manipulate and assign values to our symbols as we please ...

Everywhere we turn, we see the symbolic process at work. Feathers worn on the head or stripes on the sleeve can be made to stand for military rank; cowrie shells or rings of brass or pieces of paper can stand for wealth; crossed sticks can stand for a set of religious beliefs; buttons, elks' teeth, ribbons, special styles of ornamental haircutting or tattooing can stand for social affiliations. The symbolic process permeates human life at the most primitive and the most civilized levels alike. Warriors, medicine men, policemen, doormen, nurses, cardinals and kings wear costumes that symbolize their occupations. American Indians collected scalps, college students collect membership keys in honorary societies, to symbolize victories in their respective fields.[2]...

Food, too, is highly symbolic. Religious dietary regulations, such as those of the Catholics, Jews, and [Muslims], are observed in order to symbolize adherence to one's religion. Specific foods are used to symbolize specific festivals and observances in almost every country, for example, cherry pie on George Washington's birthday [in the United States], haggis on Burns' Nicht [in Scotland]. Eating together has been a highly symbolic act throughout all of man's known history: "companion" means one with whom you share your bread.

We select our furniture to serve as visible symbols of our taste, wealth, and social position. We often choose our residences on the basis of a feeling that it "looks well" to have a "good address". We trade in perfectly good cars for later models, not always to get better transportation, but to give evidence to the community that we can afford it.

Of all forms of symbolism, language is the most highly developed, most subtle, and most complicated. It has been pointed out that human beings, by agreement, can make anything stand for anything. Now, human beings have agreed, in the course of centuries of mutual dependency, to let the various noises that they can produce with their lungs, throats, tongues, teeth, and lips systematically stand for specified happenings in their nervous systems.

We call that system of agreements language. ... There is, as has been said, no necessary connection between the symbol and that which is symbolized. Just as men can wear yachting costumes without ever having been near a yacht, so they can make the noise "I'm hungry" without being hungry. Furthermore, just as social rank can be symbolized by feathers in the hair, by tattooing on the breast, by gold ornaments on the watch chain, or by a thousand different devices according to the culture we live in, so the fact of being hungry can be symbolized by a thousand different noises according to the culture we live in: "J'ai faim," or "Es hunger mich," or "Ho appetito," or "Hara ga hetta," and so on.

However obvious these facts may appear at first glance, they are actually not so obvious as they seem except when we take special pains to think about the subject. Symbols and things symbolized are independent of each other; nevertheless, we all have a feeling as if, and sometimes acting as if, there were necessary connections. For example, there is the vague sense we all have that foreign languages are inherently absurd: foreigners have such funny names for things, and why can't they call things by their right names? This feeling exhibits itself most strongly in those tourists who seem to believe that they can make the natives of any country understand English if they shout loud enough (Hayakawa 1964: 214-216, condensed, footnotes deleted).

In the case of symbolic human *action signs*, it is somewhat more difficult to comprehend what physical forms they take in order to understand and interpret our collective experience. Then, too, current ideas about the morphology of action signs have developed considerably over the past twenty years, (see Farnell 1995a: 1-30 for thorough discussion). Even so, the fundamental features of signs, symbols and communication that these earlier scholars discussed still holds.

For an aspiring anthropologist of human movement studies, whether of dances, the martial arts, sign languages, ceremonies, story-telling performances or any movement-based action sign system, one important over-arching issue pertaining to the field of study is the relationship between humans and animals — that is, to the *classifications* of these creatures (see Williams 1996 for relevant discussion).

Should animals be classified (thus included) in human domains or should human beings be classified (thus included) in animal domains or are there more useful ways of thinking of the matter than these?

In conclusion, we will recall the cogent statements about "cultural scenarios" that open Schieffelin's book because they reflect an important level of social anthropological thought regarding movement studies. The author's statements imply a question that is behind all the texts in this book, i.e. how do human beings conceive their situations and interpret their lives to themselves and others?

Schieffelin's answer is threefold: [i] signs and symbols constantly and actively "bring things into meaning" (see p. 221 above); [ii] this "rendering into meaning is the symbolic process by which consciousness continually works reality into intelligible forms" (p. 221) and [iii] we "are interested in the theme of reciprocity less for what it contributes to the structure and coherence of the social organization than for what it implies about the way Kaluli [or any other people] approach and conceive situations and understand their lives" (p. 222).

NOTES

Preface [pp. v-xiv]

[1] Some people use the word 'dance' by itself. Thus, the phrase might read, "more familiar kinds of literature written about dance". This usage presents serious analytical problems, thus dances (the unitary phenomena), dancing (the act) and 'the dance' (a broad category including the sum of all dances in the world) are distinctions I maintain as far as possible.

[2] Should instructors be concerned about this, *The International Encyclopedia of the Social Sciences* is an excellent reference for these and other anthropological terms.

I. Keali'inohomoku [pp. 15-33]

[1] Notice that the term 'non-literate' refers to a group which has never had a written language of their own devising. This is quite different from the term 'illiterate' which means that there is a written language, but *an illiterate* is not sufficiently educated to know the written form. Thus DeMille's statement that the primitives are illiterate is a contradiction of terms.

[2] An interesting article by Bunzel on the 'Sociology of Dance' in the 1949 edition of *Dance Encyclopedia* rejects the use of the word 'art' for these dance forms, however. In the context of his criticism, his point is well taken (1949: 437).

[3] For a critical review of the *Dance Encyclopedia* and especially of La Meri's entries see Renouf, in *Ethnomusicology*, 1969: 383-384.

[4] Harper distinguishes between ethnic and theatrical dance on the basis of "integral function of a society" vs. dance which is "deliberately organized" to be performed for a general, impersonal audience (1967: 10). This dichotomy, which is based on *genre* rather than the society, provides a good working classification. However, the distinction fails when the terms are tested. Thus one can have *ethnic dances of an ethnic society*, but not *theatrical dances of a theatrical society*. It seems clear that 'ethnic' is a more embracing category under which 'traditional' and 'theatrical' might be convenient subdivisions. In any case, Harper's discussion is thought-provoking.

III. Williams [pp. 55-63]

[1] The current fashion is for *no teaching of the kind I suggest*. I am told this kind of teaching is really hidden persuasion and influence. According to the 'exposure method' of instruction, the intellectual self of the instructor is to be kept as far out of the matter as possible, on the belief that the student will somehow find his or her own way, and that the possibility of

objectivity in teaching will be thereby increased. This is not the place to enter into a discussion of pedagogy, but I must assert that I find this method and the beliefs on which it is based both pointless and silly because in the end, it is a method of teaching which offers the student no real *choice*, thereby destroying the foundation for the development of any real individuality as a scholar. My views on teaching in any subject admittedly stem from the teaching of dancing, and from an ideal of many artists which, simply stated, is the notion of freedom through discipline, in contrast to the notion that freedom consists either of formlessness or the absence of discipline and techniques (see Best 1982 for apposite discussion).

V. Kaeppler [pp. 87-119]

[1] Research in Tonga was carried out for 20 months from 1964 to 1976 supported by Public Health Service Fellowship No. 5-F1-MH-25, 985-02 from the National Institute of Mental Health and by the Wenner-Gren Foundation for Anthropological Research, to whom I wish to express my appreciation. I also wish to thank the Government of Tonga under their majesties the late Queen Sālote Tupou III and the present King Tāufa'āhau Tupou IV, as well as the many Tongans who helped me in my work, especially Sister Tu'ifua, Tupou Posesi Fanua, the Honourable Ve'ehala, Baron Vaea, Vaisima Hopoate, Ana Malia Hopoate, and Tu'imala Ma'afu.

[2] Hanna critically reviews various definitions, but there is still something lacking (1980: 17-24).

[3] I was present at the state *kātoanga* and *taumafa kava* during which the validation of the titles of King Tupou IV and the crown prince took place (1967 and 1975).

[4] Food presentations are also given nonpublicly by bringing the gifts to the kitchen or private entrance of the receiver. This is often the case when the giver is of higher rank than the receiver. For such nonpublic presentations formalised movements or counting are not done.

[5] Apparently because on the previous day the king had stopped the *lakalaka* performances before Kolovai had their turn to perform.

[6] This is not a complete description of a kava ceremony. For more information see Collocott (1927).

[7] As will be seen below, one function of the *fakateki* head movement is to draw and hold the attention of the observers.

[8] For more defined *fakatapu* see Kaeppler 1967, 1976a, and 1976b.

[9] I am indebted to V. Huluholo Moungaloa for the text and assistance in translation. Here, as in all Tongan texts, there are many possible interpretations, all of which add to the *heliaki*.

[10] The composer of the poetry is known as *pulotu ta'anga*. The individual responsible for giving the poetry its melodic, polyphonic, and rhythmic setting is sometimes known as *pulotu hiva*; however, this is often a communal activity which can be accomplished almost spontaneously, owing to the distinctive stylistic characteristics which are well-known. An individual who can compose poetry, musical setting, and movement is known by the more elevated term *punake* — even if he or she was not responsible for all three elements of a specific composition.

[11] For a description of a set of movements that accompanies a stanza of *lakalaka* poetry see Kaeppler 1972: 212-213 and 1976a: 209-210.

VII. Notes on Comparison [pp. 151-161]

[1] This way of moving was created by Henry "Rubberlegs" Williams in the early 1900's. "Rubberlegs" was a nickname describing his particular style of dancing, and was also known as "Legamania".

[2] [Fairbank] uses the term 'pidginization' to describe the current drive to create a national Chinese dance form which is a mixture of various movement systems and vocabularies and intended to be used "principally for inter-group communication". Unfortunately the term had connotations of the 'imperialist era' for the Chinese, which she didn't wish to imply [The Editor].

VIII. Schieffelin [pp. 165-196]

[1] The phonetic symbol 'ɔ' roughly equals the sound of the English word, 'awe' [The Editor].

[2] The other ceremonies are Ilib Kuwɔ, Sæbio, Kɔluba, Iwɔ, and Heyalo (or Feyalo). More description will follow, after the Gisaro description and interpretation.

[3] Three out of fifteen ceremonies from 1966 to 1968 were performed without important social transactions.

[4] This was facilitated by the fact that the government-appointed Papuan medical orderly, who had been living in the area, departed at this time for his leave, so that there were no outsiders remaining nearby whom the Kaluli thought would inform the patrol officer.

[5] The description of what happens to the dead was given to me entirely in terms of what happens to men. When I asked about women, my informant said vaguely that "it was the same", but that it was a man who rescued the female soul from the fire, and so on.

IX. Franken [pp. 201-215]

[1] This is an important theoretical point which illustrates the essentially *social and linguistically-based* nature of human behavior with reference to assigned meanings [The Editor].

[2] An American idiomatic expression for a person in a public bar (a "drinks club") who forcibly ushers unwanted persons from the premises.

[3] Visually, the Conga line is a "follow-the-leader" line of dancers, true, but there the resemblance ends. The Conga is a West Indian freedom dance (the form to which I refer originated in Trinidad), and the spatial form is a line because former slaves were chained together in a line so they had to dance one following another. We make a point of the issue because it is just here that the *kinetic or kinological* (roughly comparable to phonetic and / or phonological) elements of danced movements (even some spatial relationships, as illustrated here) may appear to be the same, but *semasiologically*, the elements are not the same [The Editor].

X. Signs and Symbols [pp.219-231]

[1] The square-bracketed words in this and the following cited passages , e.g. White and Hayakawa are supplied so as to avoid outmoded gender distinctions and the antagonism they presently arouse. I do not hold with those, however, who would discard earlier writings because they used different forms of language than we use today. I changed the usages out of deference to modern readers, but the substance of what these authors had to say still holds [The Editor].

[2] What is 'money' if it is not relatively valueless metal coins or bits of paper with *symbols of their values and national identities* stamped or printed on them? [The Editor].

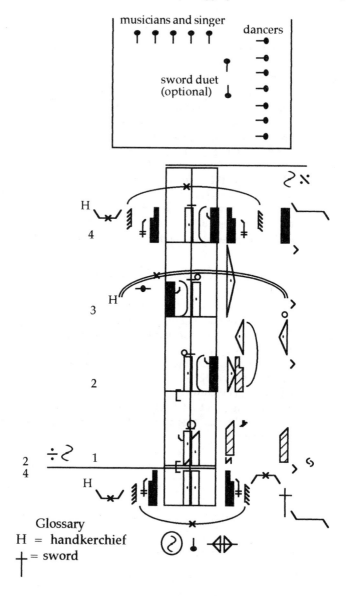

Figure 1. Waungwana Dances - Ngoma La Hazua. The
performance space is a rectangular room in a house,
or *kiwanja* (area between houses).

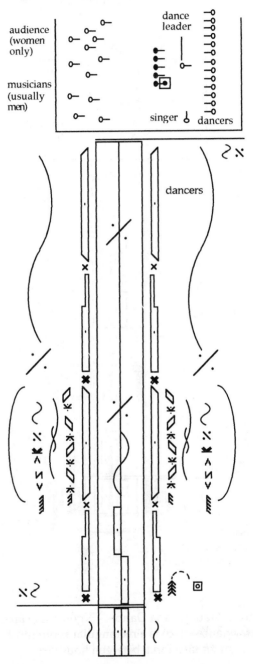

Figure 2. Waungwana Dances - Lelemama -
performance space (women covered); a tent.

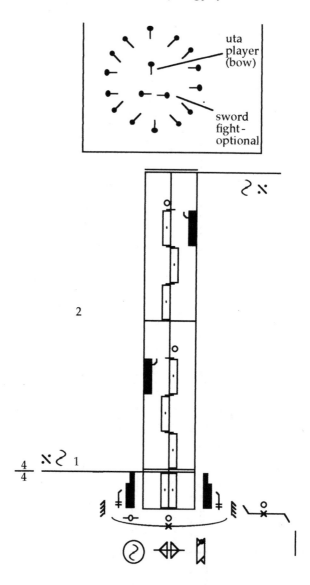

Figure 3. Watwana Dances - Uta Performance
space is out of doors in the *kiwanja*.

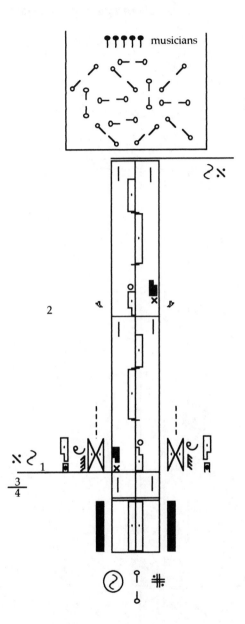

Figure 4. Watwana Dances - Mwaribe. Performance space is out of doors in the *kiwanja*.

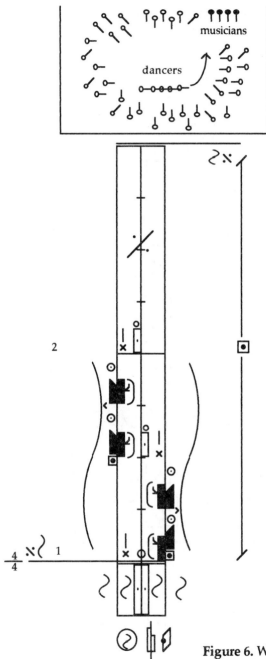

Figure 6. Women's Harem Dances
Chakacha/Ngoma Ya Ndani (var. 2)

BIBLIOGRAPHY

ALLEN, J. 1979. The Swahili House: Cultural and Ritual Concepts Underlying Its Plan and Structure. *Art and Archæology Research Papers* 9: 1-32.

ARNOLD, R. 1991. A Comparative Analysis of Some Aboriginal Dancing With Black American Jazz Dancing. *M.A. Thesis*, University of Sydney.

BATESON, G. 1973. *Steps to an Ecology of Mind*. St. Albans, Hertfordshire: Paladin.

BAYNTON, D. 1996. Savages and Deaf-Mutes. Evolutionary Theory and the Campaign Against Sign-Language. *Jour. for the Anthrop. Study of Hum. Mvmt.* [JASHM], 8(4): 139-173.

BECKWITH, M. 1906/1907. Dance Forms of the Moqui and Kwakiutl Indians. *Proceedings of the 15th International Congress of Americanists* (Quebec), 2: 79-114.

BENEDICT, R. 1934. *Patterns of Culture*. Boston: Houghton-Mifflin.

BEST, D.
>1974. *Expression in Movement and the Arts*. London: Lepus Books [H. Kimpton, Publishers].
>1982. Free Expression, or the Teaching of Techniques? *Jour. of the Anthrop. Study of Hum. Mvmt.* [JASHM], 2(2): 89-98 [Reprinted from the *Brit. Jour. of Educational Studies*, 24(3), October, 1979].

BOAS, Franz. 1944. Dance Among the Kwakiutl Indians. In *The Function of Dance in Human Society*, (Ed. Franziska Boas), New York: Dance Horizons

BOURGUIGNON, E. 1968. Trance Dance. *Dance Perspectives # 35* [no publisher listed].

BUNZEL, J.H. 1949. Sociology of the Dance. *The Dance Encyclopedia* (Chujoy, A., compiler and editor), New York: A.S. Barnes, 435-440.

CHUJOY, A. and MANCHESTER, P. (Eds.). 1967. *The Dance Encyclopedia*, New York: Simon & Schuster.

COLLOCOTT, E.E.V. 1927. Kava Ceremonial in Tonga. *Jour. of the Polynesian Society*, 36(141): 21-47.

CRICK, M. 1975. *Explorations in Language and Meaning: Towards a Semantic Anthropology*. New York: Halsted.

DEMILLE, A. 1963. *The Book of the Dance*. New York: Golden Press.

DIESING, P. 1971. *Patterns of Discovery in the Social Sciences*. New York: Aldine.

DUTTON, D. 1979. Aspects of Environmental Explanation in Anthropology and Criticism. *Experience Forms*. The Hague: Mouton.

ELLIS, H. 1920. *Studies in the Psychology of Sex*. Philadelphia: F.A. Davis.
EVANS-PRITCHARD, E.E. [Sir]
   1951. *Social Anthropology*. London: Cohen & West.
   1962. *Essays in Social Anthropology*. London: Faber & Faber.

FAIRBANK, H. 1983. Chinese Minority Dances and the Cultural Revolution. *M.A. Thesis*, New York University.
FARNELL, B.(Ed.)
   1995a. Introduction. *Human Action Signs in Cultural Context. The Visible and the Invisible in Movement and Dance*. Metuchen, N. J.: Scarecrow Press, pp. 1-30.
FARNELL, B.
   1995b. *Do You See What I Mean? Plains Indian Sign Talk and the Embodiment of Action*. Austin: University of Texas Press [with CD Rom].
FARNELL, B. and D. WILLIAMS. 1990. *The Laban Script. Movement-Writing for Non-Dancers* [with Workbook]. Canberra, A.C.T.: Australian Institute for Aboriginal and Torres Strait Islander Studies.
FLITCH, J.E.C. 1912. *Modern Dancing and Dancers*. London: Grant Richards.
FRAKE, C.O. 1964. A Structural Description of Subanun 'Religious Behavior'. *Explorations in Cultural Anthropology*. (Ed. W. Goodenough), New York: McGraw Hill.
FRANKEN, M.A.
   1986. Anyone Can Dance: A Survey and Analysis of Swahili *Ngoma*, Past and Present. *Ph.D. Thesis*, Riverside: University of California.
   1987. Women's Dances on the Swahili Coast. *UCLA Journal of Dance Ethnology*, #11.
FRAZER, J.G. [Sir]
   1911. *The Magic Art and the Evolution of Kings*. London: Macmillan.
   1947. *The Golden Bough*. New York: Macmillan.
FROBENIUS, L. 1908. *The Childhood of Man*.London: Seeley.

GARBETT, G.K. 1970. The Analysis of Social Situations. *MAN*, 5: 214-227.
GOLDFRANK, E. 1945. Socialization, Personality and the Structure of Pueblo Society (with particular reference to the Hopi and Zuni). *American Anthropologist*, 47: 516-539.
GROVE, L. 1895. *Dancing*. London: Longman, Green & Co.

HANNA, J. L. 1980. *To Dance Is Human*. Austin: University of Texas Press.
HARPER, P. 1967. Dance in a Changing Society. *African Arts/Arts d'Afrique*, 1(1): 10-80.
HARPER, W. 1973. Movement and Measurement: the Case of the Incompatible Marriage. *Quest*, June.

HASELBERGER, H. 1961. Method of Studying Ethnological Art. *Current Anthropology*, 2(4): 341-384.

HASKELL, A. 1960. *The Wonderful World of Dance.* New York: Doubleday.

HAYAKAWA, S.I. 1964. The Symbolic Process. *Custom Made. Introductory Readings for Cultural Anthropology.* (Ed. Hughes), Chicago: Rand-McNally.

HOLT, C. 1969. Two Dance Worlds. *Anthology of Impulse.* (M. van Tuyl, Ed.), New York: Dance Horizons, pp. 116-131.

HUIZINGA, J. AND A.E. JENSON. 1949. *Homo Ludens: A Story of the Play Element in Culture.* London: Routledge & Kegan Paul.

HUMPHREY, D. 1950. Dance (and related entries). *Webster's New International Dictionary,* [2nd Ed.], Springfield, Massachusetts: G. & C. Merriam.

KAEPPLER, A. L.

1967a. Folklore as Expressed in the Dance in Tonga. *Journal of American Folklore,* 80(316): 160-168.

1967b. Preservation and Evolution of Form and Function in Two Types of Tongan Dance. *Polynesian Culture History: Essays in Honor of Kenneth P. Emory.* (G. Highland, et al. Eds.). Special Publication 56. Honolulu, Hawaii: Bernice P. Bishop Museum Bishop Museum Press,

1971a. Aesthetics of Tongan Dance. *Ethnomusicology*, 15(2): 175-185.

1971b. Rank in Tonga. *Ethnology*, 10(2): 174-193.

1972. Method and Theory in Analyzing Dance Structure With an Analysis of Tongan Dance. *Ethnomusicology*, 16(2): 173-217.

1976a. Dance and Interpretation of Pacific Traditional Literature. *Directions in Pacific Traditional Literature: Essays in Honor of Katharine Luomala.* Bishop Museum Special Publication 62. Honolulu: Bishop Museum Press.

1976b. Dance in Tonga: The Communication of Social Values Through an Artistic Medium. *Communication in the Pacific.* (D. Lerner and J. Richstad, Eds.), Honolulu, Hawaii: East-West Communication Institute.

1978a. Melody, Drone, and Decoration: Underlying Structures and Surface Manifestations in Tongan Art and Society. *Art in Society: Studies in Styles, Culture and Aesthetics.* (M. Greenhalgh and V. Megaw, Eds.) London: Duckworth.

1978b. The Dance in Anthropological Perspective. *Ann. Rev. of Anthropology,* 7: 31-39.

1985. Structured Movement Systems in Tonga. *Society and the Dance.* (Ed. P. Spencer), Cambridge, U.K.: Cambridge University Press, pp. 92-118.

1986. Cultural Analysis, Linguistic Analogies and the Study of Dance in Anthropological Perspective. *Explorations in Ethnomusicology: Essays in Honor of David P. McAllester.* (Ed. Frisbie), Detroit, Michigan: Detroit Monographs on Musicology #9, pp. 25-33.

KEALI'INOHOMOKU, J.W.

1965. A Comparative Study of Dance as a Constellation of Motor Behaviors Among African and United States Negroes. *M.A. Thesis.* Evanston, Illinois: Northwestern University.

1969/1980. An Anthropologist Looks at Ballet as a Form of Ethnic Dance. *Impulse 1969-1970,* San Francisco. [Reprinted in *JASHM,* 1980, 1(2): 83-97, with permission by Marian Van Tuyl, from *Impulse 1969-1970,* the final edition of Impulse Publications].

1973. Culture Change, Functional and Dysfunctional Expressions of Dance, A Form of Affective Culture. Paper for the 9th *International Congress of Anthropological and Ethnological Sciences,* Chicago.

1974. Dance Culture as a Microcosm of Holistic Culture. *New Dimensions in Dance Research: Anthropology and Dance (The American Indian).* (Ed. T. Comstock), [CORD], New York University, pp. 245-260.

KELLER, H. 1954. *The Story of My Life.*New York: Doubleday.

KINNEY, T. and M.W. KINNEY. 1924. *The Dance.* New York: F. Stokes.

KIRSTEIN, L.

1924/1935. *Dance.* New York: Putnam's Sons.

1942. *The Book of the Dance.* New York: Doubleday.

KRIS, E. 1952. *PsychoAnalytic Explanations in Art.* New York: International University Press.

KURATH, G.P.

1960. Panorama of Dance Ethnology. *Current Anthropology,* 1(3): 233:254.

1966. Dance (and related entries). *Webster's New International Dictionary,* [3rd Ed.]. Springfield, Massachusetts: G. & C. Merriam Co.

LA MERI

1949. Ethnologic Dance. *The Dance Encyclopedia,* (Chujoy, A., Comp. and Ed.), New York: Barnes, pp. 117-178.

1967. Ethnic Dance. *The Dance Encyclopedia* (Chujoy, A., Comp. and Ed.), New York: Barnes, pp. 338-339.

LANGE, R.

1970. The Nature of Dance. *Laban Guild Magazine,* May Issue.

1975. *The Nature of Dance. An Anthropological View.* London: MacDonald & Evans.

LEEUW, G. van der. 1963. *Sacred and Profane Beauty. The Holy in Art.* (Trans. Green), New York: Holt, Rinehart & Winston.

MARTIN, J.

1939. *Introduction to the Dance.* New York: W.W. Norton.

1946. *The Dance.* New York: Tudor.

1963. [John Martin's Book of]*The Dance.* New York: Tudor.

MEAD, M. and BUNZEL, R. (Eds.) 1960. *The Golden Age of Anthropology.* New York: Braziller. [*see for Spier reference*].

MERRIAM, A. 1974. Anthropology and the Dance. *New Dimensions in Dance Research: Anthropology and Dance (The American Indian).* (Ed. T. Comstock), [CORD], New York University, pp. 928.

MIDDLETON, J.

1960. *Lugbara Religion.* London: Oxford University Press (for the International African Institute).

1963. The Yakan or Allah Water Cult Among the Lugbara of Uganda. *Jour. of the Royal Anthropological Institute,* 93(1): 80-108.

1965. *The Lugbara of Uganda.* New York: Holt, Rinehart & Winston.

1977. Ritual and Ambiguity in Lugbara Society. *Secular Ritual* (S. Moore and B. Myerhoff, Eds.), Assen: Van Gorcum.

1978. The Rainmaker Among the Lugbara of Uganda. *Systèmes de signes: textes réunis en hommage à Germaine Dieterlen.* Paris: Hermann.

1982. Lugbara Death. *Death and the Regeneration of Life.* (M. Bloch and J. Parry, Eds.), Cambridge, U.K.: Cambridge University Press.

1985. The Dance Among the Lugbara of Uganda. *Society and theDance.* (Ed. P. Spencer), Cambridge U.K.: Cambridge University Press.

MORGAN, L. 1962/1850. *League of the Ho-de-no-saun-ee, or Iroquois.* Rochester, New York: Sage and Bros.

PAGE, J. 1990. A Comparison Between Two Movement-Writing Systems: Laban and Benesh Notations. *M.A. Thesis,* University of Sydney.

POUWER, J. 1973. Signification and Fieldwork. *Journal of Symbolic Anthropology I.* The Hague: Mouton.

PROST, J. 1996. Body Language in the Context of Culture (Review Essay). *Visual Anthropology,* 8(2/3), 337-343.

RADIN, P. 1957. *Primitive Religion: Its Nature and Origin.* New York: Dover.

REDFIELD, R. 1969. *The Little Community and Peasant Society and Culture.* Chicago: University of Chicago Press.

RENOUF, R. 1969. A Book Review of *The Dance Encyclopedia. Ethnomusicology,* 13(2): 383-384.

ROSS, R. 1962. *Symbols and Civilization. Science, Morals, Religion, Art.* New York: Harcourt, Brace & World, pp. 155-157.

ROYCE, A. 1977. *The Anthropology of Dance.* Bloomington: University of Indiana Press.

SACHS, C. 1937. *The World History of the Dance.* [Trans: B. Schönberg], New York: Bonanza.

SCHIEFFELIN, E. 1976. *The Sorrow of the Lonely and the Burning of the Dancers.* New York: St. Martin's Press.

SIMMONS, J. 1983. A Matter of Interpretation. *American Way*, April, pp. 106-111.

SNYDER, A. 1974. The Dance Symbol. *New Dimensions in Dance Research: Anthropology and Dance (The American Indian)*. (Ed. T. Comstock), [CORD], New York University, pp. 213-224.

SORELL, W. 1967. *The Dance Through the Ages*. New York: Grosset and Dunlap.

SPENCER, L. and WHITE, W. 1972. Empirical Examination of Dance in Educational Institutions. *British Jour. of Physical Education*, 3(1), January.

SPENCER, P. (Ed.). 1985. *Society and the Dance*. Cambridge, U.K.: Cambridge University Press.

SPIER, L. 1921. *This reference is not in the bibliography of Royce's book.* It is included in the Mead/Bunzel reference.

STANFORD, T. 1966. *A Linguistic Analysis of Music and Dance Terms from Three Sixteenth Century Dictionaries of Mexican Indian Languages*. Institute of Latin American Studies Offprint series No. 76. Austin: University of Texas Press.

TERRY, W.

1949. History of Dance. *The Dance Encyclopedia*. (Chujoy, A., and P.W. Manchester, Comps. and Eds.), New York: Barnes, pp. 238-243.

1956. *The Dance in America*. New York: Harper & Brothers.

1967. Dance, History of. *The Dance Encyclopedia* (Chujoy, A., and P.W. Manchester, Comp. and Eds.) New York: Simon & Schuster, 255-259.

TITIEV, M. 1944. Old Oraibi. *Papers of the Peabody Museum of American Archaeology and Ethnology*, 22. Cambridge, Massachusetts: Harvard University Press.

TYLOR, E.B. 1958. [Reprint Ed.] *Religion in Primitive Culture*. New York: Harper & Row.

URCIUOLI, B. 1996. Meaning What? [Reponse to Prost]. *Visual Anthropology* 8(2/3): 365-366.

VAN VELSON, J. 1967. The Extended Case Method and Situational Analysis. *The Craft of Social Anthropology*. (A.L. Epstein, Ed.), London: Tavistock.

VARELA, C. 1996. The Prost "Review". *Visual Anthropology*, 8(2/3): 367-371.

WHITE, L. 1940. The Symbol: The Origin and Basis of Human Behavior. *Custom Made. Introductory Readings for Cultural Anthropology*. (Ed. Chas. Hughes), Chicago: Rand-McNally College Publications.

WILLIAMS, D.

1976. An Exercise in Applied Personal Anthropology. *Dance Research Journal* [CORD], 11(1), N.Y. University. [Reprinted in Williams 1991: 287-321].

1986. (Non) Anthropologists, The Dance and Human Movement. *Theatrical Movement: A Bibliographical Anthology.* (Ed. B. Fleshman), Metuchen, N.J.: Scarecrow Press, pp. 159-219.

1990. [and B. Farnell]. *The Laban Script. A Beginning Text on Movement-Writing for Non-Dancers* (with Workbook). Canberra, A.C.T.: The Australian Institute for Aboriginal and Torres Strait Islander Studies,

1991. *Ten Lectures on Theories of the Dance.* Metuchen, New Jersey: Scarecrow Press.

1995. Space, Intersubjectivity and the Conceptual Imperative: Three Ethnographic Cases. *Human Action Signs in Cultural Context: The Visible and the Invisible in Movement and Dance.* (Ed. B. Farnell), Metuchen, N.J.: Scarecrow Press, pp. 44-81.

1996. An Appreciation. *Jour. for the Anthrop. Study of Hum. Mvmt.* [JASHM], 8(4): 174-18.

WITTGENSTEIN, L.

1953. *Philosophical Investigations.* Oxford: Blackwell.

1969. *On Certainty.* Oxford: Blackwell.

SUBJECT INDEX

(empirical method cannot explain human ~, 77);
(intentional ~, 77, 79, 81);
(language-based nature of ~, 160)

Adroa, Adronga [Lugbara]
(*adro* as spirit of deceased, 131);
(~ and prophet, Rembe, 142);
(~ is Creator Divinity, 126);
(immanent aspect of ~ [*Adro*], 126)

aesthetic
(~ domain and Gisaro, 172);
(~ movement and *heliaki*, 117);
(~ principle of *heliaki*, ix, 106);
(~ principle of Tongans, ix, 126);
(~ values, 30);
(Martin doesn't define art or ~s, 21);
(western ~ [of dance], 27)

Africa (African)
(east ~, x-xi, xiii);
(fieldwork in east ~, x);
(~ican dance never existed, 18);
(~ican heritage and Islamic ideas, 213);
(~s "dance that way", 157)

ambiguity (-ous)
(~ and liminality in time/space, 142);
(~ is less in *walangaa*, 138);
(~ and paradox of disequilibrium [Lugbara] 144)
(~: a widespread claim, 158);
(*dances and resolution of* ~ [subsection: Lugbara], 142-145)

America (-ican)
(~ican and European farmers pray to God, 22);
(~ican black dance as postscript, 20);

(~ican Indian as early stage in evolution, 44);
(~ican Indian as fiction, 18);
(~ican Indian as primitive model used by Terry, 19);
(what was said about ~ican Indian dancing unreliable, 58)

ane mama [**Kaluli**]
(~ spirits, 183, 184, 186)

antagonism
(and conflict [Lugbara], 125);
(and hostility of *karule wara*, [Lugbara], 130);
(and revenge for suffering [Gisaro], 169, 242);
(and violence in Gisaro, xii; 175-76);
(consequences of prohibiting ~, [Gisaro] 178-79);

anthropology (-ical, -ists)
(~ and fieldwork, ix, x);
(~ and outdated ideas in dance scholarship, 27);
(~ of dance and what it looks for, 151);
(~ of dance lags behind main stream ~, 152);
(~ of dance, [book], 37);
(~ of human movement, v, xiv, 55);
(~ of hum. mvmt. students and exams, 63);
(applied personal ~, 62);
(Culture - Personality School of ~ in U.S., 46);
(development of ~, xiv, 161-162);
(good ~ and 'ethnics', vi);
(~ical assumptions about violence, xii, 174);
(~ical evidence, 18);
(~ical gobbledygook, 61);

ongo [Lugbara]
(~ and gender, 130);
(~ and insult, 128);
(~ and liminality of performance space, 134);
(~ and public spectacle, 131);
(~ and reversal, 138);
(~ and sites/status, 129
(~ as *abi* dances, i.e. *auwu* ~ =
  'wailing' dances and *avico* ~ =
  'playing' dances, 128);
(~ begins mourning, 132);
(~ danced for "wailing", 133);
(~ dances for mortuary rites,
  128);
(the word ~ defined, 127);
(~ dances performed in open,
  129)

opposition(s)
(~ invoked in Kaluli society,
  174, 176);
(*A Drama of Opposition* [sub-
  heading - Kaluli], 173*ff*);
(~in *miyɔwɔ* and *aa bisɔ*, 173-
  174);
(nature of [Kaluli] ~, 190);
(~s crystallize groups, 193);
(tension of ~s, 190)

origin(s)
(~ of *Heyalo* [Kaluli], 266);
(7 locations for ~ of dancing,
  57);
(~s and anthropological
  gobbledygook, 61);
(unknowable ~s of dance, 17)

pieza (Zapotec)
(~ is western social dance, 40)

Polynesia (-ian), 15, 87

précis, v, vi, vii
(~ as student aid, vi);

(~ of arguments, 63);
(~ exercises, I(1)-34, II(2)-51,
  III(3)-64, IV(4)-83, V(5)-120,
  VI(6)-145, VIII(7)-197, IX(8)-
  214)

primitive
(~ and primordium, 57);
(~ confused with primæval, 17);
(~ dance requires discussion,
  28);
(~ dancers, according to Sorell,
  18);
(~ dance, acc. to Kirstein, 18);
(no such thing as ~ dance form,
  24);
(the dance world and the term
  ~, 62);
(the term, ~, 16, 17, 18)

reciprocity, (-cal transaction)
(~ as healing, life-restoring
  process, 190);
(~ as opposition [Kaluli], 175-
  76);
(~ in New Guinea societies,
  222);
(~ pervasive in Kaluli life, 171);
(Gisaro itself is a ~cal transaction, xi, 171);

Rembe [Lugbara prophet]
(~ dance of Yakan cult, 141-142)

rite(s), (-ual)
(Lugbara dances as ~ual
  performances, 157);
(~s of transition [Lugbara], 126,
  142-43);
(~ual transitions in death
  dances described [Lugbara],
  138)

self-expression
(dance as ~, 17)